INDIAN GOVERNMENT AND POLITICS

INDIAN GOVERNMENT AND POLITICS

Ashutosh Kumar

ANMOL PUBLICATIONS PVT. LTD.
NEW DELHI-110 002 (INDIA)

ANMOL PUBLICATIONS PVT. LTD.
Regd. Office: 4360/4, Ansari Road, Daryaganj,
New Delhi-110002 (India)
Tel.: 23278000, 23261597, 23286875, 23255577
Fax: 91-11-23280289
Email: anmolpub@gmail.com
Visit us at: www.anmolpublications.com

Branch Office: No. 1015, Ist Main Road, BSK IIIrd Stage
IIIrd Phase, IIIrd Block, Bangalore-560 085 (India)
Tel.: 080-41723429 • Fax: 080-26723604
Email: anmolpublicationsbangalore@gmail.com

Indian Government and Politics

First Edition, 2010

ISBN 978-81-261-4546-1

PRINTED IN INDIA

Printed at Mehra Offset Press, Delhi.

Contents

Preface (*vii*)

1. Overview of the Indian Political System 1
2. Constitutional Provisions and Institutional Functioning 69
3. Party System and Elections 169
4. Development Process 229

Bibliography 271

Index 273

Preface

This book written on Indian Government and her Politics will serve as a standard textbook for undergraduate students of political science and public administration. It is also an incisive manual for the candidates appearing for various UPSC and civil service examinations, besides being invaluable for students and researchers of political science in general, and post-colonial contemporary Indian politics in particular.

The task of framing the Constitution of India was given to the Constituent Assembly, formed under the Cabinet Mission Plan of 1946. The inaugural meeting of the Constituent Assembly was held on December 9, 1946. Dr. Sachidananda Sinha was elected provisional Chairman of the Constituent Assembly. On December 11, 1946, Dr. Rajendra Prasad was elected as the permanent Chairman of the Constituent Assembly. The Constitution of India was enacted, signed and adopted by the Constituent Assembly on November 26, 1949.

The *Indian Government and Politics* stands out as a classic work on the Indian politics in the sense that it does not only analyse the working of the body politic but also offers practicable alternatives and suggestions within the framework of the constitution, law and politics.

—*Author*

1

Overview of the Indian Political System

Controversial Issues in the Constituent Assembly

A ticklish constitutional problem arose on 15th August, 1947 and Nehru put in jokingly: Mavalankar has vanished into thin air." He was referring to the provision in the Indian Independence Act under which the Legislative Assembly, of which G.V. Mavalankar was President, automatically dissolved on Independence Day and the Constituent Assembly became the supreme sovereign and legislative body. The question arose how Rajendra Prasad, a member of the Cabinet as well as the President of the Constituent Assembly could preside over the deliberations of that body when it functioned as a legislature.

Both Nehru and Patel felt that Prasad should continue in the Cabinet and another President should be chosen for the Constituent Assembly, when Nehru took the stand that it would be intolerable in a democracy for a Minister to preside, B. N. Rau proposed that a Deputy Speaker be elected to preside over the Assembly in the name of President of the Constituent Assembly. This led a tension between Patel and Prasad and resulted in a sharp exchange in the cabinet. A civil servant who attended the meeting observed: "These men whom we adored as giants quarrelled like children." The dispute' was referred to Gandhi, a bare week before his assassination. Prasad wanted to make a statement in the Constituent Assembly: Gandhi sent for it and modified it. Prasad accepted the changes, saying: "I stand for harmony and therefore do not press my point," Gandhi's terse comment was: "Even Rajen Babu is lured by power. I feel disillusioned."

At this point another issue was raised: "What would be Prasad's position on " the legislative side and Mavalankar's as speaker?" Reluctantly Prasad agreed to the election of another speaker, provided he was subordinate to the President of the Constituent Assembly. Mavalankar demanded equality of status and full control over his secretariat. Prasad yielded after a hard struggle, retaining the Presidentship of the Constituent Assembly, and Mavalankar took over as Speaker of the Legislative Assembly.

But the squabble' did not end there, at the instance of Gandhi, Nehru suggested that Prasad should become President of the Congress Party. Prasad objected strongly to what appeared to him an attempt to push him out of the Cabinet and Presidentship of the Constituent Assembly. For some time it appeared as though he would repudiate the agreement over Mavalankar's appointment. When Nehru dropped the proposal and Prasad's ruffed feelings had been soothed, still more difficulties were encountered. Rau took away the Legislative Assembly Secretariat, and Prasad ruled that the new staff could not be appointed without his sanction. The matter was referred to Nehru who then got Prasad to delegate to Mavalankar the authority to appoint staff. Later, a provision was written into the constitution making the Parliament Secretariat independent of the Government.

Salient Features of the Working Process of the Constituent Assembly

According to Granville Austin the success of the constitution lies principally in its having been framed by Indians, and in the excellence of the framing process itself. The members of the Assembly drafted a constitution that expressed the aspirations of the nation. They skilfully selected and modified the provisions that they borrowed, helped by the 'experts' among their number and the advice given by ministries of the Union and Provincial Governments. The Assembly members also applied to their task with great effectiveness two wholly Indian concepts, consensus and; accommodation. Accommodation was applied to the principles to be embodied in the Constitution. Consensus was the aim of the decision-making process, the single most important source of the, Constituent Assembly's effectiveness.

Decision-making by Consensus

Consensus is a manner of making decisions by unanimity. It is a recognition that majority rule may not be a successful way to decide political conflicts. Assembly leaders understood this well and bent their energies towards this goal in the hope and expectation that the constitution, framed by consensus, would work effectively and thus prove durable. According to Austin, "Consensus thus had a general appeal in the Assembly; to the leadership an ethical and effective way of reaching lasting agreement and to the rank and file as an indigenous institution that suited the framing of an Indian Constitution.

Consensus approach was adopted in a variety of ways. Most important; among them were the Congress Assembly Party meetings where each provision of the Constitution was subjected to frank and searching debates and whose approval was in fact as important as that of the Assembly itself. Everyone elected to the Assembly on the Congress ticket could attend meetings, from party stalwarts to non-congressmen like Ayyar, Ambedkar and N. G. Ayyangar, who were brought into the Assembly because the leadership believed that their talents should not be wasted. Also a part of this' process was the Assembly's committee system, the dialogue between provincial and Union. Government leaders in the Assembly, the many inter-governmental communications and the off the record discussions between Assembly leaders and dissidents among the members.

The primary, examples of decision-making by consensus were perhaps the federal and language provisions. The language question strained the Assembly's decision-making machinery to the utmost. For nearly three years the members searched for a generally acceptable solution. The Munshi-Ayyangar formula was drafted almost in desperation. Opening the final Assembly debate on language, Prasad announced that he would not put the issue to a vote. If an agreement was not acceptable to the whole country it would be most difficult to implement.

The Principle of Accommodation

According to Austin, the second of India's original contribution to constitution-making was the principle of Accommodation-the ability to reconcile apparently incompatible concepts. India's constitutional structure is a good example of the principle of accommodation on matters of substance. It has reconciled the federal and unitary system, membership of commonwealth and republican status of Government, Provisions for Panchayati Raj with the need for a strong Central Government.

The Art of Selection and Modification

According to Austin, the Constituent Assembly had discovered a new principle-the art of selection and modification. The Assembly was not merely imitative, the borrowing from different political systems did not relieve the Assembly of choice and that the borrowed provisions had to be adopted to suit Indian conditions. One example of selection and modification is the method of Constitutional amendment.

The three mechanisms of the method devised by the Assembly have made the Constitution flexible while at the same time protecting the rights of the States. They have worked better than has the amending process any other country where federalism and the British Parliamentary System jointly form the bases of the Constitution. In brief, the Assembly selected and modified the provisions from other constitutions with a great deal of professional help.

Criticism of the Constituent Assembly

The Indian Constituent Assembly, thus elected, was criticised both by some Indians and the British, as unrepresentative of the Indian people. Sri Jaya Prakash Narain referred to it as "a restricted and curbed Constituent Assembly " a creation of the British imperialism and so unable to bring freedom to the Country. Churchill said that the Assembly represented "only one major community in India"; and for Viscount Simon, it was "a body of Hindus". The working procedure, composition and status of the Constituent Assembly has been criticised on the following grounds:

Congress Domination: The Constituent Assembly was a one party body. The Assembly was the Congress and the Congress was India. The Congress had a, built-in-majority of 69 per cent in the Assembly and after partition, the congress majority jumped to 82 per cent. Prof. Shibban Lal Saxena complained that the Congress Party dominated the scene and the Constitution had very much suffered from it.

"The Congress party meetings became meetings of the real Constituent Assembly, and this real Assembly became the mock Assembly where discussions arrived at by the Congress Party meetings were registered." The Congress' overwhelming majority in the Constituent Assembly resulted from the December 1945 Provincial legislature elections and from partition, moreover, the Congress Working Committee directed the Provincial assemblies to elect some of the prominent non-congressmen so their experience and expertisation can be made available to the Assembly. Among them were A.K. Ayyar, H. K. Kunzru, N. G. Ayyangar, Ambedkar, K Santhanam, M.R. Jayakar and K.M. Munshi. In the words of K. Santhanam, "There was hardly' any shade of public opinion not represented in the Assembly."

The credit goes to the Congress Party for bringing into the proceedings of the Assembly a sense of order and discipline. As Dr. Ambedkar said, "It is because of the discipline of the Congress Party that the Drafting Committee was able to pilot the Constitution in the Assembly with the sure knowledge as to the fate of each article and each amendment. The Congress Party is, therefore, entitled to all the credit for the smooth sailing of the Draft Constitution in the Assembly."

Was it a Sovereign Assembly: The Constituent Assembly was meeting with the permission of the British Government and a fourth of the nation was represented at the Assembly's deliberations. Had such a body any power or authority of its own? Could it speak and act for India? Was it sovereign? Maulana Azad, Nehru and Prasad believed that it was sovereign because the Assembly's authority came from the people of India although they recognised that the Cabinet Mission Plan placed certain limitations on its activities.

The Assembly gave its own answer to these questions in its Rule when it arrogated to itself the authority to control its own being: "The Assembly shall not be dissolved except by a resolution assented to by at least two-thirds of the whole number of members of the Assembly." The Indian Independence Act passed by the British Parliament came into effect on 15th August; 1947, giving legally to the Constituent Assembly the status it had assumed since its inception. The Cabinet Mission Plan became outmoded, and the Constituent Assembly settled down to draft free India's Constitution. The Indian Independence Act of 1947 made it "the Sovereign Constituent Assembly for India". Pt. Nehru described it, on the midnight of August 14,1947, as "a sovereign body representing the sovereign people of India."

A Hindu Dominated Body: Although the Constituent Assembly enjoyed the confidence of a vast majority of people of India, yet some uncharitable critics dubbed it as the most unrepresentative of Constituent Assembly ever created in any democratic country of the world. British leaders like Churchill and Lord Simon named it as a Hindu Body representing the interests of the Hindus alone.

Dr. Rajendra Prasad condemned this charge as baseless and irrational. He pointed out that except the representatives of the Muslim League, the Constituent Assembly of India represented all the communities and interest. The minority communities were fully represented in the Assembly, usually by members of their own choosing. The Indian Christians had 7 representatives in the Assembly, the Anglo-Indians 3, the Parsis 3 and so on. After partition, when the composition of the Assembly had become settled, the minorities had 88 of the 235 seats allotted to the Provinces, or 37 per cent of the Provincial membership. Additionally, the ideological spectrum of the Assembly was broadened by the inclusion of non-congress 'experts' as well as by the diverse nature of the Congress membership.

An Unrepresentative Body: Another charge generally levelled against the Constituent Assembly was that it had not been directly elected by the people on the basis of universal adult franchise. As such, it did not reflect the aspirations of the masses. Socialist and

Communist leaders of India attacked the unrepresentative character of the Constituent Assembly on this account Leaders of the Congress Party while refuting this criticism pointed out that the election of a new Constituent Assembly on the basis of universal adult franchise would have been a uphill task under the special circumstances created by the partition of the country. Otherwise, too, preparation of electoral rolls and holding of national elections in a big country like India was an impossible task. Any delay in framing a suitable constitution for India would have created unformidable problem for new India. It was further pointed out that even if there had been direct elections, the result would have been the same. The same persons who happened to be members of the Constituent Assembly would have been elected by an overwhelming majority. The general composition of the Constituent Assembly would not have changed much. The representative character of the Assembly is further proved by the fact that it included all the prominent leaders of major political parties of India. Dr. Ambedkar represented the depressed classes, Hansa Mehta represented the All-India Women Conference, the landlords of India were represented by Maharaja Darbhanga, and the Hindu Mahasabha was represented by Dr. Shyama Prasad Mukerji. Frank Anthony represented the Anglo-Indians and Jndian Christians were represented by H.C. Mukerji. So was the case with Sikhs and the Muslims.

It should not be forgotten, however, that India was not the only country to adopt indirect election in this respect. The delegates of the U.S. Convention:were chosen without any popular awareness; the South African Convention was also elected by the Provincial Legislatures. Moreover, if the father of the Indian Constituent Assembly opposed its election through universal suffrage, it was more due to the practical difficulties than any theoretical consideration.

Dominated by the Legal Luminaries: Then another criticism which is made against the Constituent Assembly is that it was an Assembly which was "dominated only by the politicians and lawyers. It did not give much representation to other sections of Indian Society. The net result was that this domination gave the country a very bulky document. According to some critics the Constitution of India is a lawyer's paradise.

All said and done, the fact remains that the Constituent Assembly was guided and directed by the top leaders of the Congress. Stalwarts like Nehru, Patel, Prasad, Azad and Munshi dominated the scene. Although indirectly elected and therefore not responsible to the mass of Indians, the Constituent Assembly was a highly representative body.

Evolution of the Constituent Assembly in India

The idea of a constituent assembly, whereby Indians themselves might frame a constitution for their country, was implicit in the opposition to the 1919 Act. But, the first definite reference to a constituent assembly for India though not in those words or under that particular name-was made by Mahatma Gandhi in 1922, soon after the inauguration of the Government of India Act, 1919.

In 1922 itself, a joint meeting of members of the two Houses of the Central Legislature was held at Simla at the initiative of Mrs. Annie Besant, which decided to call a convention for the framing of a Constitution Yet another conference attended by members of the Central and Provincial Legislatures was held in Delhi in February 1923. This conference outlined essential elements of a constitution placing India on equal footing with the self-governing Dominions of the British Empire. A "National Convention" was called which met on 24 April, under the president ship of Sir Tej Bahadur Sapru. This convention drafted the "Commonwealth of India Bill". The draft Bill was submitted in slightly amended form to a committee of the All Parties Conference held at Delhi in January 1925, which was presided over by Mahatma Gandhi. Finally, the draft was submitted to a Drafting Committee which published the Bill. The Bill was sent to an influential member of the Labour Party in Britain accompanied by a memorandum signed by 43 leaders of various political parties. It found wide support in the Labour Party and was accepted with slight modifications. The Bill had the first reading after it was introduced in the House of Commons. Though with the defeat of the Labour Government the fate of the Bill was sealed, it was a major effort by the Indians to outline a constitutional system for India with the help of peaceful and constitutional means. The adoption of the famous Motilal Nehru resolution in 1924 and 1925 on the National Demand was a historic event inasmuch as the Central Legislature had, for the first time, lent its support to the growing demand that the future constitution of India should be framed by Indians themselves.

In November 1927, when the Simon Commission was appointed without any Indians represented on it, an all party meeting held at Allahabad said that apart from being virtual negation of the."National Demand", it amounted to a "deliberate insult to the people of India" for, not only did it "definitely assign to them a position of inferiority" but also denied to them "the right to participate in the determination of the constitution of their own country".

Session of the Congress on 28 December 1927. An All Parties Conference organised at Bombay on 19 May 1928 appointed a committee, under the chairmanship of Motilal Nehru "to determine the principles of the constitution of India". The report of the Committee (submitted on 10 August 1928) was later to become famous as the Nehru Report. It was the first attempt by Indians to frame a full fledged constitution for their country and has been described by Coupland as "not only an answer to the challenge that Indian nationalism was unconstructive" but "frankest attempt yet made by Indians to face squarely the difficulties of communalism". The Report embodied not only the perspective of the contemporary nationalist opinion but also an outline of a draft constitution for India. The latter was based on the principle of Dominion Status with full responsible government on the parliamentary pattern. It asserted the principle that sovereignty belongs to the Indian people, laid down a set of fundamental rights and provided for a federal system with maximum autonomy granted to the units but residuary powers vested in the Central Government and joint electorates for elections to the Federal Lower House and the Provincial Legislatures with reservation of seats for minorities in certain cases for a limited period.

It would be seen that the broad parliamentary system with a government responsible to Parliament, a chapter of justifiable fundamental rights and rights of minorities envisaged in the Nehru Report in 1928 were very largely embodied in the constitution of independent India that was adopted 21 years later, on 26 November 1949.

The White Paper issued after the third Round Table Conference outlined the British government's proposal for constitutional reforms in India. The Joint Parliamentary Committee which examined these proposals observed that "a specific grant of constituent power to authorities in India is not at the moment a practicable proposition". In June 1934, the Congress Working Committee declared that the only satisfactory alternative to the White Paper was a constitution drawn up by a constituent assembly elected on the basis of adult suffrage. This was the first time that a definite demand for a constituent assembly was formally put forward. The Working Committee of the All India Congress Committee at its meeting held at Patna on 5-7 December 1934 adopted a resolution rejecting the scheme of Indian Constitutional Reforms as recommended in the Report of the Joint Parliamentary Committee (1933-34) and reiterated the view that the only satisfactory alternative to the scheme was a constitution drawn up by a constituent assembly.

The failure of the Simon Commission and the Round Table Conference which led to the enactment of the Government of India Act, 1935 to satisfy Indian aspirations accentuated the demand for a constituent assembly of the people of India. The Congress adopted a resolution at its Lucknow Session in April 1936 in which it declared that no constitution imposed by an outside authority shall be acceptable to India; it has to be one framed by-an Indian constituent assembly elected by the people of India on adult franchise.

Since the Congress had contested elections to the Provincial Legislatures on the issues of total rejection of the Act of 1935 and the demand for a constituent assembly, following a decisive victory it adopted at Delhi on 18 March 1937 a resolution asserting the electorate's approval of the demand for a constituent assembly. It desired to frame" a constitution based on national independence, through the medium of a constituent assembly elected by adult franchise". This demand was firmly reiterated by the All India National Convention of Congress Legislators held in Delhi in March, 1937. During August-October 1937, the Central Legislative assembly and the Provincial Assemblies of each of the Provinces where the Congress held office, adopted resolutions reiterating the Congress demand to convene a constituent assembly to frame a new constitution for a free India. After the outbreak of the War in 1939, the demand for a constituent assembly was reiterated in a long statement issued by the Congress Working Committee on 14 September, 1939.

Gandhiji wrote an article entitled "The Only Way" in the Harijan of 19 November 1939 in which he expressed the view that "constituent assembly alone can produce a constitution indigenous to the country and truly and fully representing the will of the people". He declared that the only way out to arrive at a just solution of communal and other problem was a constituent assembly. The demand for a constituent assembly was for the first time authoritatively conceded by the British Government, though in an indirect way and with important reservations, in what is known as the" August Offer" of 1940.

The Cripps proposals marked an advance over the "August Offer" in that the making of the new constitution was now to rest solely and not merely "primarily" in Indian hands and a clear undertaking to accept the constitution framed by the proposed constitution-making body was given by the British Government. After the failure of the Cripps Mission, no steps were taken for the solution of the Indian constitutional problem until the War in Europe came to an end in May, 1945.

In July, with the new Labour Government coming into power in England, its Indian policy was announced on 19 September 1945 by Lord Wavell who had succeeded Lord Linlithgow as Viceroy in 1943. The Viceroy affirmed His Majesty's Government's intention to convene a constitution-making body "as soon as possible". The Cabinet Mission realised that the most satisfactory method to constitute a constitution-making body would have been by election based on adult franchise, but that would have caused" a wholly unacceptable delay" in the formulation of then C'.N constitution. "The only practicable course" according to them was, therefore, "to utilise the recently elected Provincial Legislative Assemblies as electing bodies". As what they called the "fairest and as most practicable plan" in the circumstances, the Mission recommended that the representation of the Provinces in the constitution-making body be on the basis of population, roughly in the ratio of one Member to a million and the seats allocated to the Provinces be divided among the principal communities, classified for this purpose as Sikhs, Muslims and General (all except Sikhs and Muslims), on the basis of their numerical strength. The representatives of each community were to be chosen by members of that community in the Provincial assembly and voting was to be by the method of proportional representation with single transferable vote.

The number of Members allotted to the Indian States was also to be fixed on the same basis of population as adopted for British India, but the method of their selection was to be settled later by consultation. The strength of the constitution-making body was to be 389. Of these 296 representatives were to be from British India, (292 representatives drawn from the eleven Governors' Provinces of British India and a representative each from the four Chief Commissioners' Provinces of Delhi, Ajmer-Merwara, Coorg and British Baluchistan) and 93 representatives from the Indian States. The Cabinet Mission recommended a basic framework for the constitution and laid down in some detail the procedure to be followed by the constitution-making body.

Elections for the 296 seats assigned to the British. Indian Provinces were completed by July-August 1946. The Congress won 208 seats including all the General seats except nine and the Muslim League 73 seats, that is, all but five of the seats allotted to Muslims. The party-wise break-up of the assembly's British Indian membership was as follows:

With the partition and independence of the country, on 14-15 August 1947, the constituent assembly of India could be said to have become free from the fetters of the Cabinet Mission Plan. It became a fully sovereign body and the successor to the British Parliament's plenary authority and power in the country. Moreover, following the acceptance of the Plan of 3 June, the members of the Muslim League Party from the Indian Dominion also took their seats in the assembly. The representatives of some of the Indian States had already entered the assembly on 28 April 1947. By 15 August 1947 most of the States were represented in the assembly and the remaining States also sent their representatives in due course.

The Constituent Assembly thus became a body, it was believed, fully representative of the states and provinces in India and fully sovereign of all external authority. It could abrogate or alter any law made by the British Parliament applying to India, including the Indian Independence Act itself.

The constituent assembly duly opened on the appointed day Monday, the ninth day of December, 1946 at eleven in the morning. The historic Objectives Resolution was moved in the constituent assembly by Nehru, on 13 December 1946, after it had been in session for some days. The beautifully worded draft of the Objectives Resolution cast the horoscope, so to say, of the Sovereign Democratic Republic that India was to be. The resolution envisaged a federal polity with the residuary powers vesting in the autonomous units and sovereignty belonging to the people. "Justice, social, economic and political; Equality of status, of opportunity and before the law; Freedom of thought, expression, belief, faith, worship, vocation, association and action" were to be guaranteed to all the people along with "adequate safeguards" to "minorities, backward and tribal areas and depressed and other backward classes". Thus, the Resolution gave to the assembly its guiding principles and the philosophy that was to permeate its tasks of constitution-making. It was finally adopted by the assembly on 22 January 1947.

Composition of the Constituent Assembly

In all, the Constituent Assembly was to have 389 members. As many as 296 of them were to be elected from British India and 93 were to be representatives of the native states. The Muslim League boycotted the Assembly, hence out of 296 members only 211 attended its first meeting on December 9, 1946. The electoral process itself could not have produced a representative body because it was based on the restricted franchise established by the Sixth Schedule of the 1935 Act, which excluded the mass of peasants, the majority of small shopkeepers and traders and countless others from the rolls through tax, property and educational qualifications. Only 28.5 per cent of the adult population of the provinces could vote in the provincial assembly elections of early 1946.

Working of the Constituent Assembly

The Constituent Assembly duly opened on the appointed day Monday, the day of December, 1946. It was truly a unique occasion in India's long history; the first time the representatives of the people were meeting to determine future Constitution of India. During its first four sittings on December 9, 11 and 12, the Assembly was involved with matters like the presentation of credentials and signing of the register, electing the permanent chairman, constituting a Committee for Rules of Procedure etc. On the 5th day of the First session of the Constituent Assembly-December 13, 1946-Nehru moved the historic Objectives Resolution. The Resolution said: "This Constituent Assembly declares its firm and solemn resolve to proclaim India as an Independent Sovereign Republic and to draw up for her future governance a constitution." Nehru's Objectives Resolution gave to the Assembly its guiding principles and the philosophy that was to permeate its task of constitution making.

The Assembly met in its Second plenary session from 20-26 January, 1947, and adopted the objective Resolution moved by Nehru. The Third plenary session was held from April 28 to May 2. It discussed the reports submitted by the Union Powers Committee and of the Advisory Committee on Fundamental Rights. On August 29, the Assembly adopted a resolution setting up a Drafting Committee to prepare a constitution in accordance with the decisions taken by it on the reports of the various committees. Dr. Ambedkar was appointed chairman of this Committee. The Second Draft was placed before the Assembly on February 21, 1948. After nearly three years the Assembly finally adopted the Constitution on November 26, 1949. In all, it held 11 sessions, covering 2965 days out of which 114 days were devoted to consideration of the draft Constitution.

Committees of the Constituent Assembly

The Constituent Assembly had a total of more than fifteen committees with a membership of greater than eighty individuals. Seven of them, such as the House and Staff Committee, had minor functions. The brick and mortar of the structure were provided by the reports of the Union Powers Committee, the Union Constitution Committee, the Advisory Committee on Minorities and Fundamental Rights, the Committee on Chief Commissioner's Provinces, the Committee on Financial Provisions of the Union Constitution and the Advisory Committee on Tribal Areas. These committees submitted their reports between April-August 1947, which were considered by the Constituent Assembly. On the basis of these decisions, the final shape and form were given by Dr. Ambedkar and his colleagues in the Drafting Committee.

Drafting Committee

The Assembly appointed a Drafting Committee on 29th August, 1947 to consider the Draft Constitution. Dr. Ambedkar was appointed Chairman and it had six other members. They were Sir Krishnaswami Ayyangar, N. Gopala': swami Ayyangar, K.M. Munshi, Saiyed Mohammed Sadulla, Sir B. L. Mittar and D.P. Khaitan. After the first meeting Sir B. L. Mittar ceased to be a member and in his place N. Madhava Rao was nominated by the President on December 5, 1947. The Drafting Committee, under the Chairmanship of Dr. Ambedker embodied the decision of the Assembly, with alternative and additional proposals in the form "Of a 'Draft Constitution of India' which was published in February 1948. The Drafting Committee took less than six months to prepare its Draft. In all it sat only for 141 days.

Framers of the Constitution

The members of the Constituent Assembly were not selected purely on a party basis, but were drawn from all walks of life and represented almost every section of the Indian people. They included some of the most leading personalities of Indian public life. The moving spirit of the assembly was Jawahar Lal Nehru, the first Prune Minister of free India. Rajendra Prasad was its President. Vallabhbhai Patel was one of the most important among the leading lights. While these leaders had contributed more than all others for the formulation of the basic principles of the Constitution, it was the Drafting Committee, headed by B.R. Ambedkar, which was in charge of its drafting. Dr. Ambedkar chaired the Drafting Committee and steered the document through nearly a year of debate over its various provisions. Ambedkar was ably assisted, in the task of Constitution making by the other members of the Drafting Committee among whom Alladi Krishnaswami Aiyer, N. Gopalaswami Ayyangar, K.M. Munshi and T.T Krishnamachari were the most prominent. In the words of Granville Austin, "Four leaders, Nehru, Patel, Prasad and the Congress Muslim leader Maulana Abul Kalam Azad, through their commanding grip on the Congress (Assembly Party and the Assembly's eight committees) constituted a virtual oligarchy within the Assembly. Issues were openly debated, but the influence of the Congress leaders was nearly irresistible."

In the words of Dr. Subhash Kashyap, "Nevertheless, while others fashioned its structure and shape, most significantly, Nehru gave to the Constitution of India its spirit and soul, its philosophy and its vision." At the very outset he laid down its' general outlines and he continued to influence what the Constituent Assembly did. In this, the Constitution was his handwork. Nehru was the Assembly's philosopher and its prime constitutional thinker. The President of the Constituent Assembly, Dr. Rajendra Prasad also gave credit to Nehru and Patel for the fundamentals of the Constitution. Between the two, as Austin puts it, each had his special interests-Patel was more interested in the Princely States, the public services and the working of the Home Ministry, and Nehru in Fundamental Rights, Protection of minority rights, and the social reform aspects of the Constitution and each let the other have almost free rein in these areas.

The Constituent Assembly had eight major committees-Rules, Steering, Advisory, Drafting, Union Subjects, Union Constitution,

Provincial Constitution and States-with a total membership of approximately three dozen. Either, Nehru, Patel or Prasad chaired each of these committees, and in many cases the other two or Azad were also present.

Nehru personally invited Ambedkar to become a member of his Cabinet. Ambedkar joined Cabinet because he could serve the cause of Scheduled Castes better from within the Government. One more individual, B. N. Rau, must be paced among those important in the framing of the Constitution. As Constitutional Adviser, his advice was heard in the Assembly's inner councils, although he was not an Assembly member.

Under the Rules of Procedure, the Assembly elected Dr. Rajendra Prasad as its permanent President,. and V. T. Krishnamachari and H. C. Mookheijee as Vice Presidents unanimously. Dr. Rajendra Prasad, as the President of Constituent Assembly, was indeed "a very happy choice". As a veteran political leader, he was respected by all, and was very considerate towards every member of the Assembly. While conducting the proceedings of the Assembly he never allowed "legalism to defeat the work of constitution making." He, how ever, was a more active President of the Constituent Assembly than George Washington.

The Constitution of India and Indian Polity

The task of framing the Constitution of India was given to the Constituent Assembly, formed under the Cabinet Mission Plan of 1946. The inaugural meeting of the Constituent Assembly was held on December 9, 1946. Dr Sachidananda Sinha was dected provisional Chairman of the Constituent Assembly. On December 11, 1946, Dr. Rajendra Prasad was elected as the permanent chairman of the Constituent Assembly.

The Constitution of India was enacted, signed and adopted by the Constituent Assembly on November 26, 1949.

On January 26, 1950, the Constitution of India came into force on which date India also became a Republic. Our constitution makes detailed provisions for the following:

- Citizenship,

- Fundamental Rights,
- Directive Principles of State Policy,
- Structure of the Government,
- Parliament and State Legislatures,
- Supreme Court and High Courts,
- Relationship between the Union and the States,
- Services,
- Official Language and various other matters of basic importance

Salient Features of Constitution

1. It is the longest written constitution in the world.
2. Consisting of 22 Chapters, over 395 Articles and 12 Schedules.
3. It proclaims India a Sovereign Democratic Republic.
4. Fundamental Rights are guaranteed to all citizens of India.
5. Directive Principles of State Policy are incorporated.
6. It established the parliamentary system of government, *i.e.*, the President of the Union is the constitutional head, the Council of Ministers or the Union Cabinet is the real executive and is responsible to the Lok Sabha.
7. It is federal in form (in normal times) but unitary in spirit (in emergencies).
8. It is neither too rigid (as some provisions can be amended by a simple majority) nor flexible (as some provisions require special majority for amendment).
9. It declares India a secular state.
10. It guarantees single citizenship to all citizens.
11. It introduced adult franchise, *i.e.*, every adult above 18 years has the right to vote and the system of joint electorates.
12. It established an independent judiciary; the Supreme Court acts as a guardian of the Constitution in place of the Privy Council.

The Preamble

The draft of the Preamble was prepared by Jawaharlal Nehru and is based on the American model. The 42nd Amendment added the words "Secular and Socialist" and now the preamble reads as follows.

"We the People of India, having solemnly resolved to constitute India into a Sovereign Socialist Secular Democratic Republic and to secure to all its citizens :

Justice; social, economic and political;

Liberty; of thought, expression, belief, faith and worship;

Equality; of status and of opportunity; and to promote among them all;

Fraternity; assuring the dignity of the individual and the unity and integrity of the nation;

In our Constituent Assembly, November 26, 1949, do hereby adopt, enact and give to ourselves this constitution.

Articles of the Constitution

Part	**Article**	**Deals with**
Part I	Articles 1-4	Territory of India,, admission,, establishment or formation of new states
Part II	Articles 5-11	Citizenship
Part III	Articles 12-35	Fundamental Rights
Part IV	Articles 36-51	Directive Principles of State Policy
Part IV A	Article 51-A	Duties of a citizen of India. It was added by the 42nd Amendment in 1976
Part V	Articles 52-151	Government at the Union level
Part VI	Articles 152-237	Government at the State level
Part VII	Article 238	Deals with states in Part B of the First Schedule. It was repealed by 7th Amendment in 1956
Part VIII	Articles 239-241	Administration of Union Territories
Part IX	Article 242-243	Territories in Part D of the First Scheduleand other territories. It was repealed by 7th Amendment in 1956

Part X	Articles 244-244 A	Scheduled and tribal areas
Part XI	Articles 245-263	Relations between the Union and States
Part XII	Articles 264-300	Finance,, property,, contracts and suits
Part XIII	Articles 301-307	Trade,, commerce and travel within theterritory of India
Part XIV	Articles 308-323	Services under the Union and States
Part XIV-A	Articles 323A-323B	Added by the 42nd Amendment in 1976and deals with administrative tribunals to hear disputes and other complaints
Part XV	Articles 324-329	Election and Election Commission
Part XVI	Articles 330-342	Special provision to certain classes ST/ SCand Anglo Indians
Part XVII	Articles 343-351	Official languages
Part XVIII	Articles 352-360	Emergency provisions
Part XIX	Articles 361-367	Miscellaneous provision regarding exemption of the President and governors from criminal proceedings
Part XX	Article 368	Amendment of Constitution
Part XXI	Articles 369-392	Temporary,, transitional and special provisions
Part XXII	Articles 393-395	Short title, commencement and repeal of the Constitution

Schedules

FIRST SCHEDULE : I. The State, II. The Union Territories.

SECOND SCHEDULE :

PART A. Provisions to the President and the Governors of States

PART B. (Repeated)

PART C. Provisions as to the Speaker and the Deputy Speaker of the House of the People and the Chairman and the Deputy Chairman of the Council of States and the Speaker and the Deputy Speaker of the Legislative Assembly and the Chairman and the Deputy Chairman of the Legislative Council of a State.

PART D. Provisions as to the Judges of the Supreme Court and of the High Courts.

PART E. Provisions as to the Comptroller and Auditor-General of India.

THIRD SCHEDULE : Forms of Oaths or Affirmations.

FOURTH SCHEDULE : Allocation of Seats in the Council of States.

FIFTH SCHEDULE : Provisions as to the administration and Control of Scheduled Areas and Scheduled Tribes.

PART A. General

PART B. Administration and Control of Scheduled Areas and Scheduled Tribes

PART C. Scheduled Areas

PART D. Amendment of the Schedule

SIXTH SCHEDULE : Provisions as to the administration of Tribal Areas in the States of Assam, Meghalaya, Tripura and Mizoram.

SEVENTH SCHEDULE :

LIST I. Union List

LIST II. State List

LIST III. Concurrent List

EIGHTH SCHEDULE : Languages

NINTH SCHEDULE : Article 31B

TENTH SCHEDULE : Provisions as to disqualification on the ground of defection

ELEVENTH SCHEDULE : Article 243G

TWELFTH SCHEDULE : Article 243W

Indian Polity & Constitution

What is Democracy-? "Democracy is not just about Rights. It is also about Responsibilities. Democracy is not just about asserting our own identity. It is also about respecting the identity of others.

Democracy is not just about seeking benefits. It is also about contributing to the process of nation building."

What is Politics-? Politics refers to the relationship between government and society.

What is Political Science-? Political Science is concerned with a systematic study of 'politics' in human societies. Integration and Conflict are two sides of coin "Politics."

What is State-? State is a social organisation with a fixed territory and stability in society living within that territory. State is distinguished from other forms of social organisation in terms of sovereign power exercised by it. Here Sovereignty is defined as undisputed legal authority over a territory.

In ancient India, the *Saptanga Theory of State* elaborated in *Kautilya's Arthshastra* mentions seven elements — *Swami, Amatya,* Janpada, *Durga, Kosa, Danda* and *Mitra.* In the west, writers like Harold

J. Laski and J.W. Garner have referred to four elements of state as follows-

1. Population
2. Territory
3. Government
4. Sovereignty [Central theme]

What is Government-? The state has to exercise sovereign power over the territory and the people within its jurisdiction. For doing this it needs an organisation with persons exercising power on its behalf. Government is such an organisation of the state, with defined powers and functions for the different organs [Legislature, Executive and Judiciary] of the governments. Government of a State can be democratic or non-democratic, unitary or federal and Presidential or Parliamentary.

Indian State- The origin of State in India is as old as Vedas, when Dharma was the cardinal principle of Politics in India. *Manusmiriti is* the earliest text to elaborate the principles of social life, propounds decentralization and welfare activities as the basis of the state organisation. Gradually ancient state has evolved into modern state. John Locke propounded the *Doctrine of Consent and* John Stuart Mill gave much importance to representative and responsible government.

Nation- The concept of Nation refers to sense of belongings from a particular State or Region. A society claims distinction on the basis of some common characteristics of its people. Some characteristics that form the basis of such a claim are: lineage, culture, language, religion, territory, race, and so on.

The idea of nation and the process of nationalism emphasize the sense of solidarity, and resemblances on various grounds. A sense of belonging among the people is provided by these factors either singly or in combination turned out as a Nation.

Nation Building- This is the process of consolidation of various social groups [whole population] under a common tag. It is one of the main objectives of the sate to maximize the level of integration in society which is known as Nation Building.

Political System- The political system of a state refers to the sum total of ideology or principles on which government of a State has been organised to discharge its duties or functions towards Citizens and to exercise the sovereign power of State. The political system of modern states are organised on the basis of constitution of a particular state.

Classification of Government- Government of a modern state can be classified into various forms like democratic or autocratic, unitary or federal and parliamentary or presidential etc. This classification of government usually based upon the following factors-

S. No.	Basis/Factors	Type of Government
1.	Nature of exercise of power	Democratic or Autocratic
2.	Nature of executive agency	Parliamentary or Presidential
3.	Territorial distribution of power	Federal or Unitary
4.	Nature of constitution	Hard or Soft

Political Culture- Political Culture of a country refers to a set of beliefs and attitudes prevailed in a particular political society.

Political Socialization- The process by which a particular set of attitudes, belief and orientations is passed on from one generation to another is known as political socialization. It is study of "what, when and how people learn about politics". Inter-generational continuity is the essence of political culture. The willingness of people to accept new ideas and beliefs is a matter of learnt behaviour. Thus, the learning process to acquire existing political culture is known as political socialization. Individuals acquire certain social obligations through ordinary course of interactions. Process of political socializations is not necessarily a conscious process. Various factors such as international developments, domestic transformations, historical events, and social stirrings shape the process of political socialization. There is a direct linkage between political culture and political socialization. Political socialization is the process by which political cultures are formed, maintained and changed. Thus, it is important to study the process of political socialization in order to understand political stability and development of political system. An individual acquires a particular belief, value and attitude towards politics of a state through manifest and latent transmission of information. The teaching of civics syllabus in the schools is an example of manifest political socialization. Latent political socialization process implies transmission of non-political attitudes towards prevalent institutions in a political system. It involves the fundamental aspects of culture in a political system. Political socialization takes place through a variety of institutions and situations. These are family, peer groups, educational institutions, secondary groups/such as workplace, the mass media, government and political party machineries.

Who makes Government in a State i.e. Political Parties- Political Party refers to a political or social institution with a common ideology. Party system in a state varies from state to state as one party system, two party system and multi party system

Political Participation- The study of political participation implies the study of actual involvement of people in the decision-making process rather than popular attitude of becoming involved. It refers to the involvement of mango peoples in policy making, implementing and its evaluation. In contemporary context effective participation of citizens in decision-making process has been emphasized through decentralization of power. Effective political participation is also achieved through the various emerging concepts like pressure groups, interest groups, civil society and NGO's.

Political Development- Political Development refers to gradual changes occurred into the political structure and political culture of a state during a certain time period. Political development is related to increasing governmental efficiency in the use of human and material resources of the nation for the common good. It also highlighted the notion of national political capacity or efficiency. Political development it refers to the capacity building of the government in discharging its duties or responsibilities. The concept of political capacity referred only to two basic areas of development: ability of a government to collect revenues from its subjects to implement its preferred policies and its ability to mobilize human resources.

Cardinal Theories of Politics

Liberalism- An ideology based on a commitment to individualism, consent and toleration: modern liberalism differs from classical liberalism. According to this ideology economic system is based upon Laissez-faire approach and it advocated *capitalism. Ideology also advocated the concept of free market and liberalization. Almost all developed countries on globe supported this ideology

Socialism- A political ideology based on the principle of state ownership of resources and industry along with responsibility of socioeconomic development. Socialism is a clear contrast to Laissez faire and advocated more interference from government side. Traditional Socialism is different from democratic socialism.

Marxism- This ideology was advocated and founded by Karl Marx. Marxism is based upon the principle of classless society.

*A type of economic system which precedes socialism or communism. It is based on private ownership of the means of production and on the exploitation of the wage labour.

Lenin of former USSR and Mayo of China were the main supporter of this ideology. Marx advocated replacement of capitalism by communism.

Fascism- Fascism refers to a political ideology which advocates an authoritarian hierarchical government (as opposed to democracy or liberalism). Nazi party of Germany under leadership of Adolf Hitler and Italy's Mussolini were the prime advocator of this ideology

Gandhism- One more political or economic ideology put forward by Mahatma Gandhi of India is known as Gandhism. This ideology is based upon the principle of non-violence and decentralization of power to local government

Few Important Terms in Polity

Bourgeoisie- This is a French term signifying citizen class or working class. The term is frequently used by Marxist socialists to denote the class of proprietors, capitalists, manufacturers, merchants, persons with a business of their own and members of liberal professions as opposed to the 'proletariat' who live only by selling their labour.

Proletariat- In ancient Rome the property–less class which served the state by producing children *proles*. However, the most prevalent usage refers to the one developed by Marx. In this sense proletariat includes those in industry, agriculture and intellectual posts who live by the sale of their labour, as opposed to the capitalist bourgeoisie.

Elite- This term denotes a group of persons who hold positions of eminence in society. The term is also used to refer to leaders in different fields, e.g. political elite and business elite.

Trade Union- An association of wage earners of workers for the purpose of improving their conditions and protecting their interests

Syndicalism- A movement of labour unions which favored "direct action" culminating in a revolutionary general strike to secure workers' ownership and control of industry. It originated under the influence of Robert Owen and acquired its more violent aspects in France besides getting its name from the word 'Syndicate' (union trade).

Indian Polity- The preamble of Indian constitution says that India is a *Sovereign* [undisputed legal right of Indian citizens over the state], *Socialist* [adhere to socialism ideology], *Secular* [without any religion and equal respect for all prevailed ones], *Democratic* [government by the people or by their elected representatives] *Republic* [A political system in which the supreme power lies in a body of citizens] country.

Some cardinal features of Indian Polity incorporated by Indian Constitution-

- Written
- Partially rigid and partially flexible
- Impartial Judiciary with Judicial Review
- Directive Principles of State Policy
- Universal Adult franchise
- Emergency Provisions
- Power distribution between Union and State on doctrine of "Pitch and Substance."
- Independent Agencies like UPSC, EC and CAGI
- Positive Discrimination
- PRI.

Constitution of India

The Constitution of India was drafted by the Constituent Assembly. The Constituent Assembly held its first sitting on the 9th December, 1946. It reassembled on the 14th August, 1947, as the sovereign Constituent Assembly for the Dominion of India. The proposed Constitution had been outlined by various committees of the Assembly like:

a) Union Constitution Committee

b) The Union Powers Committee

c) Committee on Fundamental Rights.

It was after a general discussion on the reports of these Committees that the Assembly appointed a Drafting Committee on the 29th August, 1947. The Drafting Committee, under the Chairmanship of Dr. Ambedkar, embodied the decision of the Assembly with alternative and additional proposals in the form of a 'Draft Constitution of India which was published in February, 1948. The Constituent Assembly next met in November, 1948, to consider the provisions of the Draft, clause by clause. After several sessions the consideration of the clauses or second reading was completed by the 17th October, 1949. The Constituent Assembly again sat on the 14th November, 1949, for the third reading and finished it on the 26th November, 1949, on which date the Constitution received the signature of the President of the Assembly and was declared as passed. The provisions relating to citizenship, elections, provisional Parliament, temporary and transitional provisions, were given immediate effect, i.e., from November 26, 1949. The rest of the Constitution came into force on the 26th January, 1950, and this date is referred to in the Constitution as the Date of its Commencement.

Preamble: WE, THE PEOPLE OF INDIA, having solemnly resolved to constitute India into a SOVEREIGN SOCIALIST SECULAR DEMOCRATIC REPUBLIC...

Fundamental Rights: Indian Government have provided six basic rights to every citizen India. So, as to provide a democratic environment for the peopel of India to live in. Here, we are describing each fundamental right in detail to help you in understanding our constitution.

Fundamental Duties: These Fundamental rights have been provided at the cost of some fundamental duties. These are considered as the duties that must be and should be performed by every citizen of India.

Official And Regional Languages of India: Subject to the provisions of articles 346 and 347, the Legislature of a State may by law adopt any one or more of the languages in use in the State or Hindi as the language or languages to be used for all or any of the official purposes...

Preamble of India

WE, THE PEOPLE OF INDIA, having solemnly resolved to constitute India into a SOVEREIGN SOCIALIST SECULAR DEMOCRATIC REPUBLIC and to secure to all its citizens:

JUSTICE, social, economic and political;

LIBERTY of thought, expression, belief, faith and worship;

EQUALITY of status and of opportunity;

and to promote among them all

FRATERNITY assuring the dignity of the individual and the unity and integrity of the Nation;

IN OUR CONSTITUENT ASSEMBLY this twenty-sixth day of November, 1949, do HEREBY ADOPT, ENACT AND GIVE TO OURSELVES THIS CONSTITUTION.

Purpose of Having a Preamble: The Preamble to our Constitution serves two purposes:-

A) It indicates the source from which the Constitution derives its authority;

B) It also states the objects, which the Constitution seeks to establish and promote.

The Preamble seeks to establish what Mahatma Gandhi described as The India of my Dreams, "...an India in which the poorest shall feel that it is their country in whose making they have an effective voice; ...an India in which all communities shall leave I perfect harmony. There can be no room in such an India for the curse of untouchability or the curse of Intoxicating drinks and drugs. Woman will enjoy as the same rights as man."

Fundamental Rights

The Fundamental Rights embodied in the Indian Constitution acts as a guarante that all Indian citizens can and will lead their lifes in peace as long as they live in Indian democracy. These civil liberties take precedence over any other law of the land. They include individual rights common to most liberal democracies, such as equality before the law, freedom of speech and expression, freedom of association and peaceful assembly, freedom of religion, and the right to constitutional remedies for the protection of civil rights such as habeas corpus.

In addition, the Fundamental Rights for Indians are aimed at overturning the inequities of past social practices. They have also been used to in sucessfully abolishing the "untouchability"; prohibit discrimination on the grounds of religion, race, caste, sex, or place of birth; and forbid trafficking in human beings and also the forced labor. They go beyond conventional civil liberties in protecting cultural and educational rights of minorities by ensuring that minorities may preserve their distinctive languages and establish and administer their own education institutions.

Originally, the right to property was also included in the Fundamental Rights; however, the Forty-fourth Amendment, passed in 1978, revised the status of property rights by stating that "No person shall be deprived of his property save by authority of law." Freedom of speech and expression, generally interpreted to include freedom of the press, can be limited "in the interests of the sovereignty and integrity of India, the security of the State, friendly relations with foreign States, public order, decency or morality, or in relation to contempt of court, defamation or incitement to an offence"

Here we have defined the six fundamental rights as per the Constitution of India:-

1. Right to Equality
2. Right to Particular Freedom
3. Cultural and Educational Rights
4. Right to Freedom of Religion
5. Right Against Exploitation and
6. Right to Constitutional Remedies

The Right to Equality

The right to equality is one of the six rights that have been granted to us. In the Indian Constitution this right have been described as:

The State shall not discriminate against any citizen on grounds only of religion, race, caste, sex, place of birth or any of them.

No citizen shall, on grounds only of religion, race, caste, sex, place of birth or any of them, be subject to any disability, liability, restriction or condition with regard to access to shops, public restaurants, hotels and places of public entertainment; or the use of wells, tanks, bathing ghats, roads and places of public resort maintained wholly or partly out of State funds or dedicated to the use of the general public.

Nothing in this article shall prevent the State from making any special provision for women and children.

Nothing in this article or in clause (2) of article 29 shall prevent the State from making any special provision for the advancement of any socially and educationally backward classes of citizens or for the Scheduled Castes and the Scheduled Tribes.

Equal opportunity for all: There shall be equality of opportunity for all citizens in matters relating to employment or appointment to any office under the State. No citizen shall, on grounds only of religion, race, caste, sex, descent, place of birth, residence or any of them, be ineligible for, or discriminated against in respect of, any employment or office under the State.

Nothing in this article shall prevent Parliament from making any law prescribing, in regard to a class or classes of employment or appointment to an office under the Government of, or any local or other authority within, a State or Union territory, any requirement as to residence within that State or Union territory prior to such employment or appointment.

Nothing in this article shall prevent the State from making any provision for reservation in matters of promotion to any class or classes of posts in the services under the State in favour of the Scheduled Castes and the Scheduled Tribes which, in the opinion of the State, are not adequately represented in the services under the State. Nothing in this article shall prevent the State from considering any unfilled vacancies of a year which are reserved for being filled up in that year in accordance with any provision for reservation made under clause (4) or clause (4A) as a separate class of vacancies to be filled up in any succeeding year or years and such class of vacancies shall not be considered together with the vacancies of the year in which they are being filled up for determining the ceiling of fifty per cent reservation on total number of vacancies of that year.

Nothing in this article shall affect the operation of any law which provides that the incumbent of an office in connection with the affairs of any religious or denominational institution or any member of the governing body thereof shall be a person professing a particular religion or belonging to a particular denomination.

The Right to Freedom

The right to freedom is one of the most important fundamental right that have been granted to us by the founders of Indian Constitution. This right allow every citizen of India to be free from the ancient form of slavery. This fundamental right is described in the constitution as:

All citizens shall have the right-

- To freedom of speech and expression;
- To assemble peaceably and without arms;
- To form associations or unions;
- To move freely throughout the territory of India;
- To reside and settle in any part of the territory of India;
- to practise any profession, or to carry on any occupation, trade or business.

Nothing in sub-clause (a) of clause (1) shall affect the operation of any existing law, or prevent the State from making any law, in so far as such law imposes reasonable restrictions on the exercise of the right conferred by the said sub-clause in the interests of [the sovereignty and integrity of India,] the security of the State, friendly relations with foreign States, public order, decency or morality, or in relation to contempt of court, defamation or incitement to an offence.

Nothing in sub-clause (b) of the said clause shall affect the operation of any existing law in so far as it imposes, or prevent the State from making any law imposing, in the interests of [the sovereignty and integrity of India or] public order, reasonable restrictions on the exercise of the right conferred by the said sub-clause.

Nothing in sub-clause (c) of the said clause shall affect the operation of any existing law in so far as it imposes, or prevent the State from making any law imposing, in the interests of _16[the sovereignty and integrity of India or] public order or morality, reasonable restrictions on the exercise of the right conferred by the said sub-clause.

Nothing in [sub-clauses (d) and (e)] of the said clause shall affect the operation of any existing law in so far as it imposes, or prevent the State from making any law imposing, reasonable restrictions on the exercise of any of the rights conferred by the said sub-clauses either in the interests of the general public or for the protection of the interests of any Scheduled Tribe.

Nothing in sub-clause (g) of the said clause shall affect the operation of any existing law in so far as it imposes, or prevent the State from making any law imposing, in the interests of the general public, reasonable restrictions on the exercise of the right conferred by the said sub-clause, and, in particular, [nothing in the said sub-clause shall affect the operation of any existing law in so far as it relates to, or prevent the State from making any law relating to,- the professional or technical qualifications necessary for practising any profession or carrying on any occupation, trade or business, or the carrying on by the State, or by a corporation owned or controlled by the State, of any trade, business, industry or service, whether to the exclusion, complete or partial, of citizens or otherwise.

The Cultural and Educational Rights

The Cultural and Educational Rights is one of the six fundamental right that have been granted to us in the Indian Constitution. This right allow every citizen of India to have a cultural and education upto where that person wants. This fundamental right is described in the constitution as:

Any section of the citizens residing in the territory of India or any part there of having a distinct language, script or culture of its own shall have the right to conserve the same.

No citizen shall be denied admission into any educational institution maintained by the State or receiving aid out of State funds on grounds only of religion, race, caste, language or any of them. All minorities, whether based on religion or language, shall have the right to establish and administer educational institutions of their choice.

In making any law providing for the compulsory acquisition of any property of any educational institution established and administered by a minority, referred to in clause (1), the State shall ensure that the amount fixed by or determined under such law for the acquisition of such property is such as would not restrict or abrogate the right guaranteed under that clause.

The State shall not, in granting aid to educational institutions, discriminate against any educational institution on the ground that it is under the management of a minority, whether based on religion or language.

The Right to Freedom of Religion

The right to freedom of religion allows Indian citizens to choose any religion that he / she wants to choose. This fundamental right was chossen after lot of thought regarding the process of person chossing his / her own religion. This fundamental right is described in the constitution as:

The right to freedom of religion is a fundamental right guaranteed under Article 25 of the Constitution of India. Article 25 reads as follows:-

Article 25. (1). Subject to public order, morality and health and to the other provisions of this Part, all persons are equally entitled to freedom of conscience and the right freely to profess, practise and propagate religion.

Article 25. (2). Nothing in this article shall affect the operation of any existing law or prevent the State from making any law:-

(a) Regulating or restricting any economic financial political or other secular activity which may be associated with religious practice;

(b) Providing for social welfare and reform or the throwing open of Hindu religious institutions of a public character to all classes and sections of Hindus.

This Article guarantees that every person in India shall have the freedom of conscience and shall have the right to profess, practise and propagate religion, subject to the restrictions that may be imposed by the State on the following grounds, namely:-

(1) Public order, morality and health;

(2) Other provisions of the Constitution;

(3) Regulation of non-religious activity associated with religious practise;

(4) Social welfare and reform;

(5) Throwing open of Hindu religious institutions of a public character to all classes of Hindus.

The Right Against Exploitation

The right against exploitation allows Indian citizens to stand up against any kind of exploitation that he/ she might be going through. This fundamental right is described in the constitution as:

Article 23. Prohibition of traffic in human beings and forced labour.-

(1) Traffic in human beings and begar and other similar forms of forced labour are prohibited and any contravention of this provision shall be an offence punishable in accordance with law.

(2) Nothing in this article shall prevent the State from imposing compulsory service for public purposes, and in imposing such service the State shall not make any discrimination on grounds only of religion, race, caste or class or any of them.

Article 24. Prohibition of employment of children in factories, etc.- No child below the age of fourteen years shall be employed to work in any factory or mine or engaged in any other hazardous employment.

The Right to Constitutional Remedies

The right to constitutional remedies allows Indian citizens to stand up for their rights against anybody even the government of India. This fundamental right is described in the constitution as:

Article 32. Remedies for enforcement of rights conferred by this Part.-

(1) The right to move the Supreme Court by appropriate proceedings for the enforcement of the rights conferred by this Part is guaranteed.

(2) The Supreme Court shall have power to issue directions or orders or writs, including writs in the nature of habeas corpus, mandamus, prohibition, quo warranto and certiorari, whichever may be appropriate, for the enforcement of any of the rights conferred by this Part.

(3) Without prejudice to the powers conferred on the Supreme Court by clauses (1) and (2), Parliament may by law empower any other court to exercise within the local limits of its jurisdiction all or any of the powers exercisable by the Supreme Court under clause (2).

(4) The right guaranteed by this article shall not be suspended except as otherwise provided for by this Constitution.

Article 33. Power of Parliament to modify the rights conferred by this Part in their application to Forces, etc.- Parliament may, by law, determine to what extent any of the rights conferred by this Part shall, in their application to:-

(a) The members of the Armed Forces; or

(b) The members of the Forces charged with the maintenance of public order; or

(c) Persons employed in any bureau or other organisation established by the State for purposes of intelligence or counter intelligence; or

(d) Persons employed in, or in connection with, the telecommunication systems set up for the purposes of any Force, bureau or organisation referred to in clauses (a) to (c), be restricted or abrogated so as to ensure the proper discharge of their duties and the maintenance of discipline among them.

Article 34. Restriction on rights conferred by this Part while martial law is in force in any area.- Notwithstanding anything in the foregoing provisions of this Part, Parliament may by law indemnify any person in the service of the Union or of a State or any other person in respect of any act done by him in connection with the maintenance or restoration of order in any area within the territory of India where martial law was in force or validate any sentence passed, punishment inflicted, forfeiture ordered or other act done under martial law in such area.

Article 35. Legislation to give effect to the provisions of this Part.- Notwithstanding anything in this Constitution,-

(a) Parliament shall have, and the Legislature of a State shall not have, power to make laws-

(i) with respect to any of the matters which under clause (3) of article 16, clause (3) of article 32, article 33 and article 34 may be provided for by law made by Parliament; and

(ii) for prescribing punishment for those acts which are declared to be offences under this Part; and Parliament shall, as soon as may be after the commencement of this Constitution, make laws for prescribing punishment for the acts referred to in sub-clause (ii)

(b) any law in force immediately before the commencement of this Constitution in the territory of India with respect to any of the matters referred to in sub-clause (i) of clause (a) or providing for punishment for any act referred to in sub-clause (ii) of that clause shall, subject to the terms thereof and to any adaptations and modifications that may be made therein under article 372, continue in force until altered or repealed or amended by Parliament.

Fundamental Duties

These Fundamental rights have been provided at the cost of some fundamental duties. These are considered as the duties that must be and should be performed by every citizen of India. These fundamental duties are defined as:

It shall be the duty of every citizens of India:-

- To abide by the Constitution and respect its ideals and institutions, the National Flag and the National Anthem;
- To cherish and follow the noble ideals which inspired our national struggle for freedom;
- To uphold and protect the sovereignty, unity and integrity of India;
- To defend the country and render national service when called upon to do so;
- To promote harmony and the spirit of common brotherhood amongst all the people of India transcending religious, linguistic and regional or sectional diversities; to renounce practices derogatory to the dignity of women;
- To value and preserve the rich heritage of our composite culture;
- To protect and improve the natural environment including forests, lakes, rivers and wild life, and to have compassion for living creatures;
- To develop the scientific temper, humanism and the spirit of inquiry and reform;
- To safeguard public property and to abjure violence;
- To strive towards excellence in all spheres of individual and collective activity so that the nation constantly rises to higher levels of endeavour and achievement.

Official Language of the Union

The part that describes the official language of the Indian democracy have to be written to promote a feeling of unity among Indian citizens. As we know that even today anywhere between 300 to 1,000 languages are spoken in India, this makes an integral part of the Indian constitution. The official language of India shall be Hindi in Devanagari script. The form of numerals to be used for the official purposes of the Union shall be the international form of Indian numerals.

Notwithstanding anything in clause (1), for a period of fifteen years from the commencement of this Constitution, the English language shall continue to be used for all the official purposes of the Union for which it was being used immediately before such commencement: Provided that the President may, during the said period, by order authorise the use of the Hindi language in addition to the English language and of the Devanagari form of numerals in addition to the international form of Indian numerals for any of the official purposes of the Union.

Notwithstanding anything in this article, Parliament may by law provide for the use, after the said period of fifteen years, of-

The English language, or

The Devanagari form of numerals, for such purposes as may be specified in the law.

Regional Languages: Article 345. Official language or languages of a State:-

Subject to the provisions of articles 346 and 347, the Legislature of a State may by law adopt any one or more of the languages in use in the State or Hindi as the language or languages to be used for all or any of the official purposes of that State:

Provided that, until the Legislature of the State otherwise provides by law, the English language shall continue to be used for those official purposes within the State for which it was being used immediately before the commencement of this Constitution.

Article 346. Official language for communication between one State and another or between a State and the Union:-

The language for the time being authorised for use in the Union for official purposes shall be the official language for communication between one State and another State and between a State and the Union: Provided that if two or more States agree that the Hindi language should be the official language for

communication between such States, that language may be used for such communication.

Article 347. Special provision relating to language spoken by a section of the population of a State:-

On a demand being made in that behalf the President may, if he is satisfied that a substantial proportion of the population of a State desire the use of any language spoken by them to be recognised by that State, direct that such language shall also be officially recognised throughout that State or any part thereof for such purpose as he may specify.

Special Directives:-

Article 350. Language to be used in representations for redress of grievances:-

Every person shall be entitled to submit a representation for the redress of any grievance to any officer or authority of the Union or a State in any of the languages used in the Union or in the State, as the case may be.

Article 350A. Facilities for instruction in mother-tongue at primary stage:-

It shall be the endeavour of every State and of every local authority within the State to provide adequate facilities for instruction in the mother-tongue at the primary stage of education to children belonging to linguistic minority groups; and the President may issue such directions to any State as he considers necessary or proper for securing the provision of such facilities.

Article 350B. Special Officer for linguistic minorities:-

There shall be a Special Officer for linguistic minorities to be appointed by the President. It shall be the duty of the Special Officer to investigate all matters relating to the safeguards provided for linguistic minorities under this Constitution and report to the President upon those matters at such intervals as the President may direct, and the President shall cause all such reports to be laid before each House of Parliament, and sent to the Governments of the States concerned.

Article 351. Directive for development of the Hindi language:-

It shall be the duty of the Union to promote the spread of the Hindi language, to develop it so that it may serve as a medium of expression for all the elements of the composite culture of India and to secure its enrichment by assimilating without interfering with its genius, the forms, style and expressions used in Hindustani and in the other languages of India specified in the Eighth Schedule, and by drawing, wherever necessary or desirable, for its vocabulary, primarily on Sanskrit and secondarily on other languages.

Directive Principles for the Establishment of the Welfare State

Part IV (Article 36-51) of the Constitution contains the directive principles of state policy. The principles reflect a unique mixture of humanitarian, socialist percepts, Gandhian ideals and democratic socialism. Though non-justiciable, they constitute the fundamental principles of governance. These directives are in nature of directions to the legislative and executive wings of government to be observed while formulating laws and policies. Most of them aim at the establishment of economic and social democracy which is pledged for in the preamble.

Our Constitution aims at bringing a synthesis between fundamental rights and directive principles between fundamental rights and directive principles of state by giving the former a pride of place and the later a place of permanence.together, not individually, they form the case and conscience of constitution

So, these principles may be classified under several groups: (i) certain ideals, particularly economic which according to the farmers of the constitution, state should strive for; (ii) certain directions to the legislature and the executive intended to show in what manner the state should exercise their legislative and executive powers and (iii) certain rights of the citizens which shall not be enforceable by the courts like the Fundamental Rights; but which the state shall nevertheless aim at securing, by regulation of its legislative and administrative policy.

By the 42nd amendments, certain changes have been introduced in part IV, adding new directives to accentuate the socialistic bias of the Constitution:

(a) Article 39 A has been inserted to enjoin the state to provide 'free legal aid' to the poor and to take other suitable steps to ensure equal justice of all, which is offered by the Preamble.

(b) Article 43 A has been inserted in order to direct the state to ensure the participation of workers in the management of industry and other undertakings. This is a positive step in advancement of socialism in the sense of economic justice.

(c) Article 48 A has been inserted in order to direct the state to protect and improve the environment and to safeguard the forests and wild life of the country.

The Janata Government sought to implement the promise of economic justice and equality of opportunity assured by the preamble, by inserting Section (2) in Article 38 (by the 44th Amendment Act, 1978) as follows:

"The state shall, in particular, strive to minimize the inequalities in income, and endeavour to eliminate inequalities in status, facilities and opportunities, not only amongst individuals but also amongst groups of people residing in different areas or engaged in different vocations."

This amendment is to be read along with the elimination of the Fundamental Right to Property. They have paved the way for confiscatory taxation and for equalizing salaries and wages for different vocations and different vocations and different categories of work, which would usher in a socialist society, even without resorting to nationalization of the mean of production.

Philosophical Bases of Directive Principles

The framers of the Constitution were in this respect influenced most by the Constitution of Irish Republic which embodies a chapter on "Directive Principles of State Policy". The Irish themselves had, however, taken the idea from the Constitution of Republican Spain which was the first ever to incorporate such principles can be traced back to such noble declarations as French declaration regarding Rights of Men, American Declaration of

Independence and the Charter of Liberal Philosophy of the 19th Century. The ideas of Jeremy Benthan, the political and social stand of the of the Liberal and Radical Parties of Western Europe, the major principles of Fabian Socialism, and to some extent those of Guild Socialism, are all akin to much of what is embodied in this part of the Constitution. The Directive Principles represent some what the pattern of instrument of instruction provided in the Government of India Act, 1935. At the same time, it will be wrong to say that the Directive Principles are all foreign borrowings. In fact, a number of these principles are entirely Indian and Gandhian in nature like setting up of village panchayat and cottage industries, prohibition, protection against cow-slaughter etc.

Classification of Directive Principles

In order to understand the comprehensiveness of the Directive Principles, it is convenient to classify them into related groups. Dr. M.P. Sharma has suggested that they can be grouped ideologically into three categories, viz., socialistic, Gandhian and liberal intellectualistic. We may classify them into following groups:

Social and Economic Justice

(a) Social order based on Justice: Article 38 (1) provides that the state shall strive to promote the welfare of the people by securing and protecting a social order based on social, economic and political justice.

Article 38 (2) further elaborated the state's duty inserted by the 44th Amendment. It provides that the state shall strive to minimize inequalities in income and endeavour to eliminate other inequalities based on status, facilities and opportunities.

(b) Distributive Justice: Distrbutive justice is the common aim of Article 38 and 39. They propose to promote equality in wider import and create circumstances to avoid injustice at the social and economic levels.

Article 39 directs the states to secure the equal right of men and women to adequate means of livelihood; distribution of the ownership and control of the material resources of the community to the common good; that the economic system does not result in the concentration of wealth and means of production; equal pay for equal work; protection of the health or workers and children and ensure that the citizens are not forced by economic necessity to enter vocations unsuited to them; and that the children and youth are protected against exploitation and against moral and material abandonment.

Ideals of Social Security

(a) Right to work, to education and public assistance in certain cases (article 41). Recently the Supreme Court declared, in Mohini Jain's Case that the right to education be equated with a fundamental right and it should be read with Article 22. This is because the right to life means a dignified life, which has no meaning without education.

(b) Free and compulsory education for children upto 14 years. (Article 45)

(c) Promotion of educational and economic interests of the weaker sections. (Article 46)

(d) Raising the standard of living and improvement of health. (Article 47)

(e) Equal justice and free legal aid. (Article 39 A).

(f) Just and human conditions of work. (Article 42)

(g) Living wage, etc. for workers in the management of industries. (Article 32(a).

Indian Polity

(3) Community Welfare ideals.

(a) Uniform Civil Code. (Article 33).

(b) Organization of agriculture and animal husbandry. (Article 48)

(c) Protection and improvement of forests and animal life. (Article 48).

(d) Protection of monuments and places and objects of national importance. (Article 49).

(e) Separation of judiciary from executive. (Article 50)

(f) Promotion of international peace and security. (Article 51)

(g) Organisation of village Panchayats. (Article 40)

Directives Contained in Other Parts

Besides the directives contained in Part IV, there are certain other directives addressed to the state in other part of the Constitution. Those directives are also non-judicial. There are:

1. Article 350 A enjoins every state and every local authority within the state to provide adequate facilities for instruction in the mother tongue at the belonging to linguistic minority groups.
2. Article 351 enjoins the union to promote the spread of the Hindi language and to develop it so that it may serve as a medium of expression of all the elements of the composite culture of India.
3. Article 335 enjoins that the claims of the members of the Scheduled Castes and Scheduled Tribes shall be taken into consideration, consistently with the maintenance of efficiency of administration, in the making of appointments to services and posts in connection with the affairs of the union or a state.

Though the Directives contained in Article 335, 305A and 351 are not included in Part IV, courts have given similar attention to them on the application of the principle, that all part of the Constitution should be read together.

Fundamental Rights Vs Directive Principles

The preamble, the Directive Principles and the Fundamental Rights constitute the more important features of our Constitution. The Directive Principals of the State Policy enshrined in Part IV and the Fundamental Rights, guaranteed in Part III of the Constitution.

Although Fundamental Rights and Directive Principles appear in the Constitution as district entities, it was the Assembly that separate them; the leaders of the freedom struggle had drawn no distinction between the positive and negative obligations of the states. Both types of rights had developed as a common demand, products of national and social revolutions, of their almost inseparable intertwining and of the character of Indian polity itself.

The directive principles, though fundamental in the governance of the country, are not enforceable by any court in terms of the express provisions of Article 37 of the Constitution, while fundamental rights are enforceable by the Supreme Court and the High Court in terms of the express provisions of Article 32 and 226 of the Constitution. This doest not, however, mean or imply any dichotomy between the two. It social aspect can, however, be amended only by legislation to carry out the objectives of the directive principles of state policy.

The directives differ from the fundamental rights in Part III of the Constitution or the ordinary laws of the land, the following ways:

1. While the fundamental rights constitute limitations upon state action, the directive principles are in the nature of instruments of instruction to the government of the day to do certain tings and to achieve certain ends by their actions.
2. Fundamental rights are justiciable, but the directive principles are non-justiciable.
3. The directives, however, require to be implanted by legislation, and so long as there is no law carrying out the policy laid down in a Directives, neither the state nor individual can violate any existing law or legal right under colour of following a Directives.
4. The fundamental rights lay down the negative obligation of the state. They are prohibitive in character and are, in fact, in the nature of injunctions requiring the state not to do certain things. Directive principles are, on the contrary, affirmative directions dealing with the positive obligations of the state towards the citizens, they declare the duty of the state to promote certain social and economic objectives.
5. The main objective of fundamental rights is to establish

political democracy, by guaranteeing equality, liberty, religious freedom and cultural rights but the aim of directive principles of state policy is to establish just social, economic and political order. MV, Pylee has rightly observed:

6. The fundamental rights are negative in negative in character, the government, the directive principles are positive as they ask the stale to endeavour to achieve certain goals.
7. Directives are implemented by the legislation sought from the legislative list contained in 7th Schedule of the Constitution. Fundamental rights are incorporated in the Constitution and are within jurisdiction of an individual.
8. The court cannot compel the state to implement the directives. They can issue writs to enforce the fundamental rights.
9. The court cannot declare any law as void on the ground that it contravenes the directives.

In the state of Madras vs Chnmpakan (1951), the Supreme Court highlighted the non-enforceable nature of the Directive Principles. It declared that no law could void on the ground of cont ravening the directive principles. However, the 25th Amendment Act (1971) introduced Article 3IC'. Which was to protect a law seeking to implement a directive under 39 (b)-(c) (ownership and control on material resources for common good; to avoid common fraction of wealth) from being declare ultra vires on the ground of contravening. The Keshvananda Bharti Case (1973) upheld the validity of the 25th Amendment Act.

The 42nd Amendment Act (1976) (Section 4) tried to further expand the scope of the directive principles through change in Article 31 A's operation. It sought to protect any laws implanting any of the directive principles from judicial review on ground of violating Article 14 and 19. However, the Minarva Mills Case (1930) foiled the attempt to accord primacy to the directives over fundamental rights. It declared the expansion of 31C as ultra vires as it tried to change the basic structure of the Constitution. The scope of Article 31C was pushed back to the pre-1976 position. The Court added 197, position. The Court added the 'reasonableness' clause to enable any Act under 31C to implement Directive Principles 39 (b)-(c), (c f. State of Tamil Nadu Vs Abu Kavur (198.1), Sec, 515).

Relative Importance

During the first sixteen years of the operation of the Constitution, the directive principles were considered subordinate to the fundamental rights: the courts track down a number of laws enacted to implement directive principles on the ground that they violated the fundamental rights. The conflict has its root in the fact that fundamental rights are enforceable by the courts, while the directive principles are not so. However, the government tried to overcome the problem by amending the Constitution. When the Supreme Court laid down in the Golaknath Case that the fundamental rights cannot be abridged to implement the directive principles, the Government tried to overcome the limitation in 1971 through the 24th Amendment which gave Parliament the right to amend fundaments rights. In the same year, the 25th Amendment Act inserted Article 31c ensuring that certain laws meant to implement Directives in clauses 39 (b) and 39 (c) will prevail even if these laws violate the rights granted in Article 14 and 19. An attempt to enhance the scope of Article 3IC was made by the 42nd Amendment Act which gave primacy to any or all the directive principles and deprived the courts of the right to look into such cases. This attempt was foiled by the Supreme Court majority judgement in Minerva'a Mills Case which asserted that such total exclusion of judicial review would offend the basic structure of the Constitution. The widening of Article 3k is restored to its pre-1976 position in that a law would be protected by this Article only if i1 has been made to implement any directive in Article 39 (b)-(c) and not any of the other directive principles in Part IV. In all other matters no fundamental rights can he violated by a law purporting to implement a directive principle.

On the whole, however, the conflict between these two features of the Constitution is meaningless as they are, in reality complementary to each other. The courts have increasingly based their judgment on a harmonious reading of Part III and IV of the Constitution.

Implementation of the Directive Principles

The Constitution has been amended, successively (e.g., first, fourth, seventeenth, twenty-:fifth, twenty-foruth 42nd and 44th Amendements), to modify those fundamental rights by reason of whose existence the state was experiencing difficulty in effecting agrarian, economic and social reforms which are envisaged by the directive principles. The unspectacular implementation of the directive principles is mainly on account of the resource crunch and lack of political will or foresight. Poverty eradication, education, betterment of the backward classes' condition are a few areas where the directives have practically failed to show results.

Though implementation has been far from satisfactory, the state is showing genuine will to implement the directive principles. In electoral politics, no government may, with impunity, ignore welfare-oriented policies with regard tee public health, education, economic equality, position of women, children and backward classes. In totality the directive principles operate well in the planning process, but still have not been fully translated into action. It cannot be denied that various governments have put in some efforts in this direction. The directive in Article 39 (b) has influenced legislation to fix land ceilings, remove intermediaries such as Zamindar, abolish hereditary proprietors, etc., and made the tiller of the soil real owners of the land. The enactment of the Hindu Marriage Act (1955) and the Hindu Succession Act (1950) have been important steps to implement the directives of Uniform Civil Code.

Gandhian Principles

Article 40: State shall organize village panchayat as unit of self-government.

Article 43: State shall try to promote cottage industries.

Article 46: State shall promote with special care the educational and economic interests at the weaker sections of the peoples: SC and ST.

Article 45: State shall provide compulsory primary education for the children upto 14 years.

Article 47: State shall try to secure the improvement of public health and the prohibition of intoxicating drinks and drugs.

Article 48: State shall preserve and improve the breeds and prohibit the slaughter of cows, calves and other cows and drought cattle.

Directives Inspired by Western Liberal Ideas

Article 44 : to secure a uniform civil code throughout the territory of India.

Article 45: Free compulsory and primary education for the children upto 14 years.

Article 50 : to work towards separating the judiciary from the executive.

Article 51: to promote international peace and amity, maintain honourable relations between nations, foster respect for international law and treaty obligation.

Article 49 : to-protect and maintain places of- historic or a rustic interests.

Directives Inspired by Socialistic Ideas

Article 38: To promote the welfare of the people and to secure a just social order.

Article 39: Adequate livelihood for all citizens; 1 distribution of ownership and control of material resources of the community to sub serve common good; an economic system which does not lead to concentration of wealth; equal pay for equal work for both men and women; health and strength of worker; opportunity and facilities for children to develop in a healthy manner and be protected from exploitation.

Article 41: To make effective provision for securing the right to work, right to education, right to public assistance in case of unemployment, old age,, sickness, and disability.

Article 42: Asks for provision for just and human condition of work, and for maternity relief.

Article 43: To secure all workers-agricultural, industrial or otherwise- living wages; in particular promote cottage industries.

Article 45: Free and compulsory education for children upto 14 years.

Article 40 has led to several laws for organising Village Panchayat; the 72nd Amendment Act seeks to organise the panchayati raj system with seats,Served for women; Article 43 is seen working in the formation of several boards to develop cottage industries legislation for compulsory education at primary level exists as directed by Article 45; various programmes to educate the tribal youth and promote the welfare of Scheduled Tribes and Scheduled Castes have hen up Various measures have been taken up to protect historical monuments, forests and wild life. The Mandal Commission has been declared Constitutional. The state is all set to provide reservation in government jobs to the socially and educationally backwards (SEB).

Non-enforceable Rights of Citizens

Article 39: Requires the state to direct its policy towards securing (a) adequate means of livelihood for all citizens (b) distribution of ownership of ownership and control of material resources of the community to usbserve common good (c) an economic system which does not lead to concentration of wealth (d) equal pay for equal work for both men and women (e) health and strength of workers (f) opportunities and facilities for children to develop in a healthy manner and be protected from exploitation.

Article 41: To make effective provision for securing the right to work, right to education, right to public assistance in case of unemployment, old age, sickness and disability.

Article 42: For just and human conditions of work and for maternity relief.

Article 43: To secure all workers – agricultural, industrial or otherwise lying wages; in particular promote cottage industries.

Article 45: To provide free and compulsory education (or children opts 14 years within a period of ten years from the commencement of the. Constitution

In 1971 fourteen major banks were nationalished and privy purses abolished. The Supreme Court's challenge to the legality of this slop prompted the government to include 31C by the 25th Amendment the directive principles 39 (b) (e) from being thrown out by the courts. Efforts have been made to organize agriculture along modern and scientific lines. Cow slaughter is banned in many states. A legal aid system has been established. Some states have legislated for public assistance in case of unemployment, old age and disability. However, on the whole, implementation of the legislations giving importance to directive principles has been slow and has not shown the do sued effect of removing economic, social and political injustices, nor h as the tendency or wealth being concentrated in a few, hands been retarded. Prohibition has proved a sad experience as states find themselves caught in the dilemma of practical difficulties and loss of revenue. Political parties are reluctant to agar to structural changes in the existing property relations because they do not want to hurl their vote banks.

- Part IV of the Constitution (Article 36-51) provides the Directive Principles of Stale Policy.
- The Philosophy of Directive Principles has been taken from the Constitution of Ireland.
- Dr. Ambedkar described the Directive Principles as the "instrument of instructions."
- Articles 38, 39, 41, 42, 43 and 45 are based on the socialistic ideas.
- Articles 39 (a), 43 (a), 48 (a) have been inserted by the 42nd Amendment to accentuate the socialistic bias of the Constitution.
- The Janata Government sought to implement the promise of economic justice and equality of opportunity assured by the Preamble by inserting section 2 in Article 38 by the 44th Amendment Act, 1978.
- Fundamental Right to property was eliminated by the 44th Amendment Act, which pared the way for confiscatory taxation, and for equalizing salaries and wages for different vocations and different categories of work.

- Directives are non-jusliceable.
- Directive Principles cannot override Fundamental Rights. Fundamental Rights air superior.
- Various Acts like Employers State Insurance Act. Minimum wages Act, Wealth Tax Act, Estate Duty Act etc. were passed to give effect to the Directive Principles.
- The attempt to confer a primacy upon the Directives as against the Fundamental Rights has been foiled by the majority of the Supreme Court, in the Minann Mills Case.
- For the promotion of cottage industries (Article 43) the central government has established several boards to help the state government.
- Legislation for compulsory primary education (Article 45) has been enacted in most of the states and in the Union Territories.

Fundamental Rights in India

Fundamental Rights is a charter of rights contained in the Constitution of India. It guarantees civil liberties such that all Indians can lead their lives in peace and harmony as citizens of India. These include individual rights common to most liberal democracies, such as equality before law, freedom of speech and expression, freedom of association and peaceful assembly, freedom to practice religion, and the right to constitutional remedies for the protection of civil rights by means of writs such as habeas corpus. Violations of these rights result in punishments as prescribed in the Indian Penal Code, subject to discretion of the judiciary.

The Fundamental Rights are defined as basic human freedoms which every Indian citizen has the right to enjoy for a proper and harmonious development of personality. These rights universally apply to all citizens, irrespective of race, place of birth, religion, caste, creed, colour or sex. They are enforceable by the courts, subject to certain restrictions. The Rights have their origins in many sources, including England's Bill of Rights, the United States Bill of Rights and France's Declaration of the Rights of Man.

The six fundamental rights recognised by the constitution are:

1. The right to equality
2. The right to freedom
3. The right to freedom from exploitation
4. The right to freedom of religion
5. Cultural and educational rights
6. The right to constitutional remedies.

Rights mean those freedoms which are essential for personal good as well as the good of the community. The rights guaranteed under the Constitution of India are fundamental as they have been incorporated into the "fundamental Law of the land" and are enforceable in a court of law. However, this does not mean that they are absolute or that they are immune from Constitutional amendment.

Fundamental rights for Indians have also been aimed at overturning the inequalities of pre-independence social practices. Specifically, they have also been used to abolish untouchability and hence prohibit discrimination on the grounds of religion, race, caste, sex, or place of birth. They also forbid trafficking of human beings and forced labour. They also protect cultural and educational rights of ethnic and religious minorities by allowing them to preserve their languages and also establish and administer their own education institutions.

Genesis

The development of constitutionally guaranteed fundamental human rights in India was inspired by historical examples such as England's Bill of Rights (1689), the United States Bill of Rights (approved on 17 September 1787, final ratification on 15 December 1791) and France's Declaration of the Rights of Man (created during the revolution of 1789, and ratified on 26 August 1789).

Under the educational system of British Raj, students were exposed to ideas of democracy, human rights and European political history. The Indian student community in England was further inspired by the workings of parliamentary democracy and British political parties.

In 1919, the Rowlatt Acts gave extensive powers to the British government and police, and allowed indefinite arrest and detention of individuals, warrantless searches and seizures, restrictions on public gatherings, and intensive censorship of media and publications. The public opposition to this act eventually led to mass campaigns of nonviolent civil disobedience throughout the country demanding guaranteed civil freedoms, and limitations on government power. Indians, who were seeking independence and their own government, were particularly influenced by the independence of Ireland and the development of the Irish constitution. Also, the directive principles of state policy in Irish constitution were looked upon by the people of India as an inspiration for the independent India's government to comprehensively tackle complex social and economic challenges across a vast, diverse nation and population.

In 1928, the Nehru Commission composing of representatives of Indian political parties proposed constitutional reforms for India that apart from calling for dominion status for India and elections under universal suffrage, would guarantee rights deemed fundamental, representation for religious and ethnic minorities, and limit the powers of the government. In 1931, the Indian National Congress (the largest Indian political party of the time) adopted resolutions committing itself to the defence of fundamental civil rights, as well as socioeconomic rights such as the minimum wage and the abolition of untouchability and serfdom. Committing themselves to socialism in 1936, the Congress leaders took examples from the constitution of the erstwhile USSR, which inspired the fundamental duties of citizens as a means of collective patriotic responsibility for national interests and challenges.

When India obtained Independence on 15 August 1947, the task of developing a Constitution for the nation was undertaken by the Constituent Assembly of India, composing of elected representatives under the presidency of Rajendra Prasad. While members of Congress composed of a large majority, Congress leaders appointed persons from diverse political backgrounds to responsibilities of developing the constitution and national laws. Notably, Bhimrao Ramji Ambedkar became the chairperson of the drafting committee, while Jawaharlal Nehru and Sardar Vallabhbhai Patel became chairpersons of committees and subcommittees responsible for different subjects. A notable development during that period having significant effect on the Indian constitution took place on 10 December 1948 when the United Nations General Assembly adopted the Universal Declaration of Human Rights and called upon all member states to adopt these rights in their respective constitutions.

The fundamental rights were included in the First Draft Constitution (February 1948), the Second Draft Constitution (17 October 1948) and final Third Draft Constitution (26 November 1949) prepared by the Drafting Committee.

Significance and Characteristics

The fundamental rights were included in the constitution because they were considered essential for the development of the personality of every individual and to preserve human dignity. The writers of the constitution regarded democracy of no avail if civil liberties, like freedom of speech and religion were not recognized and protected by the State. According to them, "democracy" is, in essence, a government by opinion and therefore, the means of formulating public opinion should be secured to the people of a democratic nation. For this purpose, the constitution guaranteed to all the citizens of India the freedom of speech and expression and various other freedoms in the form of the fundamental rights.

All people, irrespective of race, religion, caste or sex, have been given the right to move the Supreme Court and the High Courts for the enforcement of their fundamental rights. It is not necessary that the aggrieved party has to be the one to do so. Poverty stricken people may not have the means to do so and therefore, in the public interest, anyone can commence litigation in the court on their behalf. This is known as "Public interest litigation". In some cases, High Court judges have acted on their own on the basis of newspaper reports.

These fundamental rights help not only in protection but also the prevention of gross violations of human rights. They emphasize on the fundamental unity of India by guaranteeing to all citizens the access and use of the same facilities, irrespective of background. Some fundamental rights apply for persons of any nationality whereas others are available only to the citizens of India. The right to life and personal liberty is available to all people and so is the right to freedom of religion. On the other hand, freedoms of speech and expression and freedom to reside and settle in any part of the country are reserved to citizens alone, including nonresident Indian citizens. The right to equality in matters of public employment cannot be conferred to overseas citizens of India.

Fundamental rights primarily protect individuals from any arbitrary state actions, but some rights are enforceable against individuals. For instance, the Constitution abolishes untouchability and also prohibits *begar*. These provisions act as a check both on state action as well as the action of private individuals. However, these rights are not absolute or uncontrolled and are subject to reasonable restrictions as necessary for the protection of general welfare. They can also be selectively curtailed. The Supreme Court has ruled that all provisions of the Constitution, including fundamental rights can be amended. However, the Parliament cannot alter the basic structure of the Constitution. Features such as secularism and democracy fall under this category. Since the fundamental rights can only be altered by a constitutional amendment, their inclusion is a check not only on the executive branch, but also on the Parliament and state legislatures.

A state of national emergency has an adverse effect on these rights. Under such a state, the rights conferred by Article 19 (freedoms of speech, assembly and movement, etc.) remain suspended. Hence, in such a situation, the legislature may make laws which go against the rights given in Article 19. Also, the President may by order suspend the right to move court for the enforcement of other rights as well.

Right to Equality

Right to equality is an important right provided for in Articles 14, 15, 16, 17 and 18 of the constitution. It is the principal foundation of all other rights and liberties, and guarantees the following:

- Equality before law: Article 14 of the constitution guarantees that all citizens shall be equally protected by the laws of the country. It means that the State cannot discriminate against a citizen on the basis of caste, creed, colour, sex, religion or place of birth. According to the *Electricity Act* of 26 January 2003 the Parliament has the power to create special courts for the speedy trial of offences committed by persons holding high offices. Creation of special courts is not a violation of this right.

- Social equality and equal access to public areas: Article 15 of the constitution states that no person shall be discriminated on the basis of caste, colour, language etc. Every person shall have equal access to public places like public parks, museums, wells, bathing ghats and temples etc. However, the State may make any special provision for women and children. Special provisions may be made for the advancements of any socially or educationally backward class or scheduled castes or scheduled tribes.

- Equality in matters of public employment: Article 16 of the constitution lays down that the State cannot discriminate against anyone in the matters of employment. All citizens can apply for government jobs. There are some exceptions. The Parliament may enact a law stating that certain jobs can only be filled by applicants who are domiciled in the area. This may be meant for posts that require knowledge of the locality and language of the area. The State may also reserve posts for members of backward classes, scheduled castes or scheduled tribes which are not adequately represented in the services under the State to bring up the weaker sections of the society. Also, there a law may be passed which requires that the holder of an office of any religious institution shall also be a person professing that *particular religion. According to the Citizenship* (Amendment) Bill, 2003, this right shall not be conferred to Overseas citizens of India.

- Abolition of untouchability: Article 17 of the constitution abolishes the practice of untouchability. Practice of untouchability is an offence and anyone doing so is punishable by law. The *Untouchability Offences Act* of 1955 (renamed to *Protection of Civil Rights Act* in 1976) provided penalties for preventing a person from entering a place of worship or from taking water from a tank or well.

- Abolition of Titles: Article 18 of the constitution prohibits the State from conferring any titles. Citizens of India cannot accept titles from a foreign State. The British government *had created an aristocratic class known as Rai Bahadurs* and *Khan Bahadurs* in India — these titles were also abolished. However, Military and academic distinctions can be conferred on the citizens of India. The awards of *Bharat Ratna* and *Padma Vibhushan* cannot be used by the recipient as a title and do not, accordingly, come within the constitutional prohibition". The Supreme Court, on 15 December 1995, upheld the validity of such awards.

Right to Freedom

The Constitution of India contains the right to freedom, given in articles 19, 20, 21 and 22, with the view of guaranteeing individual rights that were considered vital by the framers of the constitution. The right to freedom in Article 19 guarantees the following six freedoms:

- Freedom of speech and expression, which enable an individual to participate in public activities. The phrase, "freedom of press" has not been used in Article 19, but freedom of expression includes freedom of press. Reasonable restrictions can be imposed in the interest of public order, security of State, decency or morality.
- Freedom to assemble peacefully without arms, on which the State can impose reasonable restrictions in the interest of public order and the sovereignty and integrity of India.
- Freedom to form associations or unions on which the State can impose reasonable restrictions on this freedom in the interest of public order, morality and the sovereignty and integrity of India.
- Freedom to move freely throughout the territory of India though reasonable restrictions can be imposed on this

right in the interest of the general public, for example, restrictions may be imposed on movement and travelling, so as to control epidemics.

- Freedom to reside and settle in any part of the territory of India which is also subject to reasonable restrictions by the State in the interest of the general public or for the protection of the scheduled tribes because certain safeguards as are envisaged here seem to be justified to protect indigenous and tribal peoples from exploitation and coercion. Article 370 restricts citizens from other Indian states and Kashmiri women who marry men from other states from purchasing land or property in Jammu & Kashmir.
- Freedom to practice any profession or to carry on any occupation, trade or business on which the State may impose reasonable restrictions in the interest of the general public. Thus, there is no right to carry on a business which is dangerous or immoral. Also, professional or technical qualifications may be prescribed for practicing any profession or carrying on any trade.

The constitution also guarantees the right to life and personal liberty, which in turn cites specific provisions in which these rights are applied and enforced:

- Protection with respect to conviction for offences is guaranteed in the right to life and personal liberty. According to Article 20, no one can be awarded punishment which is more than what the law of the land prescribes at that time. This legal axiom is based on the principle that no criminal law can be made retrospective, that is, for an act to become an offence, the essential condition is that it should have been an offence legally at the time of committing it. Moreover, no person accused of any offence shall be compelled to be a witness against himself. "Compulsion" in this article refers to what in law is called "Duress" (injury, beating or unlawful imprisonment to make a person do something that he does not want to do). This article is known as a safeguard against self incrimination. The other principle enshrined in this article is known as the principle of double jeopardy, that is, no person can be convicted twice for the same offence, which has been derived from Anglo Saxon law. This principle was first established in the Magna Carta.

- Protection of life and personal liberty is also stated under right to life and personal liberty. Article 21 declares that no citizen can be denied his life and liberty except by law. This means that a person's life and personal liberty can only be disputed if that person has committed a crime. However, the right to life does not include the right to die, and hence, suicide or an attempt thereof, is an offence. (Attempted suicide being interpreted as a crime has seen many debates. The Supreme Court of India gave a landmark ruling in the year 1994. The court repealed section 309 of the Indian penal code, under which people attempting suicide could face prosecution and prison terms of up to one year. In the year 1996 however another Supreme Court ruling nullified the earlier one.) "Personal liberty" includes all the freedoms which are not included in Article 19 (that is, the six freedoms). The right to travel abroad is also covered under "personal liberty" in Article 21.
- In 2002, through the 86th Amendment Act, Article 21(A) was incorporated. It made the right to primary education part of the right to freedom, stating that the State would provide free and compulsory education to children from six to fourteen years of age. Six years after an amendment was made in the Indian Constitution, the union cabinet cleared the Right to Education Bill in 2008. It is now soon to be tabled in Parliament for approval before it makes a fundamental right of every child to get free and compulsory education.
- Rights of a person arrested under ordinary circumstances is laid down in the right to life and personal liberty. No one can be arrested without being told the grounds for his arrest. If arrested, the person has the right to defend himself by a lawyer of his choice. Also an arrested citizen has to

be brought before the nearest magistrate within 24 hours. The rights of a person arrested under ordinary circumstances are not available to an enemy alien. They are also not available to persons detained under the *Preventive Detention Act*. Under preventive detention, the government can imprison a person for a maximum of three months. It means that if the government feels that a person being at liberty can be a threat to the law and order or to the unity and integrity of the nation, it can detain or arrest that person to prevent him from doing this possible harm. After three months such a case is brought before an advisory board for review.

The constitution also imposes restrictions on these rights. The government restricts these freedoms in the interest of the independence, sovereignty and integrity of India. In the interest of morality and public order, the government can also impose restrictions. However, the right to life and personal liberty cannot be suspended. The six freedoms are also automatically suspended or have restrictions imposed on them during a state of emergency.

Right against Exploitation

The right against exploitation, given in Articles 23 and 24, provides for two provisions, namely the abolition of trafficking in human beings and *Begar* (forced labor), and abolition of employment of children below the age of 14 years in dangerous jobs like factories and mines. Child labour is considered a gross violation of the spirit and provisions of the constitution. *Begar*, practised in the past by landlords, has been declared a crime and is punishable by law. Trafficking in humans for the purpose of slave trade or prostitution is also prohibited by law. An exception is made in employment without payment for compulsory services for public purposes. Compulsory military conscription is covered by this provision.

Right to Freedom of Religion

Right to freedom of religion, covered in Articles 25, 26, 27 and 28, provides religious freedom to all citizens of India. The objective of this right is to sustain the principle of secularism in India.

According to the Constitution, all religions are equal before the State and no religion shall be given preference over the other. Citizens are free to preach, practice and propagate any religion of their choice. However, certain practices like wearing and carrying of *Kirpans* in the profession of the Sikh religion, can be restricted in the interest of public order, morality and health.

Religious communities can set up charitable institutions of their own. However, activities in such institutions which are not religious are performed according to the laws laid down by the government. Establishing a charitable institution can also be restricted in the interest of public order, morality and health. No person shall be compelled to pay taxes for the promotion of a particular religion. A State run institution cannot impart education that is pro-religion. Also, nothing in this article shall affect the operation of any existing law or prevent the State from making any further law regulating or restricting any economic, financial, political or other secular activity which may be associated with religious practice, or providing for social welfare and reform.

Cultural and Educational Rights

As India is a country of many languages, religions, and cultures, the Constitution provides special measures, in Articles 29 and 30, to protect the rights of the minorities. Any community which has a language and a script of its own has the right to conserve and develop them. No citizen can be discriminated against for admission in State or State aided institutions.

All minorities, religious or linguistic, can set up their own educational institutions in order to preserve and develop their own culture. In granting aid to institutions, the State cannot discriminate against any institution on the basis of the fact that it is administered by a minority institution. But the right to administer does nct mean that the State can not interfere in case of maladministration. In a precedent-setting judgment in 1980, the Supreme Court held that "the State can certainly take regulatory measures to promote the efficiency and excellence of educational standards. It can also issue guidelines for ensuring the security of the services of the teachers or other employees of the institution.

In another landmark judgement delivered on 31 October 2002, the Supreme Court ruled that in case of aided minority institutions offering professional courses, admission could only be through a common entrance test conducted by State or a university. Even an unaided minority institution ought not to ignore the merit of the students for admission.

Right to Constitutional Remedies

Right to constitutional remedies empowers the citizens to move a court of law in case of any denial of the fundamental rights. For instance, in case of imprisonment, the citizen can ask the court to see if it is according to the provisions of the law of the country. If the court finds that it is not, the person will have to be freed. This procedure of asking the courts to preserve or safeguard the citizens' fundamental rights can be done in various ways. The courts can issue various kinds of *writs*. These writs are *habeas corpus, mandamus, prohibition, quo warranto* and *certiorari*. When a national or state emergency is declared, this right is suspended by the central government.

Critical Analysis

The fundamental rights have been criticised for many reasons. Political groups have demanded that the right to work, the right to economic assistance in case of unemployment, old age, and similar rights be enshrined as constitutional guarantees to address issues of poverty and economic insecurity, though these provisions have been enshrined in the Directive Principles of state policy. The right to freedom and personal liberty has a number of limiting clauses, and thus have been criticized for failing to check the sanctioning of powers often deemed "excessive". There is also the provision of preventive detention and suspension of fundamental rights in times of Emergency. The provisions of acts like the Maintenance of Internal Security Act (MISA) and the National Security Act (NSA) are a means of countering the fundamental rights, because they sanction excessive powers with the aim of fighting internal and cross-border terrorism and political violence, without safeguards for civil rights. The phrases "security of State", "public order" and "morality" are of wide implication. People of alternate sexuality is criminalized in India with prison term up to 10 years. The meaning of phrases like "reasonable restrictions" and "the interest of public order" have not been explicitly stated in the constitution, and this ambiguity leads to unnecessary litigation. The freedom to assemble peacably and without arms is exercised, but in some cases, these meetings are broken up by the police through the use of non-fatal methods.

"Freedom of press" has not been included in the right to freedom, which is necessary for formulating public opinion and to make freedom of expression more legitimate. Employment of child labour in hazardous job environments has been reduced, but their employment even in nonhazardous jobs, including their prevalent employment as domestic help violates the spirit and ideals of the constitution. More than 16.5 million children are employed and working in India. India was ranked 88 out of 159 in 2005, according to the degree to which corruption is perceived to exist among public officials and politicians worldwide. The right to equality in matters regarding public employment shall not be conferred to Overseas citizens of India, according to the *Citizenship (Amendment) Bill*, 2003.

Amendments

Changes to the fundamental rights require a constitutional amendment which has to be passed by a special majority of both houses of Parliament. This means that an amendment requires the approval of two-thirds of the members present and voting. However, the number of members voting should not be less than the simple majority of the house — whether the Lok Sabha or Rajya Sabha.

The right to education at elementary level has been made one of the fundamental rights under the Eighty-Sixth Amendment of 2002.

Right to Property

The Constitution originally provided for the right to property under Articles 19 and 31. Article 19 guaranteed to all citizens the right to acquire, hold and dispose off property. Article 31 provided that "no person shall be deprived of his property save by authority of law." It also provided that compensation would be paid to a person whose property has been taken for public purposes.

The provisions relating to the right to property were changed a number of times. The Forty-Forth Amendment of 1978 deleted the right to property from the list of fundamental rights A new provision, Article 300-A, was added to the constitution which provided that "no person shall be deprived of his property save by authority of law". Thus if a legislature makes a law depriving a person of his property, there would be no obligation on the part of the State to pay anything as compensation. The aggrieved person shall have no right to move the court under Article 32. Thus, the right to property is no longer a fundamental right, though it is still a constitutional right. If the government appears to have acted unfairly, the action can be challenged in a court of law by citizens.

The liberalisation of the economy and the government's initiative to set up special economic zones has led to many protests by farmers and have led to calls for the reinstatement of the fundamental right to private property. The Supreme Court has sent a notice to the government questioning why the right should not be brought back as in 2007 the supreme court unanimously said that the fundamental rights are a basic structure of the constitution and cannot be removed or diluted.

Nature of Indian State

To study the nature of any particular state, it is necessary to analyse to relation between state, power, and social classes and the purpose of the state. The reason being, modern states are generally divided into two broad forms. – liberal democratic form and totalitarian form, while the former stands on the foundation of democracy, the later is anti – thesis of the formal where power lies at the hand of few.

The other view, which also has to be analysed is the Marxists view, which analyses the state as an instrument of class.

In Studying Indian state, therefore we have to analyse the above mentioned aspects.

Indian State is a Liberal Democratic Form

The nature of Indian state can be studied from a liberal, Marxists, and Gandhi's view. The constitution of Indian declares it as a sovereign socialist republic democratic country.

Thus, Indian state is characterized as a liberal democratic model regarding the state which the powers lie the hands of people. Moreover India is a representative form of government, where elections are held on the basis of universal adult franchise, characterized by independent judiciary, rule of law and separations of powers.

Indian State is a Totalitarian Form

We have also analysed the relationship between the state and society. Though India has a federal system, it may be in relation to economic development or social change. It consists of a "Dominant political centre"

Though India is a welfare state, it is often characterized by interventionist nature. Thus in one hand, it gives freedom and in the other hand it takes away.

The Marxist view of Indian State

The Marxist view sees the Indian state as a bourgeois state– where the benefits are only with the big industrialists and rich farmers. Though this nature does not completely dominates the state it exercises a powerful influence over the Indian state.

Even someone says that India has no autonomy of its own. It is completely subservient to the elite class. The leaders in India are mostly from the elite group and they make a elitist state.

Form of Gandhi's State

1) Sovereign state: Gandhi would like the state to be absolutely free from foreign rule, domination or interference.
2) Federal state: Gandhi was against the concentration and centralization of political power, because is regarded power as a corrupting force. Therefore, he wanted federal and Panchayats.

3) Secular state: The state should be free from religious matters.
4) Democratic state: Gandhi's state means Government by the participation of the people. He agreed with Abraham Lincoln that a truly democratic government is a "Government of the people, by the people, for the people."

However, Gandhi's state is not an end in itself, but only means to the realization of a stateless society.

Criticism

India has a highly plural society marked by various ethnic groups of different language and different religion. After independence India has experienced difficulty to maintain its unity. But growth of violence, regionalism, poverty, slow development of economy has questioned the working of Indian state and its nature. Consequently the nature of Indian state has suffered a lot of criticism. In practice, democracy has not been able to meet the challenge of the poor and lower castes. These characters make the Indian state very oppressive in nature.

Conclusion

From the above analysis we see that the nature of Indian state has become a matter of controversy in contemporary discussions. However the agreed point is that the nature of Indian state has changed over this time.

The impact of social rule is visible in India.

Recently, faith in democratic, institution, redistributions, justice and secularism seems to be eroded in Indian state. However, the state continues to solve conflicting interest and development problem.

Thus today's India stands as a political and economic paradox of a rich – poor nation with a weak – strong state.

2

Constitutional Provisions and Institutional Functioning

Federalism

In the debate on India's national integration and ethnic tensions, the nature and functioning of the federal power structure occupies an important place. The foundations of federalism were laid down on the grounds of concern for the unity and integrity of a culturally diverse nation. In view of historical experiences of disruptive and disintegrative sectarian forces and the political context of partition prevailing at the time of independence, the founding fathers of the Indian Constitution wanted to strengthen the Union against possible disintegrative pressures. Introducing the draft Constitution in the Constituent Assembly, Dr Ambedkar said: though India was to be a federation, the federation was not the result of an agreement by the states to join in a federation. Not being a result of an agreement, no state has the right to secede from it. Though the country and the people may be divided into different states for convenience of administration, the country is one integral whole, its people a single people living under a single imperium derived from a single source... The Drafting Committee thought it was better to make [this] clear at the outset rather than leave it to speculation...

Thus the perceived basis of structuring the federation was "administrative convenience." Unlike the American and the (erstwhile) Soviet constitutions, the states had no inherent, not even notional, right to secede from the Union or demand self-determination. In fact the Union in India was empowered to frustrate any such separatist or secessionist pressures if and when they arose.

With administrative convenience the avowed guiding principle for designing the federation, not much weight was given to the need for reflecting India's cultural design. No specific provisions for religious or cultural minorities were incorporated, except that they were given equal rights. The principle of "preventive discrimination," applied in the case of scheduled castes and scheduled tribes, was designed more to undo their social and economic backwardness than to help them preserve and promote their cultural distinctiveness.

The Constitution's initial provisions and subsequent amendments provided for self-government under special administrative provisions for Jammu and Kashmir (Schedule IV, article 370) and to the tribal areas of North-East (Nagas, Mizos, Manipuri, Tripura, under articles 371 and 371A-I), but the Constituent Assembly refused to endorse proposals for constituting states on a linguistic basis. Nehru even went to the extent of threatening his resignation if that was to be done, as he apprehended that such a provision would endanger India's unity and integrity. Nehru was soon to revise his position on this vital issue under the force of circumstances when, in 1953, the linguistic basis of reorganizing states was accepted and Telugu-speaking Andhra emerged as the first such state. The Commission Constituted to Reorganise States in the Indian Federation nonetheless continued to emphasize that "it is the Union of India that is the basis of our nationality." Explaining the criterion of language as the basis for constituting a state, it said:

Linguistic homogeneity provides the only rational basis for reconstituting the state, for it reflects the social and cultural pattern of living obtaining in well-defined regions of the country. The congress leadership, including Nehru, which had earlier opposed the idea, conceded, saying that, being democrats, they had to respect people's wishes.

The process of linguistic reorganization of states initiated in 1953 has been carried forward under the recommendations of the

States Reorganisation Commission since 1956 and was broadly completed by the end of the 1960s. This was a major development toward incorporating cultural identities into political and administrative units. The federal devolution of power strengthened this expression of cultural diversity.

The devolution of powers between the Union (or the centre) and the states was laid down in separate lists prepared for this purpose. Accordingly, the list of the states' "exclusive" powers includes: public order; police; education; local government; roads and transport; agriculture; land and land revenue; forests; fisheries; industry and trade (limited); state Public Service Commissions; and Courts (except the Supreme Court). The states can also make laws along with the centre (provided the two do not clash), on subjects included in a "Concurrent List." These subjects include: criminal laws and their administration; economic and social planning; commercial and industrial monopolies; shipping and navigation on the inland waterways; drugs; ports (limited); courts and civil procedures. The arrangement for distribution of powers between the Union and the states has remained generally stable.

One of the controversial aspects of centre-state relations has been the allocation of economic resources by the Union to the states. Such allocation is carried out by the Planning Commission in the area of developmental expenditure and has led to complaint by the states that the resources provided are inadequate. The states also have their own power to raise revenues. The "Gadgil Plan," regarding financial relations between the Union and the states, was not acceptable to the Sarkaria Commission, which was appointed to review the whole gamut of centre-state relations in view of the state's growing unhappiness in this regard. The Commission reported in 1988, but successive Finance Commissions have gradually enlarged the scope of devolution of taxes to the states. (These later Commissions were appointed under articles 280-1 of the Constitution to decide the distribution of taxes between the Union and the states as well as grants-in-aid to the states out of the Consolidated Fund of India.) The Eighth Finance Commission raised the level of such tax revenues in favour of the states from 55 to 85 per cent.

Such an elaborate structure of power devolution has combined with the linguistic basis of federal unity to facilitate the management of cultural diversity in India and help mitigate pulls toward separatism and disintegration. Centre-state relations, whether based on ethnicity or otherwise, have not been peaceful or tension-free, but the competition has tended to focus on securing resources and greater power. States of diverse languages and cultures have often joined together to enhance their bargaining power. In some cases the Indian federal structure even provides for such bargaining through bodies such as the Inter-State and National Development Councils. Examples of bargaining coalitions include that of four Southern Chief Ministers joining in 1983 to negotiate with the centre. Similarly, in 1987 a conclave of nine opposition parties held near Delhi under the leadership of the Andhra Telugu Desham leader, N.T. Rama Rao, demanded the restoration of "cooperative federalism enshrined in the Constitution."

In 1992, the Sikkim Chief Minister and his regional party, the Sikkim Sangram Parishad, asked for membership in the North-East Council (of Northeast States and Tribal Areas) for this same purpose. Some scholars have described the federal system in India as one of "coalition and administration," or one with a "high degree of collaborative partnership." In addition, both at the central and state levels, a consciously followed approach to preserve and promote the cultural specificities of diverse groups has helped such groups identify with the national mainstream. All this has contributed to the secularization of ethnicity and has thus helped strengthen integrative forces.

It is interesting to note that most of the ethnic conflicts are between one given ethnic group and the Union of India, as if there were no ethnic contradictions and incompatibilities between individual groups. As noted earlier, the issues involved in such conflicts are invariably mixed with questions of sharing economic resources and decision-making power.

The functioning of federalism has nevertheless also had undesirable implications for the ethnic scene in India. The linguistic reorganization of the states gave impetus to various groups of specific cultural markers and ethnic identities to seek political expression and legitimacy. This was because ethnic identity was provided a territory under the scheme of reorganization. The importance of ethnic territory in ethnic conflict is very crucial, as can be gathered from recent developments in the Punjab and Kashmir and earlier events in Assam. In the Punjab and Kashmir conflicts, along with the transformation of identities and issues, the territorial base of ethnicity is being perfected by driving out Punjabi-speaking Hindus from the Punjab and Kashmiri-speaking Hindus from Kashmir. The potential for conflict formation along ethnic identity lines has thus been encouraged.

This potential has been further sharpened because linguistic reorganization in a vast and diverse country like India cannot be perfectly precise. On the periphery of the newly formed linguistic states, unassimilated linguistic minorities continued to exist. Then many other linguistic groups continued to remain in the larger Hindi-speaking states without being accommodated in the new political arrangement. The dissatisfactions of some of the unrecognized minority linguistic groups also continue to simmer. Such problems exist with regard to the Konkan region of Maharasthra/Goa, Nepali-speaking groups of Darjeeling, Sikkim, and Assam, and Maithili and Avadhi language groups in Bihar.

The possibility of political movements and conflict formation arising out of these problems cannot be ruled out. There are already several political parties which are ethnicity-based, and they will very willingly build their strength by exploiting the linguistic frustrations of their constituencies. The Sarkaria Commission (1988) clearly hinted at weaknesses of the linguistic reorganization of states in this respect when it said:

> Very often, the sub-national sentiment which is initially based on linguistic, religious or ethnic groupings, gains strength with a blend of economic issues, such as those relating to... economic backwardness. One of the most significant developments has been the rise of linguistic chauvinism, rearrangement of the boundaries of the States on linguistic basis... resulting in fissiparous tendencies.

In a very significant way, federalism has fuelled ethnic conflict through the use of the Union's special provisions over the states. The use of article 356, which provides for imposition of presidential rule in a state in the "event of the failure of constitutional machinery," has been the subject of considerable controversy and debate in this regard. Political use of this provision has been extensive, particularly by the Congress-ruled centre. It can be employed to dismiss the state government of an opposition party or to manipulate political advantages for a ruling party or a particularly favoured political leader. In such manipulative machinations, the centre-appointed governor has played a decisive role, bringing the status and integrity of the governorship into considerable disrepute. The victimized party and leaders have sought to project this abuse of power as an instance of suppression of the political rights of the dominant ethnic group in the given state.

This has been an important factor behind the alienation of the Punjab, Kashmir, and Assam. Nagaland, where presidential rule was imposed in April 1992, is a recent example of the alleged misuse of article 356. In reaction, Nagaland's Chief Minister Vamuzo, who was ousted, said:

The 'imperial character' of the Delhi government has manifested itself in its most perverted and brutal forms in the northeastern states. The latest act of perfidy by the Congress government has come at a time when, with the knowledge and approval of Delhi, I was engaged in an effort to persuade the underground insurgents in Nagaland to give up arms and join the political process. Obviously, such efforts were not to the liking of certain sections of the political leadership in the state who have a vested interest in a violent underground movement...

Let me, however, sound a note of warning. The entire North-East is in a state of turmoil. Frustration because of unemployment is driving the educated youth of this region to desperation. The sense of alienation due to the overbearing presence of the army is being compounded by the lack of opportunity. And the denial to the people of their right to govern themselves in accordance with the Constitution is creating situations that will ultimately convince the people of the entire Northeast, from Arunachal to Mizoram, that they have no hope of a life of peace and dignity under the present dispensation.

While the abuse of some constitutional provisions by the centre against the states has tended to alienate the states-based ethnic leadership, the creation and use of other specific provisions at the local level by the army, state governments, or police have resulted in distancing the common people from the Union. (Such provisions include the Disturbed Areas Act, the Armed Forces Special Powers Act of 1958 for the Eastern region and of 1983 for Punjab and Chandigarh, and the act relating to "Terrorist Affected Disturbed Areas.") As a consequence of their application, the social bases of ethnic conflicts have widened and deepened. The Sarkaria Commission blamed those in charge of the centre for this misuse and centralization of power in the Union, saying:

> Those in power at the centre, have been obliged to use diverse strategies and tactics which were not always sound from [a] long-term [point of view] to maintain their control over state level forces. Many a time, the actions of the centre, its discriminatory approach towards some states, its lack of understanding of local problems, its abject insensitiveness (sic) and the blatant misuse of authority vis-à-vis the states, have all distanced it from the people. This in turn has, it is believed, reversed the process of national integration...

Based on federal experience in India, it may not be out of place to assume that the structure of federalism and its inherent resilience can cope with the pressures of ethnicity and conflicts. It can even help resolve, or at least contain, some of these pressures, if the imperatives of federal devolution of power and obligations of mutual accommodation and adjustments are observed sincerely. The diffusion of Tamil militancy and separatism during the 1960s and instances of moderation of tribal insurgencies in the Northeast and Assam during the 1980s may be recalled in this regard. Against this, politically motivated distortions and manipulation of federal powers and institutions can worsen ethnic conflicts.

Punjab and Kashmir are painful illustrations of this. In the case of Punjab, if the political expediency of appeasing Haryana had not hamstrung the centre (irrespective of the party in power), the Rajiv-Longowal Agreement of 1985 would have been implemented to ease the conflict there, if not completely resolve it. The statement of the dismissed Nagaland Chief Minister Vamuzo cited earlier is also relevant here.

In an important way, federal relations have been vitiated by the breakdown of the Congress Party's dominance of the centre and the states since the 1960s and the emergence of political incompatibility and competition between the party ruling at the centre and in the various states. As these incompatibilities have grown, demands for redefining and restructuring these relations have been most pronounced, because the forum consisting of a single party in power everywhere could not be utilized to sort out federal tensions.

Reacting to distortions in federal relations and the abuse of powers devolved under the constitutional arrangement, some scholars have called for restructuring Indian federalism. That may be neither practical nor offer a real panacea, because the structure so redefined may also be misused or manipulated for political purposes. The remedy lies in the evolution and strict observance of healthy guidelines and norms in the operational aspects of federalism, which have to become a reliable instrument for containing, moderating, and resolving ethnic conflicts.

Parliamentary Constitutions with Proportional Elections

In this constitutional setting the main actors are, as we have seen, likely to be cohesive and disciplined political parties. Some of these actors or parties are furthermore likely to form an executive, and they are also likely, to rely to a considerable extent on instructions, and bundles of instructions or programs, in their efforts to get votes.

Now, when discussing the formation of an executive it is essential that the number of main actors, although they are few, most likely are more than two. Each party therefore knows that in all likelihood it will have to make deals with other parties. Thus, the main actors must adopt strategies which are instrumental in bringing them into coalitions, and in affecting the policies of those coalitions. What kind of strategies are these? What kind of matters are the parties to a coalition likely to agree about? In part 9 we concluded tentatively that the parties to a large extent will rely on instructions in their electoral strategies. This topic will finally be discussed in part 12, but assuming so far that the tentative conclusion is correct, the coalition agreements are likely to be about instructions as well. But what kind of instructions?

A first point is that specific instructions, rather than general, are likely to be particularly important in these agreements. There are two reasons for this contention. The first one is that it is easier for political parties to make deals about specific instructions than about general ones. If, for instance, one party is committed to a particular specific instruction, and another party to another one, they can easily agree about supporting each other-if you support my instruction, I support yours. General instructions, on the contrary, are often in conflict with each other and, if so, not easily reconciled. This first reason is thus related to the compatibility of various political positions as such.

The second reason, on the other hand, has to do with the acceptability for those concerned of a reconciliation. This problem, as it happens, is the subject matter of a theorem saying that a coalition executive cannot have a purely ideological foundation (Moberg, 2000). Following the terminology used here it may also be said that a reconciliation of two general instructions, even if such a reconciliation, in spite of the technical difficulties, is reached, is not likely to be accepted by the parties concerned.

But even if compromises based only on general instructions from the different parties are unlikely, there may be deals in which a general instruction of one party is knit together with a specific instruction of another party. They may agree that the first party supports the second party's specific instruction, if the second party supports, or perhaps just tolerates, the first party's general instruction.

This, however, requires that the general instruction involved is not too offensive but rather attenuated or pragmatic enough. It may also be argued that general instructions, which give a prominent and far-reaching role to the state, are more easily reconciled with specific instructions than those giving a limited role to the state. The reason is that specific instructions often are natural parts of state interventionism. From these general arguments we can now infer the following hypotheses about the parties' programs:

- Specific instructions are likely to be frequent in all parties' programs.
- All parties do not necessarily have general instructions in their programs, and when such instructions appear they are likely to be pragmatic or attenuated.

We also get these hypotheses about the executive coalitions likely to emerge, and about their governmental programs:

- A governmental program containing only specific instructions is perfectly possible.
- A small party may be committed to some general instructions, but it is not likely to get them included in a governing coalition's program.
- If a governmental program contains general instructions, and in that sense has an ideological inclination, those instructions are likely to have come directly from a big, dominating party's program. Either that party has been able to form an executive of its own, or it is the main participant in an executive involving one or a few small extra coalition members. In this latter case there may be a deal saying that the dominating party will support some specific instructions of the smaller parties, if they support, or tolerate, the dominating party's general instructions.
- Parties with articulated (in contrast to pragmatic or attenuated) and conflicting general instructions on their programs are not likely to be able to make deals about specific instructions with each other. The freedom of such parties is thus somewhat restricted.
- A party not having any general instruction in its program is completely free in choosing its partners, irrespective of their general instructions. Such a party is often able to play a pivotal role in coalition building processes. It can, for example, credibly threaten to leave, and thereby destroy, a coalition to which it presently belongs in order to join another one. Such threats can be used for enforcing

concessions from the other members of the first coalition, or from the members of the second potential coalition, and thus for giving favours to the supporters of the party itself. For operating in that way a party need not be very big-in fact a moderate size may by an advantage since the party, thereby, fits into more places and thus gets more opportunities to have its specific instructions implemented.

- A party with strongly held, articulated and controversial general instructions in its program, for example a party with an extreme ideological inclination, may affront most other parties. If so the party may be excluded from all possible coalitions, and thus from all influence.

The purpose of the negotiating parties is, as I have mentioned above, to form a durable executive. This means that, in this constitutional setting, the main actor interaction, and thereby also the real decision making, to a large extent occurs in the government formation process. After that the executive will just go on presenting its agreed upon program, bit by bit, for the legislature. The real decision making is thus a batch process rather than a continuous process. The interval between the batches may be as long as the whole election period. This obviously also means that the majorities are fairly constant over the same long time periods. There is no constant recomposition of decisive majorities. Matters may, however, turn out somewhat differently if a minority executive, rather than a majority executive, is formed. Even such an executive depends, for its existence, on the support of a majority, but that majority, by definition, will contain parties which do not belong to the executive proper, and therefore the membership of that majority may shift to some extent, for example from decision to decision in the legislature, or from time to time. This means that the decision-making will become somewhat more of a continuous process, and also that the composition of the majorities may change to some extent.

Another conclusion is that a big party may dominate the politics of its country for a long period even if it suffers occasional electoral recessions and, indeed, even if it never has a majority of its own. The party can stay in the executive all the time just by making deals about some specific instructions favored by one or two small parties, and then govern together with them. Most likely such a party continuously appoints the prime minister and the heads of a number of key ministries. This possibility for ideological influence may, in fact, be an important driving force for big parties to suppress internal divisions, or to live with them in one way or another, in order to remain big. If so we should expect to find an important ideological component in the programs of big parties like that.

We may also conclude that an organized opposition, in the form of for instance a shadow cabinet, is unlikely. The reason is that a new governing coalition, since the parties can combine in many ways, not necessarily consists exclusively of the former outsiders. Rather, some former outsiders may join some former incumbents in a new executive. In order not to jeopardize any such possibilities the present outsiders are therefore not likely to form an organized group and thereby link their destinies. For a party aiming to develop and keep a pivotal position this consideration is particularly important. Finally it may be concluded that the executive coalitions formed are likely to be minimal winning in William Riker's sense (Riker, 1962). The reason is the important roles played by interests and specific instructions in the coalition agreements. Thus, and in other words, the executive coalitions are likely to exploit their outside minorities.

Some Conditions for the System's Proper Functioning

A parliamentary system depends, for its proper functioning on cohesive, disciplined political parties. Therefore some constitutional elements or constructions, which from a logical point may seem possible are, nevertheless, destructive in real politics.

First, it is important that the proportional technique used for appointing the legislators is of a pure list character, or at least rather close to that. A system without any lists at all-such as the Finish system is hardly useful in a purely parliamentary setting. The reason, of course, is that it may be difficult for the party leaderships to maintain party discipline within such a system..

Second, it is important that the popular techniques of primaries, referendums and initiatives are not frequently used. The reason is that these techniques, as explained in part 6.6, are detrimental to party discipline. Still, and in some particular and rare cases, referendums may be used for upholding party discipline, as is also mentioned in part 6.6.

The Impossibility of a Coalition with a Purely Ideological Foundation

In previous part I said that a coalition executive cannot have a purely ideological foundation. This, in fact, is a theorem which says that it is impossible to account for the formation of the executive only in terms of a simple a left-right scale, or, in somewhat more technical terms, that it is impossible to account for the formation of the executive within the framework of the spatial model, at least in its one-dimensional version.

In the figure below we see a situation which can be used for proving the theorem. The figure represents a legislature with six political parties, P1-P6, each one with a certain position on the left-right scale and with a certain number of representatives in the assembly with altogether 300 members. Now, we may at first assume that there is no executive at all. If so the decisions taken by the legislature will be determined by the median voter theorem. This means that the decisions will become m, which is the ideological position of the party P3 and also the median position.

For proving the theorem we may compare this situation with one in which there is an executive. Clearly, if the executive is to make any difference at all, and thus to be of any interest for its members, its policy must diverge somewhat from m. We may for example think about an executive which has the policy indicated by l, and thus a leftist inclination, and which is supported by the majority composed of P2 and P3.

Now, it is easy to see that l is worse than m for P3. P3 is therefore in fact disfavored by belonging to the executive. Therefore, contrary to our assumption, P3 will not be member of the executive or support it. Our assumption that P3 belongs to the executive, since it is advantageous to do so, thus leads to a contradiction. This kind of argument is usually called a reductio ad absurdum. If it is possible to show that an assumption leads to a contradiction, then it is also fair to conclude that the assumption is unreasonable or absurd.

So far I have only dealt with the particular example in the particular figure above. Obviously we have to ask if other examples, with other possible party constellations in the legislature, also lead to contradictions for the same reasons. The answer is in the affirmative since the examples, however they are varied, will always have two crucial properties. First, the executive's policy must always diverge from m since otherwise the executive would not matter at all and, consequently, it would not be important to be a member of it. Second, since the constellation supporting the executive has to be a majority, it necessarily includes the median member of the assembly. (This, of course, presupposes that the coalition supporting the executive is connected, but departing from this assumption does hardly add anything of interest.) Thus, contrary to our assumptions, the executive will always include at least one party member for whom the membership is a unfavourable. We are thus entitled to draw the general conclusion that it is impossible to account for the formation of the executive within the framework of a simple, one-dimensional ideological model. As a contrast, it is easy to account for a coalition executive in terms of interests. Thus, the parties belonging to an executive can, for instance, agree to tax those outside the coalition and share the spoils between themselves.

Let us consider the following scenario. A party A tries, in an election campaign, to attract a particular group of voters by offering them some advantages at the expense of other voters. This offer, or proposal, which we can call P, is thus a specific instruction. Then some members of the target group, who appreciate the proposal, vote for A, which thereby becomes somewhat bigger than it otherwise would be. After the election A will be considered a possible executive member and, in the negotiations preceding the formation of the executive, A promises to support important points in the other prospective member parties' programs in return for their support of P. The parties reach an agreement along these lines and form an executive. P thus becomes part of the executive's program and will, accordingly, become implemented. Is this kind of scenario, we may ask, likely, or even typical, of a parliamentary democracy with proportionalism? My answer is in the affirmative. A first prerequisite for this answer is that the parties are able to deliver in the way described, and this condition, as we have seen, is fulfilled. This, however, does not settle the issue. It is obviously not sufficient for the parties to be able to act in the way described-they must also find it expedient to do so, it must pay in terms of votes. More exactly, the behaviour must be expected to result in a net gain in votes-the number of voters attracted from other parties must be greater than the number of voters repelled.

In principle this is quite possible. The negative effects may for example be spread out so thinly, and over so many people, that those hit hardly notice. With some shrewd manoeuvring it may even be possible to allocate the negative effects mainly on voters who would not have voted for the party anyway. This is so since the campaigning politicians, in a setting in which specific interests are important, are likely to be able to recognize "their own people" to a considerable extent. In a presidential setting with plurality, on the contrary, and as I will later argue, such a behaviour is hardly imaginable. There, as we will see, it is imperative for all campaigners not to hurt anybody. In addition to these problems about the management of the negative effects it is, however, also necessary to consider the reactions of those favored by the proposal. Are they really likely to feel attracted and thus to change their minds in favour of the proposing party? Some may perhaps do so immediately, but there may also be those in the target group who, although favored by the particular proposal, generally dislike the system of politically distributed goods and clientelism, and therefore want to change the system rather than to use it. Such a voter, according to the terminology used here, favours some general instruction rather than the specific instruction at issue. But perhaps there is no party committed to the general instruction which the voter endorses, or if there is such a party its chances of becoming big enough for getting the instruction into a governmental program may be slim. Such dilemmas are, in fact, as we saw in part 11, quite likely. Our voter may thus find it best to play safe and vote for the party offering the favours. Voting for the second best may, after all, seem more prudent since it may give a payoff even if the favored party, after the election, still is quite small.

- The conclusion thus is that electoral strategies including specific instructions about favours to particular target groups may be quite profitable in the parliamentary, proportional setting.

From a methodological point of view it is, I think, important to note that I have not assumed any kind of rational ignorance among the voters in order to reach this conclusion. Rational ignorance, we remember, is the kind of ignorance that ordinary citizens have about public matters, since it does not pay to keep informed. The likelihood that a particular citizen voter will become pivotal in a general election is infinitesimal, and therefore the efforts needed for finding out about the campaigners programs are not worthwhile. The idea put forward here, that small target groups of voters may be favored at the expense of others, may thus be supported by the assumption that these others are rationally ignorant, and that, in fact, is often done. That assumption is however not necessary. The redistribution can, in fact, as I have shown, be explained as a consequence of perfectly enlightened and rational voter behaviour within the institutional structures present. Such an explanation tells as much more about the situation than one relying on rational ignorance, and is therefore much more interesting. It is therefore, I would say, a good research strategy to avoid assumptions about rational ignorance as long as possible. In addition to this I would like to argue that ignorance, in the situation described, with several parties and a lot of interests involved, is more limited than usually assumed. People, in particular since they are not only voters but often also rent-seekers, are likely to know quite a lot about the favours offered by the political system. Another interesting point is that relations between voters and campaigners in the particular setting discussed here have important similarities with a market type contract relation.

Having said this it is however also important to emphasize, since we are dealing with compound voting, that other approaches to the voters than the one illustrated are by no means excluded.

The campaigning parties may, for instance, try to attract ideologically committed voters with various ideological arguments, they may support various general instructions, or they may just refer to their achievements in the past hoping to get the voters confidence.

But even if various strategies thus may be useful, they can usually not be used without due regards. A party may for example be hurt if its various messages and promises do not form a reasonably coherent totality. If, for instance, some promise given to a group of marginal voters is to strikingly at odds with the party's ideology, some voters belonging to the party's core may leave the party. This importance of coherence has been emphasized by, among others, Downs (1957, pp 109 ff).

The Quasi Contractual Relations between Parties and Voters

In the constitutional setting discussed here, the parties have a considerable capacity for delivering. It may also be said that they have a considerable capacity for credible commitment towards the voters, and from there it is not long to think about tacit deals, or quasi contracts, between the parties and their voters in various target groups. In a real deal, or a contract, as we know, each of the parties undertakes to do something in return for the undertakings of the other parties. Here we may think of a contract like this: The party says that it will give favours to the members of the target group in return for their votes, and the members of the target group say that they will vote for the party in return for the favours. Obviously there is no contract like this, but there is something that may be considered as an approximation, and it is interesting to see how this approximation differs from the imagined real contract.

In the imagined real contract situation the party would not go ahead fulfilling its promises without making sure that the voters had fulfilled theirs. In the political situation there is obviously no such possibility-voting is anonymous and the party has no way of controlling the voters. A main rationale for anonymity, in fact, is to prevent parties and voters from bargaining. Joseph Schlesinger, for instance, writes (1991, p 146) that "... benefit seekers need some mechanisms to assert their claims.... One of the principal arguments for the secret ballot is that it makes it difficult for benefit seekers to prove their support and be paid for their vote". But even if anonymity certainly makes real contracts impossible it cannot prevent quasi contracts universally. In such a quasi contract situation the party, in its own interest, is likely to go ahead in good faith once it has made its commitment. It will try to get into the executive, and it will try to get the promise incorporated in the executive's program. Or, in short, it will behave as in a real contract situation and thereby, for future needs, enhance its own credibility. The voters, in contrast to the party, have not even made a public commitment, but just listened to the party. Still, even they, to the extent they are attracted by the offer, are likely to behave as in a real contract situation, and thus vote for the party. True, a voter might speculate that she will get the favour anyway, and therefore use her vote for some other purpose. But that means taking a risk and if the voter really wants to add the party in its efforts to fulfil its part of the deal, the best the voter can do is to vote for the party and thereby contribute to its chances of becoming a member of the executive, and to get the proposal included in the governmental program.

Obviously there is no real contract in the situation described. There is no formal agreement, no control, and no enforcement. Still the parts are likely to behave as if they were parts to a real contract, and it is therefore quite reasonable to talk about a quasi contract between the party and the attracted voters in the target group. The factor which mainly accounts for the possibility of such a quasi contract is the party's capacity for delivering, or for credible commitment. That capacity is linked to the particular constitutional setting dealt with here.

According to the discussion the main actors are the likely targets for lobbying. In this constitutional setting, it is thus the political parties, which essentially means the party leaderships at the summits of the party hierarchies, which will be approached by the lobbyists. Since these targets are few and powerful the lobbying will become a very concentrated, and possibly closed, activity. Furthermore, and since this constitutional setting to such a large extent is tuned towards interest politics, it should be a very fertile ground for lobbying activities. The lobbying is thus also likely to very effective.

- Our first conclusion thus is that the lobbying activities are likely to be concentrated, possibly closed, and very effective. I argued that the lobbyists are likely to demand what they can reasonably get. Here, since that is possible, the lobbyists are likely to ask for changes of status quo-they will not be confined to merely blocking.
- From this-and following the argument in part 10-it may be concluded that the interest organizations are likely to be long lasting and formed before the laws, which support their interests, are created. One interesting possibility is that trade unions, which are formed for negotiating with their counterparts about wages and other conditions of labor, are likely to become important lobbyists as well. Since the unions are likely to be able to influence the voting behaviour of their members to some extent, they may even, by playing a mediating role, enforce the contract character of the relation between parties and voters.
- Another conclusion, which follows form the fact that the prerequisites for organizational ties between parties and organizations as stated in part 10 are fulfilled, is that such ties are quite possible-and perhaps even likely.

This conclusion, it should be noted, is further supported by the fact that politics in the constitutional setting at issue here is likely to be strongly interest oriented. Thus not only the organizational prerequisites for alliances between parties and interest organizations are present, but also strong positive incentives for that kind of collaboration.

Parliamentary Constitutions with Proportional Elections: In this constitutional setting we are likely to get several political parties since the elections for the legislature are proportional. Furthermore it is important for the parties to get into the executive, since in a parliamentarian system most decisive constellations include the executive. Since there are numerous parties the executive is likely to be a coalition.

A party aspiring for a place in a coalition executive is greatly helped by being cohesive and disciplined, and therefore the parties will be so, if effective means for discipline are available. In a proportional system that is the case, and thus the parties are likely to become cohesive and disciplined. The main actors will consequently be party main actors.

As for their policies the basic important fact is that the parties are capable of delivering, or, in other words, have a capacity for credible commitment towards the voters. In their relations to the voters they are therefore likely to strive for instruction rather than delegation. Furthermore, and since it is much easier to agree about specific instructions than about general ones when forming a coalition executive, specific instructions are likely to be particularly important components of policies. Politics will to a large extent be interest politics. Since lobbyists are expected to approach the main actors they will, in this constitutional setting, turn to the leaderships of the cohesive political parties.

The lobbying activities will thus be very concentrated, and to some extent perhaps also closed or secret. Since politics to such a large extent is tuned towards interests, lobbying is also likely to be quite effective. The interest organizations, which may have organizational ties with the parties, are likely to get interests satisfied in exchange for votes from their members. This, so far, is a short summary of some earlier main points. In addition to this a few further conclusions may be added. I will start from the contention that the main actors, in this constitutional setting, are political parties, and that politics therefore, on the whole, is party politics. It may also be said that we are dealing with a partyocracy.

- Now, since the parties are just parties, this means that there is no democratically appointed main actor with a responsibility for the common good. All actors represent primarily, and basically, their own interests.
- Another related conclusion is that all proposals for decisions are made by those directly interested in them. The making of proposals, and of decisions, are in a sense inseparable aspects of one and the same process. Almost everything is done when the executive is formed, and by

the parties taking part in that process. The fact that the main actors are parties, does not, of course, mean that individuals are unimportant. The parties do obviously consist of individual human beings and this fact should certainly, and in accordance with methodological individualism, be recognized. The individuals do however almost exclusively play their roles within, or on behalf of, the parties. Thus, and when it comes to dealings with actors outside the party, for example with other parties, or with the electorate in campaigns, or with lobbyists, it is usually the individuals belonging to the party leaderships which acts on behalf of their parties. Party positions on political issues are of course also determined by the individuals who belong to the party, usually with more influence the higher up in the party hierarchy they are:

- An important conclusion of this, since the individuals essentially play their roles within, or on behalf of, the parties, is that political careers, in this type of system, always are party careers. Since the parties are likely to be well developed organizations, and to have an easily recognized identity over time, they will be able to develop successively, and to harbour, more and more elaborated, and more and more comprehensive, party programs.
- Furthermore, since the programs are likely to favour the interests of particular groups of voters, long-lasting, mutually supportive relations between parties and voters tend to develop. The party leaderships will thus to a large extent be able to recognise their own people in the electorate. I have already said several times that politics in this constitutional setting tends to be focused on special interests.
- Another formulation of this conclusion, which alludes to the well known Gresham's law in economics ("cheap money drives out good"), is that specific instructions drive out general ones. This does not mean that general instructions are altogether eradicated-we have for example seen that general instructions in a big party's program may prevail.

Specific instructions are, however, much less threatened, and even encouraged by the system. Most parties, as it seems, will have to deal extensively with specific instructions in order to survive. Specific instructions are thus, in a sense, forced upon politics. This may also impede the voters from favouring ideological positions, and reduce them to interest seekers. All of this, it may be noted, is to a large extent in agreement with Buchanan's contention (1993) that "Political players who might seek to further some conception of an all-encompassing general, or public, interest cannot survive". Buchanan is however discussing democratic constitutions in general, whereas the focus here is on parliamentary constitutions with proportional elections.

- One implication of this focussing on special interests is that the turnout in elections is likely to be high. Since people are stimulated to pursue their own private or personal interests by political means, the turnout is likely to be greater than in other types of democratic systems.
- Another implication is that the system is likely to exhibit the kind of properties which are usually associated with the so called "tragedy of the commons". There, we remember, the single farmer, since he is unable to affect the general handling of the common pasture, will have to put his cow on the pasture as quickly as possible if it shall get any grass at all. Consequently, and since all farmers are driven to behave in the same way, the pasture will be destroyed. In the political system discussed here the incentives of politicians and voters will bring them to treat common societal resources in a similar destructive way.

Parliamentary Constitutions with Majoritarian Elections

As I mentioned in previous part, there may also be more than two parties. Here, in this part, and in the following parts, I will however concentrate on the two-party case. The reason is that this case has important unique properties, since there will not be any coalition building. If, on the contrary, there are more than two parties we are likely to get coalition politics, and the analysis, although different in some respects, will also have important similarities with the analysis of proportional, parliamentary systems.

The most important fact in the two-party case is that there is normally no interaction at all between the main actors. The biggest party, that is the party which won the last general election, is likely have a safe majority of its own. That party will thus form the executive single-handedly. There will not be any need for the party to cooperate with the other party. The governing party will act alone. In this respect the system differs starkly from the three other main types of constitutional systems we are considering here.

There may, however, be exceptions to this general rule. Thus, if the biggest party's majority is narrow, relatively strong and independent, individual legislators of the governing party may be able to challenge the party leadership. Such legislators may for example force the party leadership to change some proposal in some way, or to deliver some other kind of favour, for example for the legislators' local constituencies. In these situations individual main actors thus become important, and the governing party main actor will have to deal with them. This, of course, is tantamount to main actor interaction.

Here, after having said what there is to say about main actor interaction in a narrow sense, I could end this part. It does, however, seem fitting to add a few consequences of the general rule of no main actor interaction at all, since they constitute contrasts to the preceding proportional variety of parliamentarism. Here are two consequences of that kind.

- First, the governmental process may be more continuous, and less of a batch process, than in the proportional variety of parliamentarism. The reason is that the proposals, which are presented for the legislature, are prepared by the governing party alone. The governmental program may therefore develop gradually during the electoral period.
- Second, in this system, there is always a clear-cut opposition. The party which does not govern is the

opposition. There is no ambiguity in that sense, and there is nothing to be lost, such as valuable pivotal positions, by organizing the opposition. The establishment of a shadow cabinet should therefore cause no surprise.

The President, the Prime Minister and the Cabinet

The President and Vice-President

52. The President of India.-

There shall be a President of India.

53. Executive power of the Union.-

(1) The executive power of the Union shall be vested in the President and shall be exercised by him either directly or through officers subordinate to him in accordance with this Constitution.

(2) Without prejudice to the generality of the foregoing provision, the supreme command of the Defence Forces of the Union shall be vested in the President and the exercise thereof shall be regulated by law.

(3) Nothing in this article shall-

(a) be deemed to transfer to the President any functions conferred by any existing law on the Government of any State or other authority; or

(b) prevent Parliament from conferring by law functions on authorities other than the President.

54. Election of President.- The President shall be elected by the members of an electoral college consisting of-

(a) the elected members of both Houses of Parliament; and

(b) the elected members of the Legislative Assemblies of the States.

Explanation.-In this article and in article 55, "State" includes the National Capital Territory of Delhi and the Union territory of Pondicherry.

55. Manner of election of President.-

(1) As far as practicable, there shall be uniformity in the scale

of representation of the different States at the election of the President.

(2) For the purpose of securing such uniformity among the States inter se as well as parity between the States as a whole and the Union, the number of votes which each elected member of Parliament and of the Legislative Assembly of each State is entitled to cast at such election shall be determined in the following manner:-

(a) every elected member of the Legislative Assembly of a State shall have as many votes as there are multiples of one thousand in the quotient obtained by dividing the population of the State by the total number of the elected members of the Assembly;

(b) if, after taking the said multiples of one thousand, the remainder is not less than five hundred, then the vote of each member referred to in sub-clause (a) shall be further increased by one;

(c) each elected member of either House of Parliament shall have such number of votes as may be obtained by dividing the total number of votes assigned to the members of the Legislative Assemblies of the States under sub-clauses (a) and (b) by the total number of the elected members of both Houses of Parliament, fractions exceeding one-half being counted as one and other fractions being disregarded.

(3) The election of the President shall be held in accordance with the system of proportional representation by means of the single transferable vote and the voting at such election shall be by secret ballot.

Explanation.- In this article, the expression "population" means the population as ascertained at the last preceding census of which the relevant figures have been published: Provided that the reference in this Explanation to the last preceding census of which the relevant figures have been published shall, until the relevant figures for the first census taken after the year 2026 have been published, be construed as a reference to the 1971 census.

56. Term of office of President.-

(1) The President shall hold office for a term of five years from the date on which he enters upon his office:

Provided that-

(a) the President may, by writing under his hand addressed to the Vice-President, resign his office;

(b) the President may, for violation of the Constitution, be removed from office by impeachment in the manner provided in article 61;

(c) the President shall, notwithstanding the expiration of his term, continue to hold office until his successor enters upon his office.

(2) Any resignation addressed to the Vice-President under clause (a) of the proviso to clause (1) shall forthwith be communicated by him to the Speaker of the House of the People.

57. Eligibility for re-election.-A person who holds, or who has held, office as President shall, subject to the other provisions of this Constitution, be eligible for re-election to that office.

58. Qualifications for election as President.-

(1) No person shall be eligible for election as President unless he-

(a) is a citizen of India,

(b) has completed the age of thirty-five years, and

(c) is qualified for election as a member of the House of the People.

(2) A person shall not be eligible for election as President if he holds any office of profit under the Government of India or the Government of any State or under any local or other authority subject to the control of any of the said Governments.

Explanation.-For the purposes of this article, a person shall not be deemed to hold any office of profit by reason only that he is the President or Vice- President of the Union or the Governor of any State or is a Minister either for the Union or for any State.

59. Conditions of President's office.-

(1) The President shall not be a member of either House of Parliament or of a House of the Legislature of any State, and if a member of either House of Parliament or of a House of the Legislature of any State be elected President, he shall be deemed to have vacated his seat in that House on the date on which he enters upon his office as President.

(2) The President shall not hold any other office of profit.

(3) The President shall be entitled without payment of rent to the use of his official residences and shall be also entitled to such emoluments, allowances and privileges as may be determined by Parliament by law and, until provision in that behalf is so made, such emoluments, allowances and privileges as are specified in the Second Schedule.

(4) The emoluments and allowances of the President shall not be diminished during his term of office.

60. Oath or affirmation by the President.-Every President and every person acting as President or discharging the functions of the President shall, before entering upon his office, make and subscribe in the presence of the Chief Justice of India or, in his absence, the senior-most Judge of the Supreme Court available, an oath or affirmation in the following form, that is to say-

"I, A.B., do swear in the name of God that I will faithfully execute solemnly affirm the office of President (or discharge the functions of the President) of India and will to the best of my ability preserve, protect and defend the Constitution and the law and that I will devote myself to the service and well-being of the people of India.".

61. Procedure for impeachment of the President.-

(1) When a President is to be impeached for violation of the Constitution, the charge shall be preferred by either House of Parliament.

(2) No such charge shall be preferred unless-

(a) the proposal to prefer such charge is contained in a resolution which has been moved after at least fourteen days' notice in writing signed by not less than one-fourth of the total number of members of the House has been given of their intention to move the resolution, and

(b) such resolution has been passed by a majority of not less than two-thirds of the total membership of the House.

(3) When a charge has been so preferred by either House of Parliament, the other House shall investigate the charge or cause the charge to be investigated and the President shall have the right to appear and to be represented at such investigation.

(4) If as a result of the investigation a resolution is passed by a majority of not less than two-thirds of the total membership of the House by which the charge was investigated or caused to be investigated, declaring that the charge preferred against the President has been sustained, such resolution shall have the effect of removing the President from his office as from the date on which the resolution is so passed.

62. Time of holding election to fill vacancy in the office of President and the term of office of person elected to fill casual vacancy.-

(1) An election to fill a vacancy caused by the expiration of the term of office of President shall be completed before the expiration of the term.

(2) An election to fill a vacancy in the office of President occurring by reason of his death, resignation or removal, or otherwise shall be held as soon as possible after, and in no case later than six months from, the date of occurrence of the vacancy; and the person elected to fill the vacancy shall, subject to the provisions of article 56, be entitled to hold office for the full term of five years from the date on which he enters upon his office.

63. The Vice-President of India.- There shall be a Vice-President of India.

64. The Vice-President to be ex officio Chairman of the Council of States.- The Vice-President shall be ex officio Chairman of the Council of States and shall not hold any other office of profit: Provided that during any period when the Vice-President acts as President or discharges the functions of the President under article 65, he shall not perform the duties of the office of Chairman of the Council of States and shall not be entitled to any salary or allowance payable to the Chairman of the Council of States under article 97.

65. The Vice-President to act as President or to discharge his functions during casual vacancies in the office, or during the absence, of President.-

(1) In the event of the occurrence of any vacancy in the office of the President by reason of his death, resignation or removal, or otherwise, the Vice-President shall act as President until the date on which a new President elected in accordance with the provisions of this Chapter to fill such vacancy enters upon his office.

(2) When the President is unable to discharge his functions owing to absence, illness or any other cause, the Vice-President shall discharge his functions until the date on which the President resumes his duties.

(3) The Vice-President shall, during, and in respect of, the period while he is so acting as, or discharging the functions of, President, have all the powers and immunities of the President and be entitled to such emoluments, allowances and privileges as may be determined by Parliament by law and, until provision in that behalf is so made, such emoluments, allowances and privileges as are specified in the Second Schedule.

66. Election of Vice-President.-

(1) The Vice-President shall be elected by the members of an electoral college consisting of the members of both Houses of Parliament in accordance with the system of proportional representation by means of the single transferable vote and the voting at such election shall be by secret ballot.

(2) The Vice-President shall not be a member of either House of Parliament or of a House of the Legislature of any State, and if a member of either House of Parliament or of a House of the Legislature of any State be elected Vice-President, he shall be deemed to have vacated his seat in that House on the date on which he enters upon his office as Vice-President.

(3) No person shall be eligible for election as Vice-President unless he-

(a) is a citizen of India;

(b) has completed the age of thirty-five years; and

(c) is qualified for election as a member of the Council of States.

(4) A person shall not be eligible for election as Vice-President if he holds any office of profit under the Government of India or the Government of any State or under any local or other authority subject to the control of any of the said Governments.

Explanation.- For the purposes of this article, a person shall not be deemed to hold any office of profit by reason only that he is the President or Vice- President of the Union or the Governor of any State or is a Minister either for the Union or for any State.

67. Term of office of Vice-President.-The Vice-President shall hold office for a term of five years from the date on which he enters upon his office:

Provided that-

(a) a Vice-President may, by writing under his hand addressed to the President, resign his office;

(b) a Vice-President may be removed from his office by a resolution of the Council of States passed by a majority of all the then members of the Council and agreed to by the House of the People; but no resolution for the purpose of this clause shall be moved unless at least fourteen days' notice has been given of the intention to move the resolution;

(c) a Vice-President shall, notwithstanding the expiration of his term, continue to hold office until his successor enters upon his office.

68. Time of holding election to fill vacancy in the office of Vice-President and the term of office of person elected to fill casual vacancy.-

(1) An election to fill a vacancy caused by the expiration of the term of office of Vice-President shall be completed before the expiration of the term.

(2) An election to fill a vacancy in the office of Vice-President occurring by reason of his death, resignation or removal, or otherwise shall be held as soon as possible after the occurrence of the vacancy, and the person elected to fill the vacancy shall, subject to the provisions of article 67, be entitled to hold office for the full term of five years from the date on which he enters upon his office.

69. Oath or affirmation by the Vice-President.-Every Vice-President shall, before entering upon his office, make and subscribe before the President, or some person appointed in that behalf by him, an oath or affirmation in the following form, that is to say-

"I, A.B., do swear in the name of God that I will bear true faith and solemnly affirm allegiance to the Constitution of India as by law established and that I will faithfully discharge the duty upon which I am about to enter."

70. Discharge of President's functions in other contingencies.-Parliament may make such provisions as it thinks fit for the discharge of the functions of the President in any contingency not provided for in this Chapter.

71. Matters relating to, or connected with, the election of a President or Vice-President.-

(1) All doubts and disputes arising out of or in connection with the election of a President or Vice-President shall be inquired into and decided by the Supreme Court whose decision shall be final.

(2) If the election of a person as President or Vice-President is declared void by the Supreme Court, acts done by him in the exercise and performance of the powers and duties of the office of President or Vice-President, as the case may be, on or before the date of the decision of the Supreme Court shall not be invalidated by reason of that declaration.

(3) Subject to the provisions of this Constitution, Parliament may by law regulate any matter relating to or connected with the election of a President or Vice-President.

(4) The election of a person as President or Vice-President shall not be called in question on the ground of the existence of any vacancy for whatever reason among the members of the electoral college electing him.

72. Power of President to grant pardons, etc., and to suspend, remit or commute sentences in certain cases.-

(1) The President shall have the power to grant pardons, reprieves, respites or remissions of punishment or to suspend, remit or commute the sentence of any person convicted of any offence-

(a) in all cases where the punishment or sentence is by a Court Martial;

(b) in all cases where the punishment or sentence is for an offence against any law relating to a matter to which the executive power of the Union extends;

(c) in all cases where the sentence is a sentence of death.

(2) Nothing in sub-clause (a) of clause (1) shall affect the power conferred by law on any officer of the Armed Forces of the Union to suspend, remit or commute a sentence passed by a Court Martial.

(3) Nothing in sub-clause (c) of clause (1) shall affect the power to suspend, remit or commute a sentence of death exercisable by the Governor of a State under any law for the time being in force.

73. Extent of executive power of the Union.-

(1) Subject to the provisions of this Constitution, the executive power of the Union shall extend-

(a) to the matters with respect to which Parliament has power to make laws; and

(b) to the exercise of such rights, authority and jurisdiction as are exercisable by the Government of India by virtue of any treaty or agreement: Provided that the executive power referred to in sub-clause (a) shall not, save as expressly provided in this Constitution or in any law made by Parliament, extend in any State to matters with respect to which the Legislature of the State has also power to make laws.

(2) Until otherwise provided by Parliament, a State and any officer or authority of a State may, notwithstanding anything in this article, continue to exercise in matters with respect to which Parliament has power to make laws for that State such executive power or functions as the State or officer or authority thereof could exercise immediately before the commencement of this Constitution.

Council of Ministers

74. Council of Ministers to aid and advise President.-

(1) There shall be a Council of Ministers with the Prime Minister at the head to aid and advise the President who shall, in the exercise of his functions, act in accordance with such advice: Provided that the President may require the Council of Ministers to reconsider such advice, either generally or otherwise, and the President shall act in accordance with the advice tendered after such reconsideration.

(2) The question whether any, and if so what, advice was tendered by Ministers to the President shall not be inquired into in any court.

75. Other provisions as to Ministers.-

(1) The Prime Minister shall be appointed by the President and the other Ministers shall be appointed by the President on the advice of the Prime Minister.

(1A) The total number of Ministers, including the Prime Minister, in the Council of Ministers shall not exceed fifteen per cent. of the total number of members of the House of the People.

(1B) A member of either House of Parliament belonging to any political party who is disqualified for being a member of that House under paragraph 2 of the Tenth Schedule shall also be disqualified to be appointed as a Minister under clause (1) for duration of the period commencing from the date of his disqualification till the date on which the term of his office as such member would expire or where he contests any election to either House of Parliament before the expiry of such period, till the date on which he is declared elected, whichever is earlier.

(2) The Ministers shall hold office during the pleasure of the President.

(3) The Council of Ministers shall be collectively responsible to the House of the People.

(4) Before a Minister enters upon his office, the President shall administer to him the oaths of office and of secrecy according to the forms set out for the purpose in the Third Schedule.

(5) A Minister who for any period of six consecutive months is not a member of either House of Parliament shall at the expiration of that period cease to be a Minister.

(6) The salaries and allowances of Ministers shall be such as Parliament may from time to time by law determine and, until Parliament so determines, shall be as specified in the Second Schedule.

The Attorney-General for India

76. Attorney-General for India.-

(1) The President shall appoint a person who is qualified to be appointed a Judge of the Supreme Court to be Attorney-General for India.

(2) It shall be the duty of the Attorney-General to give advice

to the Government of India upon such legal matters, and to perform such other duties of a legal character, as may from time to time be referred or assigned to him by the President, and to discharge the functions conferred on him by or under this Constitution or any other law for the time being in force.

(3) In the performance of his duties the Attorney-General shall have right of audience in all courts in the territory of India.

(4) The Attorney-General shall hold office during the pleasure of the President, and shall receive such remuneration as the President may determine.

Conduct of Government Business

77. Conduct of business of the Government of India.-

(1) All executive action of the Government of India shall be expressed to be taken in the name of the President.

(2) Orders and other instruments made and executed in the name of the President shall be authenticated in such manner as may be specified in rules to be made by the President, and the validity of an order or instrument which is so authenticated shall not be called in question on the ground that it is not an order or instrument made or executed by the President.

(3) The President shall make rules for the more convenient transaction of the business of the Government of India, and for the allocation among Ministers of the said business.

78. Duties of Prime Minister as respects the furnishing of information to the President, etc.-It shall be the duty of the Prime Minister-

(a) to communicate to the President all decisions of the Council of Ministers relating to the administration of the affairs of the Union and proposals for legislation;

(b) to furnish such information relating to the administration of the affairs of the Union and proposals for legislation as the President may call for; and

(c) if the President so requires, to submit for the consideration of the Council of Ministers any matter on which a decision has been taken by a Minister but which has not been considered by the Council.

Legislative Powers of the President

123. Power of President to promulgate Ordinances during recess of Parliament.-

(1) If at any time, except when both Houses of Parliament are in session, the President is satisfied that circumstances exist which render it necessary for him to take immediate action, he may promulgate such Ordinances as the circumstances appear to him to require.

(2) An Ordinance promulgated under this article shall have the same force and effect as an Act of Parliament, but every such Ordinance-

(a) shall be laid before both Houses of Parliament and shall cease to operate at the expiration of six weeks from the reassembly of Parliament, or, if before the expiration of that period resolutions disapproving it are passed by both Houses, upon the passing of the second of those resolutions; and

(b) may be withdrawn at any time by the President.

Explanation.-Where the Houses of Parliament are summoned to reassemble on different dates, the period of six weeks shall be reckoned from the later of those dates for the purposes of this clause.

(3) If and so far as an Ordinance under this article makes any provision which Parliament would not under this Constitution be competent to enact, it shall be void.

The Union Judiciary

124. Establishment and constitution of Supreme Court.-

(1) There shall be a Supreme Court of India consisting of a Chief Justice of India and, until Parliament by law prescribes a larger number, of not more than seven other Judges.

(2) Every Judge of the Supreme Court shall be appointed by the President by warrant under his hand and seal after consultation with such of the Judges of the Supreme Court and of the High Courts in the States as the President may deem necessary for the purpose and shall hold office until he attains the age of sixty-five years: Provided that in the case of appointment of a Judge other than the Chief Justice, the Chief Justice of India shall always be consulted: Provided further that-

(a) a Judge may, by writing under his hand addressed to the President, resign his office;

(b) a Judge may be removed from his office in the manner provided in clause (4).

(2A) The age of a Judge of the Supreme Court shall be determined by such authority and in such manner as Parliament may by law provide.

(3) A person shall not be qualified for appointment as a Judge of the Supreme Court unless he is a citizen of India and-

(a) has been for at least five years a Judge of a High Court or of two or more such Courts in succession; or

(b) has been for at least ten years an advocate of a High Court or of two or more such Courts in succession; or

(c) is, in the opinion of the President, a distinguished jurist.

Explanation I.-In this clause "High Court" means a High Court which exercises, or which at any time before the commencement of this Constitution exercised, jurisdiction in any part of the territory of India.

Explanation II.-In computing for the purpose of this clause the period during which a person has been an advocate, any period during which a person has held judicial office not inferior to that of a district judge after he became an advocate shall be included.

(4) A Judge of the Supreme Court shall not be removed from his office except by an order of the President passed after an address by each House of Parliament supported by a

majority of the total membership of that House and by a majority of not less than two-thirds of the members of that House present and voting has been presented to the President in the same session for such removal on the ground of proved misbehaviour or incapacity.

(5) Parliament may by law regulate the procedure for the presentation of an address and for the investigation and proof of the misbehaviour or incapacity of a Judge under clause (4).

(6) Every person appointed to be a Judge of the Supreme Court shall, before he enters upon his office, make and subscribe before the President, or some person appointed in that behalf by him, an oath or affirmation according to the form set out for the purpose in the Third Schedule.

(7) No person who has held office as a Judge of the Supreme Court shall plead or act in any court or before any authority within the territory of India.

125. Salaries, etc., of Judges.-

(1) There shall be paid to the Judges of the Supreme Court such salaries as may be determined by Parliament by law and, until provision in that behalf is so made, such salaries as are specified in the Second Schedule.

(2) Every Judge shall be entitled to such privileges and allowances and to such rights in respect of leave of absence and pension as may from time to time be determined by or under law made by Parliament and, until so determined, to such privileges, allowances and rights as are specified in the Second Schedule: Provided that neither the privileges nor the allowances of a Judge nor his rights in respect of leave of absence or pension shall be varied to his disadvantage after his appointment.

126. Appointment of acting Chief Justice.- When the office of Chief Justice of India is vacant or when the Chief Justice is, by reason of absence or otherwise, unable to perform the duties of his office, the duties of the office shall be performed by such one of the other Judges of the Court as the President may appoint for the purpose.

127. Appointment of ad hoc Judges.-

(1) If at any time there should not be a quorum of the Judges of the Supreme Court available to hold or continue any session of the Court, the Chief Justice of India may, with the previous consent of the President and after consultation with the Chief Justice of the High Court concerned, request in writing the attendance at the sittings of the Court, as an ad hoc Judge, for such period as may be necessary, of a Judge of a High Court duly qualified for appointment as a Judge of the Supreme Court to be designated by the Chief Justice of India.

(2) It shall be the duty of the Judge who has been so designated, in priority to other duties of his office, to attend the sittings of the Supreme Court at the time and for the period for which his attendance is required, and while so attending he shall have all the jurisdiction, powers and privileges, and shall discharge the duties, of a Judge of the Supreme Court.

128. Attendance of retired Judges at sittings of the Supreme Court.- Notwithstanding anything in this Chapter, the Chief Justice of India may at any time, with the previous consent of the President, request any person who has held the office of a Judge of the Supreme Court or of the Federal Court or who has held the office of a Judge of a High Court and is duly qualified for appointment as a Judge of the Supreme Court to sit and act as a Judge of the Supreme Court, and every such person so requested shall, while so sitting and acting, be entitled to such allowances as the President may by order determine and have all the jurisdiction, powers and privileges of, but shall not otherwise be deemed to be, a Judge of that Court: Provided that nothing in this article shall be deemed to require any such person as aforesaid to sit and act as a Judge of that Court unless he consents so to do.

129. Supreme Court to be a court of record.- The Supreme Court shall be a court of record and shall have all the powers of such a court including the power to punish for contempt of itself.

130. Seat of Supreme Court.- The Supreme Court shall sit in Delhi or in such other place or places, as the Chief Justice of India may, with the approval of the President, from time to time, appoint.

131. Original jurisdiction of the Supreme Court.- Subject to the provisions of this Constitution, the Supreme Court shall, to the exclusion of any other court, have original jurisdiction in any dispute-

(a) between the Government of India and one or more States; or

(b) between the Government of India and any State or States on one side and one or more other States on the other; or

(c) between two or more States, if and in so far as the dispute involves any question (whether of law or fact) on which the existence or extent of a legal right depends: Provided that the said jurisdiction shall not extend to a dispute arising out of any treaty, agreement, covenant, engagement, sanad or other similar instrument which, having been entered into or executed before the commencement of this Constitution, continues in operation after such commencement, or which provides that the said jurisdiction shall not extend to such a dispute.

131A. [Exclusive jurisdiction of the Supreme Court in regard to questions as to constitutional validity of Central laws.] Rep. by the Constitution (Forty-third Amendment) Act, 1977, s. 4 (w.e.f. 13-4-1978).

132. Appellate jurisdiction of Supreme Court in appeals from High Courts in certain cases.-

(1) An appeal shall lie to the Supreme Court from any judgment, decree or final order of a High Court in the territory of India, whether in a civil, criminal or other proceeding, if the High Court certifies under article 134A that the case involves a substantial question of law as to the interpretation of this Constitution.

(3) Where such a certificate is given, any party in the case may appeal to the Supreme Court on the ground that any such question as aforesaid has been wrongly decided.

Explanation.- For the purposes of this article, the expression "final order" includes an order deciding an issue which, if decided in favour of the appellant, would be sufficient for the final disposal of the case.

133. Appellate jurisdiction of Supreme Court in appeals from High Courts in regard to civil matters.-

(1) An appeal shall lie to the Supreme Court from any judgment, decree or final order in a civil proceeding of a High Court in the territory of India if the High Court certifies under article 134A-

(a) that the case involves a substantial question of law of general importance; and

(b) that in the opinion of the High Court the said question needs to be decided by the Supreme Court.

(2) Notwithstanding anything in article 132, any party appealing to the Supreme Court under clause (1) may urge as one of the grounds in such appeal that a substantial question of law as to the interpretation of this Constitution has been wrongly decided.

(3) Notwithstanding anything in this article, no appeal shall, unless Parliament by law otherwise provides, lie to the Supreme Court from the judgment, decree or final order of one Judge of a High Court.

134. Appellate jurisdiction of Supreme Court in regard to criminal matters.-

(1) An appeal shall lie to the Supreme Court from any judgment, final order or sentence in a criminal proceeding of a High Court in the territory of India if the High Court-

(a) has on appeal reversed an order of acquittal of an accused person and sentenced him to death; or

(b) has withdrawn for trial before itself any case from any court subordinate to its authority and has in such trial convicted the accused person and sentenced him to death; or

(c) certifies under article 134A that the case is a fit one for appeal to the Supreme Court: Provided that an appeal under sub-clause (c) shall lie subject to such provisions as may be made in that behalf under clause (1) o f article 145 and to such conditions as the High Court may establish or require.

(2) Parliament may by law confer on the Supreme Court any further powers to entertain and hear appeals from any judgment, final order or sentence in a criminal proceeding of a High Court in the territory of India subject to such conditions and limitations as may be specified in such law.

134A. Certificate for appeal to the Supreme Court.-Every High Court, passing or making a judgment, decree, final order, or sentence, referred to in clause (1) of article 132 or clause (1) of article 133, or clause (1) of article 134,-

(a) may, if it deems fit so to do, on its own motion; and

(b) shall, if an oral application is made, by or on behalf of the party aggrieved, immediately after the passing or making of such judgment, decree, final order or sentence, determine, as soon as may be after such passing or making, the question whether a certificate of the nature referred to in clause (1) of article 132, or clause (1) of article 133 or, as the case may be, sub-clause (c) of clause (1) of article 134, may be given in respect of that case.

135. Jurisdiction and powers of the Federal Court under existing law to be exercisable by the Supreme Court.- Until Parliament by law otherwise provides, the Supreme Court shall also have jurisdiction and powers with respect to any matter to which the provisions of article 133 or article 134 do not apply if jurisdiction and powers in relation to that matter were exercisable by the Federal Court immediately before the commencement of this Constitution under any existing law.

136. Special leave to appeal by the Supreme Court.-

(1) Notwithstanding anything in this Chapter, the Supreme Court may, in its discretion, grant special leave to appeal from any judgment, decree, determination, sentence or order in any cause or matter passed or made by any court or tribunal in the territory of India.

(2) Nothing in clause (1) shall apply to any judgment, determination, sentence or order passed or made by any court or tribunal constituted by or under any law relating to the Armed Forces.

137. Review of judgments or orders by the Supreme Court.- Subject to the provisions of any law made by Parliament or any rules made under article 145, the Supreme Court shall have power to review any judgment pronounced or order made by it.

138. Enlargement of the jurisdiction of the Supreme Court.-

(1) The Supreme Court shall have such further jurisdiction and powers with respect to any of the matters in the Union List as Parliament may by law confer.

(2) The Supreme Court shall have such further jurisdiction and powers with respect to any matter as the Government of India and the Government of any State may by special agreement confer, if Parliament by law provides for the exercise of such jurisdiction and powers by the Supreme Court.

139. Conferment on the Supreme Court of powers to issue certain writs.- Parliament may by law confer on the Supreme Court power to issue directions, orders or writs, including writs in the nature of habeas corpus, mandamus, prohibition, quo warranto and certiorari, or any of them, for any purposes other than those mentioned in clause (2) of article 32.

139A. Transfer of certain cases.-

(1) Where cases involving the same or substantially the same questions of law are pending before the Supreme Court and one or more High Courts or before two or more High Courts and the Supreme Court is satisfied on its own motion or on an application made by the Attorney-General of India or by a party to any such case that such questions are substantial questions of general importance, the Supreme Court may withdraw the case or cases pending before the High Court or the High Courts and dispose of all the cases itself:

Provided that the Supreme Court may after determining the said questions of law return any case so withdrawn together with a copy of its judgment on such questions to the High Court from which the case has been withdrawn, and the High Court shall on receipt thereof, proceed to dispose of the case in conformity with such judgment.

(2) The Supreme Court may, if it deems it expedient so to do for the ends of justice, transfer any case, appeal or other proceedings pending before any High Court to any other High Court.

140. Ancillary powers of Supreme Court.- Parliament may by law make provision for conferring upon the Supreme Court such supplemental powers not inconsistent with any of the provisions of this Constitution as may appear to be necessary or desirable for the purpose of enabling the Court more effectively to exercise the jurisdiction conferred upon it by or under this Constitution.

141. Law declared by Supreme Court to be binding on all courts. The law declared by the Supreme Court shall be binding on all courts within the territory of India.

142. Enforcement of decrees and orders of Supreme Court and orders as to discovery, etc.-

(1) The Supreme Court in the exercise of its jurisdiction may pass such decree or make such order as is necessary for doing complete justice in any cause or matter pending before it, and any decree so passed or order so made shall be enforceable throughout the territory of India in such manner as may be prescribed by or under any law made by Parliament and, until provision in that behalf is so made, in such manner as the President may by order prescribe.

(2) Subject to the provisions of any law made in this behalf by Parliament, the Supreme Court shall, as respects the whole of the territory of India, have all and every power to make any order for the purpose of securing the attendance of any person, the discovery or production of any documents, or the investigation or punishment of any contempt of itself.

143. Power of President to consult Supreme Court.-

(1) If at any time it appears to the President that a question of law or fact has arisen, or is likely to arise, which is of such a nature and of such public importance that it is expedient to obtain the opinion of the Supreme Court upon it, he may refer the question to that Court for consideration and the Court may, after such hearing as it thinks fit, report to the President its opinion thereon.

(2) The President may, notwithstanding anything in the proviso to article 131, refer a dispute of the kind mentioned in the said proviso to the Supreme Court for opinion and the Supreme Court shall, after such hearing as it thinks fit, report to the President its opinion thereon.

144. Civil and judicial authorities to act in aid of the Supreme Court.- All authorities, civil and judicial, in the territory of India shall act in aid of the Supreme Court.

144A. [Special provisions as to disposal of questions relating to constitutional validity of laws.] Rep. by the Constitution (Forty-third Amendment) Act, 1977, s. 5 (w.e.f. 13-4-1978).

145. Rules of Court, etc.-

(1) Subject to the provisions of any law made by Parliament, the Supreme Court may from time to time, with the approval of the President, make rules for regulating generally the practice and procedure of the Court including-

(a) rules as to the persons practising before the Court;

(b) rules as to the procedure for hearing appeals and other matters pertaining to appeals including the time within which appeals to the Court are to be entered;

(c) rules as to the proceedings in the Court for the enforcement of any of the rights conferred by Part III;

(cc) rules as to the proceedings in the Court under article 139A;

(d) rules as to the entertainment of appeals under sub-clause (c) of clause (1) of article 134;

(e) rules as to the conditions subject to which any judgment pronounced or order made by the Court may be reviewed and the procedure for such review including the time within which applications to the Court for such review are to be entered;

(f) rules as to the costs of and incidental to any proceedings in the Court and as to the fees to be charged in respect of proceedings therein;

(g) rules as to the granting of bail;

(h) rules as to stay of proceedings;

(i) rules providing for the summary determination of any appeal which appears to the Court to be frivolous or vexatious or brought for the purpose of delay;

(j) rules as to the procedure for inquiries referred to in clause (1) of article 317.

(2) Subject to the provisions of clause (3), rules made under this article may fix the minimum number of Judges who are to sit for any purpose, and may provide for the powers of single Judges and Division Courts.

(3) The minimum number of Judges who are to sit for the purpose of deciding any case involving a substantial question of law as to the interpretation of this Constitution or for the purpose of hearing any reference under article 143 shall be five: Provided that, where the Court hearing an appeal under any of the provisions of this Chapter other than article 132 consists of less than five Judges and in the course of the hearing of the appeal the Court is satisfied that the appeal involves a substantial question of law as to the interpretation of this Constitution the determination of which is necessary for the disposal of the appeal, such Court shall refer the question for opinion to a Court constituted as required by this clause for the purpose of deciding any case involving such a question and shall on receipt of the opinion dispose of the appeal in conformity with such opinion.

(4) No judgment shall be delivered by the Supreme Court save in open Court, and no report shall be made under

article 143 save in accordance with an opinion also delivered in open Court.

(5) No judgment and no such opinion shall be delivered by the Supreme Court save with the concurrence of a majority of the Judges present at the hearing of the case, but nothing in this clause shall be deemed to prevent a Judge who does not concur from delivering a dissenting judgment or opinion.

146. Officers and servants and the expenses of the Supreme Court.-

(1) Appointments of officers and servants of the Supreme Court shall be made by the Chief Justice of India or such other Judge or officer of the Court as he may direct: Provided that the President may by rule require that in such cases as may be specified in the rule, no person not already attached to the Court shall be appointed to any office connected with the Court, save after consultation with the Union Public Service Commission.

(2) Subject to the provisions of any law made by Parliament, the conditions of service of officers and servants of the Supreme Court shall be such as may be prescribed by rules made by the Chief Justice of India or by some other Judge or officer of the Court authorised by the Chief Justice of India to make rules for the purpose: Provided that the rules made under this clause shall, so far as they relate to salaries, allowances, leave or pensions, require the approval of the President.

(3) The administrative expenses of the Supreme Court, including all salaries, allowances and pensions payable to or in respect of the officers and servants of the Court, shall be charged upon the Consolidated Fund of India, and any fees or other moneys taken by the Court shall form part of that Fund.

147. Interpretation.-In this Chapter and in Chapter V of Part VI, references to any substantial question of law as to the interpretation of this Constitution shall be construed as including references to any substantial question of law as to the interpretation

of the Government of India Act, 1935 (including any enactment amending or supplementing that Act), or of any Order in Council or order made thereunder, or of the Indian Independence Act, 1947, or of any order made thereunder.

The States

General

152. Definition.- In this Part, unless the context otherwise requires, the expression "State" does not include the State of Jammu and Kashmir.

The Executive

The Governor

153. Governors of States.- There shall be a Governor for each State: Provided that nothing in this article shall prevent the appointment of the same person as Governor for two or more States.

154. Executive power of State.-

(1) The executive power of the State shall be vested in the Governor and shall be exercised by him either directly or through officers subordinate to him in accordance with this Constitution.

(2) Nothing in this article shall-

(a) be deemed to transfer to the Governor any functions conferred by any existing law on any other authority; or

(b) prevent Parliament or the Legislature of the State from conferring by law functions on any authority subordinate to the Governor.

155. Appointment of Governor.- The Governor of a State shall be appointed by the President by warrant under his hand and seal.

156. Term of office of Governor.-

(1) The Governor shall hold office during the pleasure of the President.

(2) The Governor may, by writing under his hand addressed to the President, resign his office.

(3) Subject to the foregoing provisions of this article, a Governor shall hold office for a term of five years from the date on which he enters upon his office: Provided that a Governor shall, notwithstanding the expiration of his term, continue to hold office until his successor enters upon his office.

157. Qualifications for appointment as Governor.- No person shall be eligible for appointment as Governor unless he is a citizen of India and has completed the age of thirty-five years.

158. Conditions of Governor's office.-

(1) The Governor shall not be a member of either House of Parliament or of a House of the Legislature of any State specified in the First Schedule, and if a member of either House of Parliament or of a House of the Legislature of any such State be appointed Governor, he shall be deemed to have vacated his seat in that House on the date on which he enters upon his office as Governor.

(2) The Governor shall not hold any other office of profit.

(3) The Governor shall be entitled without payment of rent to the use of his official residences and shall be also entitled to such emoluments, allowances and privileges as may be determined by Parliament by law and, until provision in that behalf is so made, such emoluments, allowances and privileges as are specified in the Second Schedule.

(3A) Where the same person is appointed as Governor of two or more States, the emoluments and allowances payable to the Governor shall be allocated among the States in such proportion as the President may by order determine.

(4) The emoluments and allowances of the Governor shall not be diminished during his term of office.

159. Oath or affirmation by the Governor.- Every Governor and every person discharging the functions of the Governor shall, before entering upon his office, make and subscribe in the presence of the Chief Justice of the High Court exercising jurisdiction in

relation to the State, or, in his absence, the senior most Judge of that Court available, an oath or affirmation in the following form, that is to say-

"I, A. B., do swear in the name of God that I will solemnly affirm faithfully execute the office of Governor (or discharge the functions of the Governor) of.............(name of the State) and will to the best of my ability preserve, protect and defend the Constitution and the law and that I will devote myself to the service and well-being of the people of..........(name of the State)."

160. Discharge of the functions of the Governor in certain contingencies.- The President may make such provision as he thinks fit for the discharge of the functions of the Governor of a State in any contingency not provided for in this Chapter.

161. Power of Governor to grant pardons, etc., and to suspend, remit or commute sentences in certain cases.- The Governor of a State shall have the power to grant pardons, reprieves, respites or remissions of punishment or to suspend, remit or commute the sentence of any person convicted of any offence against any law relating to a matter to which the executive power of the State extends.

162. Extent of executive power of State.- Subject to the provisions of this Constitution, the executive power of a State shall extend to the matters with respect to which the Legislature of the State has power to make laws: Provided that in any matter with respect to which the Legislature of a State and Parliament have power to make laws, the executive power of the State shall be subject to, and limited by, the executive power expressly conferred by this Constitution or by any law made by Parliament upon the Union or authorities thereof.

Council of Ministers

163. Council of Ministers to aid and advise Governor.-

(1) There shall be a Council of Ministers with the Chief Minister at the head to aid and advise the Governor in the exercise of his functions, except in so far as he is by or under this Constitution required to exercise his functions or any of them in his discretion.

(2) If any question arises whether any matter is or is not a matter as respects which the Governor is by or under this Constitution required to act in his discretion, the decision of the Governor in his discretion shall be final, and the validity of anything done by the Governor shall not be called in question on the ground that he ought or ought not to have acted in his discretion.

(3) The question whether any, and if so what, advice was tendered by Ministers to the Governor shall not be inquired into in any court.

164. Other provisions as to Ministers.-

(1) The Chief Minister shall be appointed by the Governor and the other Ministers shall be appointed by the Governor on the advice of the Chief Minister, and the Ministers shall hold office during the pleasure of the Governor:

Provided that in the States of Bihar, Madhya Pradesh and Orissa, there shall be a Minister in charge of tribal welfare who may in addition be in charge of the welfare of the Scheduled Castes and backward classes or any other work.

(1A) The total number of Ministers, including the Chief Minister, in the Council of Ministers in a State shall not exceed fifteen per cent. of the total number of members of the Legislative Assembly of that State: Provided that the number of Ministers, including the Chief Minister in a State shall not be less than twelve:

Provided further that where the total number of Ministers including the Chief Minister in the Council of Ministers in any State at the commencement of the Constitution (Ninety-first Amendment) Act, 2003 exceeds the said fifteen per cent. or the number specified in the first proviso, as the case may be, then the total number of Ministers in that State shall be brought in conformity with the provisions of this clause within six months from such date* as the President may by public notification appoint.

(1B) A member of the Legislative Assembly of a State or either House of the Legislature of a State having Legislative

Council belonging to any political party who is disqualified for being a member of that House under paragraph 2 of the Tenth Schedule shall also be disqualified to be appointed as a Minister under clause (1) for duration of the period commencing from the date of his disqualification till the date on which the term of his office as such member would expire or where he contests any election to the Legislative Assembly of a State or either House of the Legislature of a State having Legislative Council, as the case may be, before the expiry of such period, till the date on which he is declared elected, whichever is earlier.

(2) The Council of Ministers shall be collectively responsible to the Legislative Assembly of the State.

(3) Before a Minister enters upon his office, the Governor shall administer to him the oaths of office and of secrecy according to the forms set out for the purpose in the Third Schedule.

(4) A Minister who for any period of six consecutive months is not a member of the Legislature of the State shall at the expiration of that period cease to be a Minister.

(5) The salaries and allowances of Ministers shall be such as the Legislature of the State may from time to time by law determine and, until the Legislature of the State so determines, shall be as specified in the Second Schedule.

The Advocate-General for the State

165. Advocate-General for the State.-

(1) The Governor of each State shall appoint a person who is qualified to be appointed a Judge of a High Court to be Advocate-General for the State.

(2) It shall be the duty of the Advocate-General to give advice to the Government of the State upon such legal matters, and to perform such other duties of a legal character, as may from time to time be referred or assigned to him by the Governor, and to discharge the functions conferred on him by or under this Constitution or any other law for the time being in force.

(3) The Advocate-General shall hold office during the pleasure of the Governor, and shall receive such remuneration as the Governor may determine.

Conduct of Government Business

166. Conduct of business of the Government of a State.-

(1) All executive action of the Government of a State shall be expressed to be taken in the name of the Governor.

(2) Orders and other instruments made and executed in the name of the Governor shall be authenticated in such manner as may be specified in rules to be made by the Governor, and the validity of an order or instrument which is so authenticated shall not be called in question on the ground that it is not an order or instrument made or executed by the Governor.

(3) The Governor shall make rules for the more convenient transaction of the business of the Government of the State, and for the allocation among Ministers of the said business in so far as it is not business with respect to which the Governor is by or under this Constitution required to act in his discretion.

167. Duties of Chief Minister as respects the furnishing of information to Governor, etc.- It shall be the duty of the Chief Minister of each State-

(a) to communicate to the Governor of the State all decisions of the Council of Ministers relating to the administration of the affairs of the State and proposals for legislation;

(b) to furnish such information relating to the administration of the affairs of the State and proposals for legislation as the Governor may call for; and

(c) if the Governor so requires, to submit for the consideration of the Council of Ministers any matter on which a decision has been taken by a Minister but which has not been considered by the Council.

The State Legislature

General

168. Constitution of Legislatures in States.-

(1) For every State there shall be a Legislature which shall consist of the Governor, and-

(a) in the States of Bihar, Maharashtra, Karnataka and Uttar Pradesh, two Houses;

(b) in other States, one House.

(2) Where there are two Houses of the Legislature of a State, one shall be known as the Legislative Council and the other as the Legislative Assembly, and where there is only one House, it shall be known as the Legislative Assembly.

169. Abolition or creation of Legislative Councils in States.-

(1) Notwithstanding anything in article 168, Parliament may by law provide for the abolition of the Legislative Council of a State having such a Council or for the creation of such a Council in a State having no such Council, if the Legislative Assembly of the State passes a resolution to that effect by a majority of the total membership of the Assembly and by a majority of not less than two-thirds of the members of the Assembly present and voting.

(2) Any law referred to in clause (1) shall contain such provisions for the amendment of this Constitution as may be necessary to give effect to the provisions of the law and may also contain such supplemental, incidental and consequential provisions as Parliament may deem necessary.

(3) No such law as aforesaid shall be deemed to be an amendment of this Constitution for the purposes of article 368.

170. Composition of the Legislative Assemblies.-

(1) Subject to the provisions of article 333, the Legislative Assembly of each State shall consist of not more than five hundred, and not less than sixty, members chosen by direct election from territorial constituencies in the State.

(2) For the purposes of clause (1), each State shall be divided into territorial constituencies in such manner that the ratio between the population of each constituency and the number of seats allotted to it shall, so far as practicable, be the same throughout the State.

Explanation.-In this clause, the expression "population" means the population as ascertained at the last preceding census of which the relevant figures have been published: Provided that the reference in this Explanation to the last preceding census of which the relevant figures have been published shall, until the relevant figures for the first census taken after the year 2026 have been published, be construed as a reference to the 2001 census.

(3) Upon the completion of each census, the total number of seats in the Legislative Assembly of each State and the division of each State into territorial constituencies shall be readjusted by such authority and in such manner as Parliament may by law determine: Provided that such readjustment shall not affect representation in the Legislative Assembly until the dissolution of the then existing Assembly: Provided further that such readjustment shall take effect from such date as the President may, by order, specify and until such readjustment takes effect, any election to the Legislative Assembly may be held on the basis of the territorial constituencies existing before such readjustment: Provided also that until the relevant figures for the first census taken after the year 2026 have been published, it shall not be necessary to readjust-

(i) the total number of seats in the Legislative Assembly of each State as readjusted on the basis of the 1971 census; and

(ii) the division of such State into territorial constituencies as may be readjusted on the basis of the 2001 census, under this clause.

171. Composition of the Legislative Councils.-

(1) The total number of members in the Legislative Council of a State having such a Council shall not exceed one third

of the total number of members in the Legislative Assembly of that State: Provided that the total number of members in the Legislative Council of a State shall in no case be less than forty.

(2) Until Parliament by law otherwise provides, the composition of the Legislative Council of a State shall be as provided in clause (3).

(3) Of the total number of members of the Legislative Council of a State-

(a) as nearly as may be, one-third shall be elected by electorates consisting of members of municipalities, district boards and such other local authorities in the State as Parliament may by law specify;

(b) as nearly as may be, one-twelfth shall be elected by electorates consisting of persons residing in the State who have been for at least three years graduates of any university in the territory of India or have been for at least three years in possession of qualifications prescribed by or under any law made by Parliament as equivalent to that of a graduate of any such university;

(c) as nearly as may be, one-twelfth shall be elected by electorates consisting of persons who have been for at least three years engaged in teaching in such educational institutions within the State, not lower in standard than that of a secondary school, as may be prescribed by or under any law made by Parliament;

(d) as nearly as may be, one-third shall be elected by the members of the Legislative Assembly of the State from amongst persons who are not members of the Assembly;

(e) the remainder shall be nominated by the Governor in accordance with the provisions of clause (5).

(4) The members to be elected under sub-clauses (a), (b) and (c) of clause (3) shall be chosen in such territorial constituencies as may be prescribed by or under any law made by Parliament, and the elections under the said sub-

clauses and under sub-clause (d) of the said clause shall be held in accordance with the system of proportional representation by means of the single transferable vote.

(5) The members to be nominated by the Governor under sub-clause (e) of clause (3) shall consist of persons having special knowledge or practical experience in respect of such matters as the following, namely:-

Literature, science, art, cooperative movement and social service.

172. Duration of State Legislatures.-

(1) Every Legislative Assembly of every State, unless sooner dissolved, shall continue for five years from the date appointed for its first meeting and no longer and the expiration of the said period of five years shall operate as a dissolution of the Assembly:

Provided that the said period may, while a Proclamation of Emergency is in operation, be extended by Parliament by law for a period not exceeding one year at a time and not extending in any case beyond a period of six months after the Proclamation has ceased to operate.

(2) The Legislative Council of a State shall not be subject to dissolution, but as nearly as possible one-third of the members thereof shall retire as soon as may be on the expiration of every second year in accordance with the provisions made in that behalf by Parliament by law.

173. Qualification for membership of the State Legislature.- A person shall not be qualified to be chosen to fill a seat in the Legislature of a State unless he-

(a) is a citizen of India, and makes and subscribes before some person authorised in that behalf by the Election Commission an oath or affirmation according to the form set out for the purpose in the Third Schedule;

(b) is, in the case of a seat in the Legislative Assembly, not less than twenty-five years of age and, in the case of a seat in the Legislative Council, not less than thirty years of age; and

(c) possesses such other qualifications as may be prescribed in that behalf by or under any law made by Parliament.

174. Sessions of the State Legislature, prorogation and dissolution.-

(1) The Governor shall from time to time summon the House or each House of the Legislature of the State to meet at such time and place as he thinks fit, but six months shall not intervene between its last sitting in one session and the date appointed for its first sitting in the next session.

(2) The Governor may from time to time-

(a) prorogue the House or either House;

(b) dissolve the Legislative Assembly.

175. Right of Governor to address and send messages to the House or Houses.-

(1) The Governor may address the Legislative Assembly or, in the case of a State having a Legislative Council, either House of the Legislature of the State, or both Houses assembled together, and may for that purpose require the attendance of members.

(2) The Governor may send messages to the House or Houses of the Legislature of the State, whether with respect to a Bill then pending in the Legislature or otherwise, and a House to which any message is so sent shall with all convenient despatch consider any matter required by the message to be taken into consideration.

176. Special address by the Governor.-

(1) At the commencement of the first session after each general election to the Legislative Assembly and at the commencement of the first session of each year, the Governor shall address the Legislative Assembly or, in the case of a State having a Legislative Council, both Houses assembled together and inform the Legislature of the causes of its summons.

(2) Provision shall be made by the rules regulating the procedure of the House or either House for the allotment

of time for discussion of the matters referred to in such address.

177. Rights of Ministers and Advocate-General as respects the Houses.- Every Minister and the Advocate-General for a State shall have the right to speak in, and otherwise to take part in the proceedings of, the Legislative Assembly of the State or, in the case of a State having a Legislative Council, both Houses, and to speak in, and otherwise to take part in the proceedings of, any committee of the Legislature of which he may be named a member, but shall not, by virtue of this article, be entitled to vote.

Officers of the State Legislature

178. The Speaker and Deputy Speaker of the Legislative Assembly.-Every Legislative Assembly of a State shall, as soon as may be, choose two members of the Assembly to be respectively Speaker and Deputy Speaker thereof and, so often as the office of Speaker or Deputy Speaker becomes vacant, the Assembly shall choose another member to be Speaker or Deputy Speaker, as the case may be.

179. Vacation and resignation of, and removal from, the offices of Speaker and Deputy Speaker.-A member holding office as Speaker or Deputy Speaker of an Assembly-

(a) shall vacate his office if he ceases to be a member of the Assembly;
(b) may at any time by writing under his hand addressed, if such member is the Speaker, to the Deputy Speaker, and if such member is the Deputy Speaker, to the Speaker, resign his office; and
(c) may be removed from his office by a resolution of the Assembly passed by a majority of all the then members of the Assembly:

Provided that no resolution for the purpose of clause (c) shall be moved unless at least fourteen days' notice has been given of the intention to move the resolution:

Provided further that, whenever the Assembly is dissolved, the Speaker shall not vacate his office until immediately before the first meeting of the Assembly after the dissolution.

180. Power of the Deputy Speaker or other person to perform the duties of the office of, or to act as, Speaker.-

(1) While the office of Speaker is vacant, the duties of the office shall be performed by the Deputy Speaker or, if the office of Deputy Speaker is also vacant, by such member of the Assembly as the Governor may appoint for the purpose.

(2) During the absence of the Speaker from any sitting of the Assembly the Deputy Speaker or, if he is also absent, such person as may be determined by the rules of procedure of the Assembly, or, if no such person is present, such other person as may be determined by the Assembly, shall act as Speaker.

181. The Speaker or the Deputy Speaker not to preside while a resolution for his removal from office is under consideration.-

(1) At any sitting of the Legislative Assembly, while any resolution for the removal of the Speaker from his office is under consideration, the Speaker, or while any resolution for the removal of the Deputy Speaker from his office is under consideration, the Deputy Speaker, shall not, though he is present, preside, and the provisions of clause (2) of article 180 shall apply in relation to every such sitting as they apply in relation to a sitting from which the Speaker or, as the case may be, the Deputy Speaker, is absent.

(2) The Speaker shall have the right to speak in, and otherwise to take part in the proceedings of, the Legislative Assembly while any resolution for his removal from office is under consideration in the Assembly and shall, notwithstanding anything in article 189, be entitled to vote only in the first instance on such resolution or on any other matter during such proceedings but not in the case of an equality of votes.

182. The Chairman and Deputy Chairman of the Legislative Council.- The Legislative Council of every State having such

Council shall, as soon as may be, choose two members of the Council to be respectively Chairman and Deputy Chairman thereof and, so often as the office of Chairman or Deputy Chairman becomes vacant, the Council shall choose another member to be Chairman or Deputy Chairman, as the case may be.

183. Vacation and resignation of, and removal from, the offices of Chairman and Deputy Chairman.-A member holding office as Chairman or Deputy Chairman of a Legislative Council-

(a) shall vacate his office if he ceases to be a member of the Council;

(b) may at any time by writing under his hand addressed, if such member is the Chairman, to the Deputy Chairman, and if such member is the Deputy Chairman, to the Chairman, resign his office; and

(c) may be removed from his office by a resolution of the Council passed by a majority of all the then members of the Council:

Provided that no resolution for the purpose of clause (c) shall be moved unless at least fourteen days' notice has been given of the intention to move the resolution.

184. Power of the Deputy Chairman or other person to perform the duties of the office of, or to act as, Chairman.-

(1) While the office of Chairman is vacant, the duties of the office shall be performed by the Deputy Chairman or, if the office of Deputy Chairman is also vacant, by such member of the Council as the Governor may appoint for the purpose.

(2) During the absence of the Chairman from any sitting of the Council the Deputy Chairman or, if he is also absent, such person as may be determined by the rules of procedure of the Council, or, if no such person is present, such other person as may be determined by the Council, shall act as Chairman.

185. The Chairman or the Deputy Chairman not to preside while a resolution for his removal from office is under consideration.-

(1) At any sitting of the Legislative Council, while any resolution for the removal of the Chairman from his office is under consideration, the Chairman, or while any resolution for the removal of the Deputy Chairman from his office is under consideration, the Deputy Chairman, shall not, though he is present, preside, and the provisions of clause (2) of article 184 shall apply in relation to every such sitting as they apply in relation to a sitting from which the Chairman or, as the case may be, the Deputy Chairman is absent.

(2) The Chairman shall have the right to speak in, and otherwise to take part in the proceedings of, the Legislative Council while any resolution for his removal from office is under consideration in the Council and shall, notwithstanding anything in article 189, be entitled to vote only in the first instance on such resolution or on any other matter during such proceedings but not in the case of an equality of votes.

186. Salaries and allowances of the Speaker and Deputy Speaker and the Chairman and Deputy Chairman.- There shall be paid to the Speaker and the Deputy Speaker of the Legislative Assembly, and to the Chairman and the Deputy Chairman of the Legislative Council, such salaries and allowances as may be respectively fixed by the Legislature of the State by law and, until provision in that behalf is so made, such salaries and allowances as are specified in the Second Schedule.

187. Secretariat of State Legislature.-

(1) The House or each House of the Legislature of a State shall have a separate secretarial staff:

Provided that nothing in this clause shall, in the case of the Legislature of a State having a Legislative Council, be construed as preventing the creation of posts common to both Houses of such Legislature.

(2) The Legislature of a State may by law regulate the recruitment, and the conditions of service of persons appointed, to the secretarial staff of the House or Houses of the Legislature of the State.

(3) Until provision is made by the Legislature of the State under clause (2), the Governor may, after consultation with the Speaker of the Legislative Assembly or the Chairman of the Legislative Council, as the case may be, make rules regulating the recruitment, and the conditions of service of persons appointed, to the secretarial staff of the Assembly or the Council, and any rules so made shall have effect subject to the provisions of any law made under the said clause.

Conduct of Business

188. Oath or affirmation by members.-Every member of the Legislative Assembly or the Legislative Council of a State shall, before taking his seat, make and subscribe before the Governor, or some person appointed in that behalf by him, an oath or affirmation according to the form set out for the purpose in the Third Schedule.

189. Voting in Houses, power of Houses to act notwithstanding vacancies and quorum.-

(1) Save as otherwise provided in this Constitution, all questions at any sitting of a House of the Legislature of a State shall be determined by a majority of votes of the members present and voting, other than the Speaker or Chairman, or person acting as such.

The Speaker or Chairman, or person acting as such, shall not vote in the first instance, but shall have and exercise a casting vote in the case of an equality of votes.

(2) A House of the Legislature of a State shall have power to act notwithstanding any vacancy in the membership thereof, and any proceedings in the Legislature of a State shall be valid notwithstanding that it is discovered subsequently that some person who was not entitled so to do sat or voted or otherwise took part in the proceedings.

(3) Until the Legislature of the State by law otherwise provides, the quorum to constitute a meeting of a House of the Legislature of a State shall be ten members or one-tenth of the total number of members of the House, whichever is greater.

(4) If at any time during a meeting of the Legislative Assembly or the Legislative Council of a State there is no quorum, it shall be the duty of the Speaker or Chairman, or person acting as such, either to adjourn the House or to suspend the meeting until there is a quorum.

Disqualifications of Members

190. Vacation of seats.-

(1) No person shall be a member of both Houses of the Legislature of a State and provision shall be made by the Legislature of the State by law for the vacation by a person who is chosen a member of both Houses of his seat in one house or the other.

(2) No person shall be a member of the Legislatures of two or more States specified in the First Schedule and if a person is chosen a member of the Legislatures of two or more such States, then, at the expiration of such period as may be specified in rules made by the President, that person's seat in the Legislatures of all such States shall become vacant, unless he has previously resigned his seat in the Legislatures of all but one of the States.

(3) If a member of a House of the Legislature of a State-

(a) becomes subject to any of the disqualifications mentioned in clause (1) or clause (2) of article 191; or

(b) resigns his seat by writing under his hand addressed to the speaker or the Chairman, as the case may be, and his resignation is accepted by the Speaker or the Chairman, as the case may be, his seat shall thereupon become vacant:

Provided that in the case of any resignation referred to in sub-clause (b), if from information received or otherwise and after making such inquiry as he thinks fit, the Speaker or the Chairman, as the case may be, is satisfied that such resignation is not voluntary or genuine, he shall not accept such resignation.

(4) If for a period of sixty days a member of a House of the Legislature of a State is without permission of the House

absent from all meetings thereof, the House may declare his seat vacant: Provided that in computing the said period of sixty days no account shall be taken of any period during which the House is prorogued or is adjourned for more than four consecutive days.

191. Disqualifications for membership.-

(1) A person shall be disqualified for being chosen as, and for being, a member of the Legislative Assembly or Legislative Council of a State-

(a) if he holds any office of profit under the Government of India or the Government of any State specified in the First Schedule, other than an office declared by the Legislature of the State by law not to disqualify its holder;

(b) if he is of unsound mind and stands so declared by a competent court;

(c) if he is an undischarged insolvent;

(d) if he is not a citizen of India, or has voluntarily acquired the citizenship of a foreign State, or is under any acknowledgment of allegiance or adherence to a foreign State;

(e) if he is so disqualified by or under any law made by Parliament.

Explanation.-For the purposes of this clause, a person shall not be deemed to hold an office of profit under the Government of India or the Government of any State specified in the First Schedule by reason only that he is a Minister either for the Union or for such State.

(2) A person shall be disqualified for being a member of the Legislative Assembly or Legislative Council of a State if he is so disqualified under the Tenth Schedule.

192. Decision on questions as to disqualifications of members.-

(1) If any question arises as to whether a member of a House of the Legislature of a State has become subject to any of

the disqualifications mentioned in clause (1) of article 191, the question shall be referred for the decision of the Governor and his decision shall be final.

(2) Before giving any decision on any such question, the Governor shall obtain the opinion of the Election Commission and shall act according to such opinion.

193. Penalty for sitting and voting before making oath or affirmation under article 188 or when not qualified or when disqualified.- If a person sits or votes as a member of the Legislative Assembly or the Legislative Council of a State before he has complied with the requirements of article 188, or when he knows that he is not qualified or that he is disqualified for membership thereof, or that he is prohibited from so doing by the provisions of any law made by Parliament or the Legislature of the State, he shall be liable in respect of each day on which he so sits or votes to a penalty of five hundred rupees to be recovered as a debt due to the State.

Powers, Privileges and Immunities of State Legislatures and their Members

194. Powers, privileges, etc., of the Houses of Legislatures and of the members and committees thereof.-

(1) Subject to the provisions of this Constitution and to the rules and standing orders regulating the procedure of the Legislature, there shall be freedom of speech in the Legislature of every State.

(2) No member of the Legislature of a State shall be liable to any proceedings in any court in respect of anything said or any vote given by him in the Legislature or any committee thereof, and no person shall be so liable in respect of the publication by or under the authority of a House of such a Legislature of any report, paper, votes or proceedings.

(3) In other respects, the powers, privileges and immunities of a House of the Legislature of a State, and of the members and the committees of a House of such Legislature, shall be such as may from time to time be defined by the

Legislature by law, and, until so defined, shall be those of that House and of its members and committees immediately before the coming into force of section 26 of the Constitution (Forty-fourth Amendment) Act, 1978.

(4) The provisions of clauses (1), (2) and (3) shall apply in relation to persons who by virtue of this Constitution have the right to speak in, and otherwise to take part in the proceedings of, a House of the Legislature of a State or any committee thereof as they apply in relation to members of that Legislature.

195. Salaries and allowances of members.-Members of the Legislative Assembly and the Legislative Council of a State shall be entitled to receive such salaries and allowances as may from time to time be determined, by the Legislature of the State by law and, until provision in that respect is so made, salaries and allowances at such rates and upon such conditions as were immediately before the commencement of this Constitution applicable in the case of members of the Legislative Assembly of the corresponding Province.

Legislative Procedure

196. Provisions as to introduction and passing of Bills.-

(1) Subject to the provisions of articles 198 and 207 with respect to Money Bills and other financial Bills, a Bill may originate in either House of the Legislature of a State which has a Legislative Council.

(2) Subject to the provisions of articles 197 and 198, a Bill shall not be deemed to have been passed by the Houses of the Legislature of a State having a Legislative Council unless it has been agreed to by both Houses, either without amendment or with such amendments only as are agreed to by both Houses.

(3) A Bill pending in the Legislature of a State shall not lapse by reason of the prorogation of the House or Houses thereof.

(4) A Bill pending in the Legislative Council of a State which has not been passed by the Legislative Assembly shall not lapse on a dissolution of the Assembly.

(5) A Bill which is pending in the Legislative Assembly of a State, or which having been passed by the Legislative Assembly is pending in the Legislative Council, shall lapse on a dissolution of the Assembly.

197. Restriction on powers of Legislative Council as to Bills other than Money Bills.-

(1) If after a Bill has been passed by the Legislative Assembly of a State having a Legislative Council and transmitted to the Legislative Council-

(a) the Bill is rejected by the Council; or

(b) more than three months elapse from the date on which the Bill is laid before the Council without the Bill being passed by it; or

(c) the Bill is passed by the Council with amendments to which the Legislative Assembly does not agree; the Legislative Assembly may, subject to the rules regulating its procedure, pass the Bill again in the same or in any subsequent session with or without such amendments, if any, as have been made, suggested or agreed to by the Legislative Council and then transmit the Bill as so passed to the Legislative Council.

(2) If after a Bill has been so passed for the second time by the Legislative Assembly and transmitted to the Legislative Council-

(a) the Bill is rejected by the Council; or

(b) more than one month elapses from the date on which the Bill is laid before the Council without the Bill being passed by it; or

(c) the Bill is passed by the Council with amendments to which the Legislative Assembly does not agree; the Bill shall be deemed to have been passed by the Houses of the Legislature of the State in the form in which it was passed by the Legislative Assembly for the second time with such amendments, if any, as have been made or suggested by the Legislative Council and agreed to by the Legislative Assembly.

(3) Nothing in this article shall apply to a Money Bill.

198. Special procedure in respect of Money Bills.-

(1) A Money Bill shall not be introduced in a Legislative Council.

(2) After a Money Bill has been passed by the Legislative Assembly of a State having a Legislative Council, it shall be transmitted to the Legislative Council for its recommendations, and the Legislative Council shall within a period of fourteen days from the date of its receipt of the Bill return the Bill to the Legislative Assembly with its recommendations, and the Legislative Assembly may thereupon either accept or reject all or any of the recommendations of the Legislative Council.

(3) If the Legislative Assembly accepts any of the recommendations of the Legislative Council, the Money Bill shall be deemed to have been passed by both Houses with the amendments recommended by the Legislative Council and accepted by the Legislative Assembly.

(4) If the Legislative Assembly does not accept any of the recommendations of the Legislative Council, the Money Bill shall be deemed to have been passed by both Houses in the form in which it was passed by the Legislative Assembly without any of the amendments recommended by the Legislative Council.

(5) If a Money Bill passed by the Legislative Assembly and transmitted to the Legislative Council for its recommendations is not returned to the Legislative Assembly within the said period of fourteen days, it shall be deemed to have been passed by both Houses at the expiration of the said period in the form in which it was passed by the Legislative Assembly.

199. Definition of "Money Bills".-

(1) For the purposes of this Chapter, a Bill shall be deemed to be a Money Bill if it contains only provisions dealing with all or any of the following matters, namely:-

   (a) the imposition, abolition, remission, alteration or regulation of any tax;

(b) the regulation of the borrowing of money or the giving of any guarantee by the State, or the amendment of the law with respect to any financial obligations undertaken or to be undertaken by the State;

(c) the custody of the Consolidated Fund or the Contingency Fund of the State, the payment of moneys into or the withdrawal of moneys from any such Fund;

(d) the appropriation of moneys out of the Consolidated Fund of the State;

(e) the declaring of any expenditure to be expenditure charged on the Consolidated Fund of the State, or the increasing of the amount of any such expenditure;

(f) the receipt of money on account of the Consolidated Fund of the State or the public account of the State or the custody or issue of such money; or

(g) any matter incidental to any of the matters specified in sub-clauses (a) to (f).

(2) A Bill shall not be deemed to be a Money Bill by reason only that it provides for the imposition of fines or other pecuniary penalties, or for the demand or payment of fees for licences or fees for services rendered, or by reason that it provides for the imposition, abolition, remission, alteration or regulation of any tax by any local authority or body for local purposes.

(3) If any question arises whether a Bill introduced in the Legislature of a State which has a Legislative Council is a Money Bill or not, the decision of the Speaker of the Legislative Assembly of such State thereon shall be final.

(4) There shall be endorsed on every Money Bill when it is transmitted to the Legislative Council under article 198, and when it is presented to the Governor for assent under article 200, the certificate of the Speaker of the Legislative Assembly signed by him that it is a Money Bill.

200. Assent to Bills.- When a Bill has been passed by the Legislative Assembly of a State or, in the case of a State having a Legislative Council, has been passed by both Houses of the

Legislature of the State, it shall be presented to the Governor and the Governor shall declare either that he assents to the Bill or that he withholds assent therefrom or that he reserves the Bill for the consideration of the President: Provided that the Governor may, as soon as possible after the presentation to him of the Bill for assent, return the Bill if it is not a Money Bill together with a message requesting that the House or Houses will reconsider the Bill or any specified provisions thereof and, in particular, will consider the desirability of introducing any such amendments as he may recommend in his message and, when a Bill is so returned, the House or Houses shall reconsider the Bill accordingly, and if the Bill is passed again by the House or Houses with or without amendment and presented to the Governor for assent, the Governor shall not withhold assent therefrom: Provided further that the Governor shall not assent to, but shall reserve for the consideration of the President, any Bill which in the opinion of the Governor would, if it became law, so derogate from the powers of the High Court as to endanger the position which that Court is by this Constitution designed to fill.

201. Bills reserved for consideration.- When a Bill is reserved by a Governor for the consideration of the President, the President shall declare either that he assents to the Bill or that he withholds assent therefrom: Provided that, where the Bill is not a Money Bill, the President may direct the Governor to return the Bill to the House or, as the case may be, the Houses of the Legislature of the State together with such a message as is mentioned in the first proviso to article 200 and, when a Bill is so returned, the House or Houses shall reconsider it accordingly within a period of six months from the date of receipt of such message and, if it is again passed by the House or Houses with or without amendment, it shall be presented again to the President for his consideration.

Panchayati Raj System

The Three-tier Panchayati Raj

The Panchayati Raj is a three-tier system. It has Panchayats at the root or village level, Block Samitis at the Block or Tehsil level and the Zilla Parishads at the district level. In the previous chapter, you have read about the Village Panchayats, which are the basic units of Panchayati Raj. The Block Samiti or the Khand Samiti is the second layer of the three-tier system of Panchayati Raj. The Zilla Parishad or the District Council is the top layer in the three-tier system of Panchayati Raj. All the three institutions together look after the needs and problems of the rural areas and they are together called the Panchayati Raj.

The Block Samitis

The Block Samitis in some areas are also called the Khand Samitis, while in others they are also called the Prakhand Samitis. The Block Samiti is an important link between the village Panchayat on the one side and the Zilla Parishad on the other.

Composition: The members of the Block Samitis are not elected directly. The Pradhans and the Panchas of the Village Panchayats within the Block choose their representatives to the Block Samitis. Besides these elected representatives, there are other members of the Block Samitis as well. They are:

(i) Chairmen of the Town Area Committees and the Notified Area Committees within the Block.

(ii) All the-members of the Lok Sabha, the Rajya Sabha, the Legislative Assembly and the Legislative Council elected from the Block concerned.

(iii) If there are no representatives of women and' Scheduled Castes in the Block Samiti then these members are appointed by the District Officer concerned. There must be two women members and four members as representatives of the Scheduled Castes and Scheduled Tribes in a Block Samiti.

The members of the Block Samiti elect a Block Chairman or the Block Pramukh and a Vice-Chairman. The Chairman or the Block Pramukh looks after the work of the Block Samiti and if the members are not satisfied with his work they have the right to remove him by passing a vote of No-Confidence against him. In his absence, the Vice-Chairman looks after the work of the Block Samiti. The term of a Block Samiti is five years.

Functions: One of the main functions of the Block Samiti is to obtain money from the Government for various programmes to develop the Block.

The Block Samitis also provide services of experts to village Panchayats of their area who give advice to the Panchayat Committees for their development. For this purpose, the Block Samitis have various experts such as agricultural experts, an engineer, an educational expert, a veterinary doctor and many other experts to give advice on various works of rural development. These experts frequently visit the villages and tell the people how to get more production by using improved seeds and manures, how to improve the breed of their cattle, how to learn scientific methods of cultivation and how to make use of the different family welfare programmes. Sources of Income-Broadly, the income of the Block Samitis comes from two sources(i) Taxes, (ij) Government assistance. The Block Samitis levy taxes on lands and houses, cattle and fairs and raise funds from the village for providing them expert services. The government assistance comes in the form of grants-in-aid from the State Governments.

The Zilla Parishad

The Zilla Parishad or the District Council is the highest institution of the Panchayati Raj in India. Just as the Block Samitis coordinate the development activities of all the Panchayats in their areas, similarly the Zilla Parishads coordinate the activities of the Block Samitis in the whole district.

Composition: The composition of the Zilla Parishad is somewhat similar to the composition of a Block Samiti, though on a bigger scale. It is composed of the following members:

(i) The Chairmen of the Block Samitis in the district.

(ii) Members of the Lok Sabha and the Rajya Sabha represent the district.

(iii) Members of the Vidhan Sabha and Vidhan Parishkd from the district.

(iv) Representatives of the Scheduled Castes and Scheduled Tribes.

(v) Representatives of women.

The Zilla Parishad elects its Chairman and a Vice-Chairman. The Chairman presides over the meetings.

The Zilla Parishad and the Block Samitis appoint different committees for efficient and smooth functioning of various 'programmes. These subcommittees are composed from among the members themselves to look after such developmental works as education, sanitation, public health, agricultural production, finance, social welfare and family planning.

The Government appoints a Secretary of the Zilla Parishad who is a permanent employee of the Parishad. He maintains records and accounts.

Functions of the Zilla Parishad: The Zilla Parishad is the apex organisation of the three tier system of Panchayati Raj. Its main function is to help the village panchayats and the Block Samitis and to coordinate their work. It also gives advice to the government on the work of the Panchayats and the Block Samitis. It prepares plans for the comprehensive development of the whole district. It takes steps to increase agricultural production and to improve sanitation in the rural areas. It constructs good roads in villages.

Implementation of five-year Plans and other plans for rural development are the responsibility of the Zilla Parishad.

Sources of Income: Its main sources of income are the following:

1. Financial grants from the Government.
2. Rent from the property owned by the Zilla Parishad.
3. Taxes levied on properties and fairs, etc.

Significance of Panchayati Raj

The Panchayati Raj has many achievements to its credit:

(1) The Panchayati Raj system has brought about political awakening in rural India.

(2) The Panchayati Raj has brought the government close to the people.

(3) The Panchayats have succeeded in improving the condition of their respective villages by taking up welfare activities.

(4) Primary and adult schools run by the Panchayats have spread literacy and education among the rural people.

(5) The Panchayats have succeeded in drawing the attention of the government officials to their problems.

Gram Sabha

Gram Sabha is a body consisting of persons registered in the electoral rolls of a village or a group of villages which elect a Panchayat. A vibrant and enlightened Gram Sabha is central to the success of the Panchayati Raj system. The year 1999-2000 has thus been declared as the "Year of the Gram Sabha". State Governments have been urged:

- o To vest in the Gram Sabha, powers on the lines envisaged in the Provisions of the Panchayats (Extension to the Scheduled Areas) Act, 1996.
- o To make a mandatory provision in the Panchayati Raj Act for holding Gram Sabha meetings throughout the country on the occasion of the Republic Day, Labour Day, Independence Day and Gandhi Jayanti.
- o To make a mandatory provision in the Panchayati Raj Act specifying separately, the quorum for Gram Sabha meetings, for ordinary meetings, meetings convened for special purposes and re-convened meetings due to cancellation of and earlier meeting for want of quorum.
- o To make members of the Gram Sabhas aware of their powers and responsibilities with a view to ensuring mass participation, particularly of the hitherto marginalised, groups, such as women and SCs/STs.
- o To lay down procedures for the Gram Sabha to effectively carry out social audit of beneficiary oriented development programmes of the Ministry or Rural Development, particularly the legal powers of the Gram Sabha to order recovery or punishment for financial mismanagement.
- o To evolve a plan of action for generating wide publicity for Gram Sabha meetings.
- o To evolve guidelines/procedures for holding Gram Sabha meetings and a model list of business for such meetings.

- o To generate awareness as to the rights of the Gram Sabha with respect to control over natural resources, land records and conflict resolution.

The Constitution (Seventy-third Amendment) Act, 1992 envisages empowered Panchayats as institutions of self-government at the village level capable of:

- o Planning and executing village level public works and their maintenance.
- o Ensuring welfare of the people at the village level including health, education, communal harmony, social justice particularly gender and caste based discrimination, dispute resolution, welfare of children, especially the girl child.

The Constitution (Seventy-third Amendment) Act, 1992 also envisages empowered Gram Sabhas as the Parliament of the People at the grassroots level to whom the Gram Panchayats are solely accountable.

Office Bearers of the Panchayats

Village Pradhan or Sarpanch: The members of the Village Panchayat elect one of their members as Sarpanch or the Pradhan who is the Head-Panch or the President of the Panchayat. It is his duty to call the meetings of the Panchayat and to preside over these meetings.

The Panchayat Secretary: The District Magistrate or the Deputy Commissioner appoints The Panchayat Secretary. He is a salaried officer who maintains the records and the registers of the work done by the Panchayat. He also prepares accounts, etc. He is a permanent employee. Generally, he looks after the work of two or three Panchayats.

Functions of the Village Panchayat

The functions of a Village Panchayat can be divided into two categories:

(i) Essential or Compulsory, and

(ii) Optional or Voluntary.

Essential or Compulsory Functions: The essential or compulsory functions of the Village Panchayats are as follows:

1. Construction and maintenance of village roads and waterways.
2. Construction of culverts and roads.
3. Planting of trees.
4. Construction and repair of village wells and tanks.
5. Provision of clean drinking water.
6. Provision of lights on roads and streets.
7. Sanitation and public health.
8. Supervision over the work of the government servants such as the Patwari, the Lekhpal, the police constable, the chowkidar, the vaccinator or the peon, and to report any complaint against them to the higher authorities.
9. Supervision of the Primary Schools.

Optional or Voluntary Functions

The optional or voluntary functions of the Panchayats are as follows:

1. Management of hospitals and maternity centers.
2. Management of village markets.
3. Management of veterinary hospitals for the treatment of cattle.
4. Supply of good seeds and fertilizers.
5. Organizing recreation and entertainment programmes, such as Akharas, or village sports.
6. Opening and maintaining libraries.
7. Holding of village fairs.

Sources of Income:

For all these functions, the Panchayat needs money. The various sources of its income are the following:

1. Taxes on houses and shops.
2. Taxes on fairs and markets.

3. Fees realized from registration of sale and purchase of cattle.
4. Income from the sale of public property.
5. Government grants

The Nyaya Panchayat

Generally, there is one Nyaya Panchayat for three or four villages. Each Village Panchayat elects some members to the Nyaya Panchayat. No person can be a member of both the Panchayat Samiti and the Nyaya Panchayat at the same time. The Nyaya Panchayats can hear only such petty cases as tress pass, minor thefts and other cases of simple nature, whether civi I or criminal. They can impose fines up to one hundred rupees. If a party is not satisfied with its judgement, it can go in appeal to the High Court. The \ ~yaya Panchayat cannot send a person to prison. The establishment of the Nyaya Panchayats has a great significance for the poor people because they save them from undue expenditure and litigation on minor disputes. The cases tried by these Panchayats are decided quickly and there is little chance of misleading the panchayat by telling lie

Panchayati Raj Institutions since 1959

As the working of Panchayati Raj Institutions since 1959 has been argued as successful in a few states and a failure in most of the states. It means that the system has been experiencing ups and downs. Although, the concept of Panchayati Raj is a State subject but basically each state is free to evolve its own system depending upon Local needs, circumstances administrative conveniences and experiences. With the result, we have a variety of Panchayati Raj institutions with all kinds of combinations and permutations. In fact, their success or failure depends upon their structure, powers, function leadership, finances and state control. In a big country like India, changes in different aspects of these bodies have been taking place as per the changing circumstances. Although the whole activities of Panchayati Raj institutions are broad based but their resource base are very weak. As things stand today, the local economy is very weak which indicates that Panchayati Raj

Institutions have very limited scope to impose taxes in their jurisdiction.

Introduction of Panchayati Raj was hailed as one of the most important political innovations in independent India. It was also considered as a revolutionary step. Panchayati Raj is a system of local self-government where in the people take upon themselves the responsibility for development. It is also a system of institutional arrangement for achieving rural Development through people's initiative and participation. Panchayati Raj involves a three-tier structure of democratic institutions at district, block and village levels namely, Zilla Parishad, Panchayat Samiti and Village Panchayats respectively. These institutions are considered as training ground for democracy and gives political education to the masses. These institutions were established in 1959 based on the philosophy of decentralization 4 and gram swaraj. Rural development plans and programmes are implemented at this level so that fruits of development can accrue to the community directly.

Both the Central and State Governments have appointed several Committees and Commissions for reviewing and recommending reforms to strengthen Panchayati Raj during the last three decades. Panchayati Raj that emerged in the states is substantially in tune with Balwant Rai Mehta team recommendations though there are distinguishing differences from state to state. Another Committee of Panchayati Raj appointed by the Central Government under the Chairmanship of Shri Ashok Mehta in 1978 is very important as it reviewed the system of Panchayati Raj in different states in the country and recommended a different structure of Panchayati Raj.

Starting with Rajstahan several states introduced Panchayati Raj in quick succession. In a handsome tribute, Prof. Maddick 7 describing the Mehta report "as an outstanding document and model of the way in which the growth of democratic institutitons in the country one of vital importance while inaugurating Panchayati Raj at Nagour, Rajstahan on October 2, 1959, Nehru 8 said with understandable enthusiasm, "we are going to lay the foundation of democracy or Panchayati Raj in India,".

The focus was still on community projects and N.E.S and he thought that the reason for slow progress was dependence on official Machinary, a situation which would be remedied, by Panchayati Raj. At a Seminar in Jaipur in Dec, 1964 Balwant Rai Mehta clearly stated that community development is the object, the purpose, and Panchayati Raj is the instrument for implementing the programme.

The draft fifth plan stated "The basic concept behind establishing Panchayati Raj was to create rural local self government agencies reasonable for discharging certain selected functions pertaining to development. Panchayati Raj is the instrument of community development, the apparatus of rural local self government a means of reorganising district administration not adequately people oriented in its traditional form and an agent of state government for certain purposes. After the death of Nehru both national and inter national problems, and understandable anxiety over performance on the development front; served to weaken this faith and Panchayati Raj came under attack.

During that time Hanson clearly stated, "if Panchayati Raj was to function effectively, within a reasonably short span of time, as a development institution, its introduction had to be accompanied by revolutionary changes in the social and economic structure of the village. However, a little later, Panchayati Raj is hailed as the most important political invention of independent India, because through it, the massess of Indian people are beginning, for the first time in their history, to experience the realities of democracy, in however, contradictory of distorted form.

Process of Decline

After the mid sixties, the process of decline started. In many states a tendency to postpone the Panchayati Raj elections indefinitely was noticeable. In some states, parallel bodies came to be set up at the district level, thus reducing the role of Panchayati Raj in development planning & implementation.

Main Problems

Started with great hope and enthusiasm some of the major problems and short comings that devoted in the working Panchayati Raj institutions can be identified as:

(i) Election not being held on a regular basis.

(ii) Lack of adequate transfer of powers and resources to Panchayati institutions.

(iii) Lack of Panchayati Raj bodies to generate their own resources such as tax on sale land.

(iv) Non-Representation of woman and weaker sections in the elected bodies.

Revival of Panchayati Raj

The G.V.K. Rao committee 10 appointed by the Planning Commission in 1985 to review the existing administrative arrangements for rural development strongly recommended for the revival of Panchayati Raj institutitons all over the Country & highlighting the need to transfer power of state to democratic bodies at the Local level. The government of India their set up committee in June 1986 headed by L.M. Singvi. To prepare a concept paper on the revitalization of the Panchayati Raj institutions, the Committee recommended that the Panchayati Raj should be constitutionally recognized, protected and preserved by the inclusion of a new chapter in the constitution. It also suggested a constitutional provision to ensure regular, free and fair elections for Panchayati Raj institutions. Accepting these recommendations of the Committee the central government headed by late Rajiv Gandhi brought in the Constitution 12 64th amendment Bill which was passed by the Lok Sabha on the 16th August 1989. This was comprehensive Bill covering all vital aspects of PRI 'S. Unfortunately, this Bill could not be enacted as it was not approved by the Rajya Sabha. In the year 1990, the issues relating to strengthening of Panchayati Raj institutions were considered afresh and based on detailed discussions in the Cabinet committee set up for this purpose.

It was considered that a constitution Amendment Bill may be drawn up afresh. The matter was brought up before a Conference of Chief Ministers held in June, 1990 presided over by the then Prime Minister. The Conference endorsed the proposals for the introduction of Constitution Amendment Bill and also the model guidelines with the modification that the number of tiers in the

Panchayati Raj structure, may be left to be decided by the State governments and the arrangement for conduct of elections for PRI's may also be left to be made by the state themselves.

The Constitutitons Amendment Bill and model guidelines were approved by the Cabinet in July 1990 and it was decided that there should be a Common Constitution Amendment Bill both for PRI's and Urban Local bodies.13 Further modifications were made in the Bill on the basis of the discussions with the leaders of various political parties.

73rd and 74th Constitution Amendment perspective & Rebirth of Panchayati Raj: The Constitution 74th Amendment Bill introduced in the Lok Sabha on September 7, 1990 it could not however, be taken up in view of the political changes. A Comprehensive amendment was introduced in the form of Constitution Seventy Second Amendment Bill 1991 by the then government. The Constitution 72nd Amendment Bill was passed in the Lok Sabha on Dec. 23, 1992. 73rd Amendment Act 1992 has came into effect from April 24, 1993. The Constitution 73rd 14 Amendment Act 1992 indicates states to establish three tier system of strong viable and responsive panchayats at the Village, intermediate and district levels.

The Constitution (73rd Amendment) Act, 1992 and the Constitution (74th Amendment) Act, 1992 have added new Parts IX and IX A to the Constitution. Under these two parts, we have as many as 34 new articles-243 to 243ZG-and two new schedules viz. schedules 11 and 12. The 73rd Amendment gives constitutional recognition to the Panchayats and the 74th Amendment to the Municipalities. Thus, to the Union and the States, a third tier of governmental instrumentalities has been added. There is nothing entirely new about the institutions of Panchayats and Municipalities. Both these have existed for long. There were local self government and Panchayati Raj laws in many parts of India. But, unfortunately these institutions were not able to function satisfactorily for any length of time. Often, they stood superceded. Despite the Gandhian approach of treating the villages as units of polity and Gandhi's love for Panchayati Raj institutions, Dr. Ambedkar in the Constituent Assembly did not favour them and even said some very harsh things like their being dens of corruption, localism, backwardness etc. Finally, as a compromise or a concession to Gandhi's views, article 40 was included under the non-enforceable Part V on the Directive Principles of State Policy. It said that the state shall take steps to organize Village Panchayats and endow them with necessary authority "to function as units of self-government".

Hardly any attention was paid to article 40 until Prime Minister Rajiv Gandhi took serious interest and initiative to bring forward a constitutional amendment. It was, however opposed on grounds of its being an effort to reach the Panchayats directly, bypassing the States. The amendment finally became a reality during Narasirnha Rao's time. The seventy-third and seventy-fourth constitutional amendments have made some fundamental changes in our political structure and in the status of local institutions. These institutions now have constitutional protection. The two amendments provide for the state legislatures making their own laws under the constitutional provisions for establishing Panchayats, Municipalities, etc. and conferring on them such powers and authority as may be necessary to enable them to function as institutions of self-government. In every State, a three-tier system is envisaged. Panchayats are to be established at the Village and district levels and at the intermediate level. States which have a population of less than two million, need not have the intermediate level Panchayats.

The important thing is that now Panchayats have to be elected directly by the people in the same manner as members of the popular houses at the Union and State levels are elected i.e. through territorial constituencies. For a Village Panchayat, the electorate would be the Gram Sabha which would consist of those registered in the electoral rolls. These Panchayats cannot remain superceded for long; fresh elections would have to be held within six months of the dissolution of a Panchayat. Secondly, in all panchayats, seats would be reserved for women, Scheduled Castes and Scheduled Tribes. There shall be a fixed five year term for all Panchayats. They shall have their own budget, power of taxation and list of items in their jurisdiction. In their respective areas, the Panchayats shall be able to formulate their own development plans and implement them. Every State shall have a State Election. Commissioner for conducting Panchayat elections and I every five years a State Finance commission shall be constituted to take stock of the economic condition of the Panchayats.

Similarly, in the 74th Amendment, there are provisions for the setting up of Nagar Palikas and Nagar Panchayats. In the matter of reservations, elections, power of taxation, formulation and implementation of development projects, constitution of a Finance Commission, fixed term, etc., the provisions are very similar to those in the 73rd Amendment in respect of Panchayats

Under the distribution of legislative powers between ! the Union and the States, local government in both rural and urban areas has been in the exclusive State List. As it is, all the States-some reluctantly-have already passed legislation as required under the new constitutional provisions. Elections to local bodies have also been held in almost all the States. Bihar is an exception. Also; the 73rd and 74th Amendments do not apply to the States of Meghalaya, Mizoram, Nagaland and Jammu and Kashmir, the Union Territory of Delhi, hill areas in Manipur and Darjeeling in W. Bengal. Also, these do not apply unless extended to Scheduled Areas and Tribal Areas under article 244. The Constitution (Eighty-third Amendment of the year 2000 has added a clause to article 243M to provide that reservation of seats for the Scheduled Castes under article 243D shall not apply to the State of Arunachal Pradesh. It was hoped that the new Panchayats and Municipalities would begin a new era of real representative and participatory democracy with nearly three and a half million elected representatives-one third of them women-involved in the business of governance all over India thereby bringing power to the people where it belonged. As things stood, matters causing some concern were:

(i) The Constitution (87th Amendment) Bill, 1999 introduced by the Minister for Rural Development on 16 December 1999 seeks to amend article 243 C of the Constitution with a view to give discretion to State Legislatures to provide that all the seats in panchayats at the intermediate and district levels shall be filled by persons elected as

Chairpersons at the village level panchayats and intermediate level panchayats and also to provide discretion in the manner in which the Chairpersons of the panchayats at the intermediate level or the district level have to be elected as has been allowed in case of panchayats at the village level.

The Amendment Bill followed a request contained in a resolution passed by the Andhra Assembly. The pending Bill is being used as an alibi for postponing elections to the district and intermediate level panchayats.

(ii) The Area Development Scheme which places at the disposal of every member of Union Parliament a sum of Rupees two crares every year for being spent in his! her area on his/her recommendation on items mentioned in the guide list. There are similar schemes placing funds at the disposal of MLAs at the level of States. All the Items on which these large funds can be spent at the discretion of MPs and MLAs are covered by the eleventh and twelfth schedules of the Constitution listing schemes to be entrusted to the Panchayats, Municipalities etc. The Area Development Schemes and the like are tantamount to legislators' foray into the area of executive functions. Secondly, this may seem to be an affront to and a violation of the federal scheme as also of the basic spirit of Panchayati Raj institutions.

(iii) Much can be said for and against the ex-officio membership of local Lok Sabha members and M.L.A.s on the district and intermediate level panchayats.

(iv) The ground realities indicate that, for their own reasons, those elected to Parliament and State Legislatures-the M.P.s, M.L.A.s and M.L.C.s-have not

(v) The details of functioning of the Local Government institutions are largely left to the initiative of the State Governments and are to be settled by them. The States have passed vastly varied laws according to their own perception of what and how much can be devolved on the local authorities. While the States naturally want the Union to transfer more of effective legislative, executive and financial powers in wider areas to them, the question is to what extent they would be themselves willing to decentralise further down and share effective power with local self-government institutions. So far as the 73rd and 74th Constitution Amendments are concerned, these do not themselves confer any powers on panchayats and Municipalities

Reservation for Woman in Panchayati Raj Institutions

The Constitution 73rd Amendment Act in order to revive the existing Panchayati Raj system due to its structural and functional inadequacies has made mandatory on the part of the states that they would reserve a minimum of 30 per cent of seats to woman in their Panchayati Raj institutions so as to involve actively in the decision making process. In accordance with the 73rd Amendment 33 per cent of seats have been reserved for rural woman in the Panchayati Raj Institutions. The Statutory reservation of seats for woman in Panchayati Raj bodies has provided an opportunity for their formal involvement in the development and political processes at the grass root level thereby to enabling them to influence the decision making process in the local governments.

Implications of constitutional 73rd & 74 Amendment: The 73rd & 74th Constitutional Amendment 16 has been made to many weakness. It has certain features which are binding on the state legislature where they can go to discretion:

I. Constitutional Status to Panchayati Raj Institutions.

II. Reservation of Seats for Weaker Section of Society.

III. Direct Election of Panchayati Raj, every five years at all levels.

IV. Finance Commission to be set up by State Government to devolve funds and suggest ways of financing

V. Election Commission at State Level to Conduct Panchayati Raj Elections.

All these elected bodies have now, been in position for more than five years. It is thus, important to verify whether the aims and objectives of the Constitutional amendment and the aspirations generated by it have been met and if so, to what extent. Various discussions, debates, conferences are being organized to see and many issues are debated for new experience.

Panchayati Raj Institutions

I. Devolution of finances to PRI's bodies.

II. Exercise of Power and responsibility by Panchayati Raj Institution.

III. What has been the impact of the reservations especially for woman and to what extant this has helped the weaker section of society.

IV. Whether the PRI's in the new set up have improved their position regarding devolution of powers and financial resources in view of setting up State Finance and Election Commissions.

V. What sort of training and orientation 18 would be required for the newly elected Panchayati Raj bodies.

In a net-shell the 73rd Amendment had aroused a lot of expectations and it is to be expected that it would usher Panchayati Raj Institutions in a new and dynamic role. The PRI in the district comprises of one Zilla Parishad at the district level, 7 Panchayat Samitis/ 4 Block Advisory Committee (BAC) at the Block level and 155-Gram Panchayats/ 167 ADC Villages at the village level. The Chief Executive Officer (DM & Collector) Zilla Parishad, Additional Chief Executive Officer (ADM & Collector) Zilla Parishad and Secretary Zilla Parishad (Member Secretary) are the Official Members in the Executive Committee of Zilla Parishad. The Executive Officer (Block Development Officer) Panchayat Samiti and the Secretary (Panchayat Extension Officer-Member Secretary) are the Official Members in the Executive committee of the Panchayat Samitis.

It consists of 21 directly elected members and 24 Ex-officio members. The Chairman of the different Panchayat Samitis/ BACs of the district, the MLAs elected from the constituencies falling under District and MPs of the two parliamentary constituencies constitute the Ex-officio members. All the Panchayat Samitis in the district is being constituted from 22 directly elected members and 29 Ex-officio members. Each Panchayat Samiti and Zilla Parishad consist of 7 Standing Committees.

(i) Finance, Audit and Planning Committee (to be known as Finance Committee).

(ii) Education, Environment, Cultural, Health and Sports Affairs Committee (to be known as Education and Health Committee).

(iii) Communication, Rural Electrification and non-conventional Energy Committee (to be known as Works Committee)

(iv) Industries including Cottage Industry and Sericultlural Committee (to be known as Industries Committee).

(v) Social Justice Committee.

(vi) Agricultural, Food, Irrigation, Cooperation, Fisheries and Animal Husbandry Committee (to be known as Agriculture Committee).

(vii) Poverty Alleviation Programme, Social and Farm Forestry, Rural Housing and Drinking Water Committee (to be known as Poverty alleviation Committee).

The number of members to be elected for each standing committee and the Zilla Parishad has been notified by the State Government. The Chairman and the Vice Chairman of the Panchayat Samiti and the Sabhadhipati and the Sahakari Sabhadhipati of the Zilla Parishad are the Ex-officio members of the Standing Committees of the Panchayat Samities or the Zilla Parishad as the case may be. Also, the Chairman of the Panchayat Samiti and the Sabhadhipati of Zilla Parishad shall be the President of the Standing Committee in Finance, Audit and Planning of the Panchayat Samiti or the Zilla Parishad, as the case may be.

In case of Hrishyamukh Panchayat Samiti and Amarpur Panchayat Samiti, a member of the Panchayat Samiti other than the Chairman and the Vice-Chairman shall be eligible to serve on maximum 3 Standing Committees. In case of other Panchayat Samitis, no member other than the Chairman and the Vice-Chairman shall be eligible to serve on more than 2 Standing

Committees. Similarly, in case of DTZP, no member other than the Sabhadhipati and the Sahakari Sabhadhipati shall be eligible to serve on more than 2 Standing Committees. The Ex-officio members of the Panchayat Samiti or Zilla Parishad could be elected as Members and Presidents of Standing Committees of Panchayat Samiti or Zilla Parishad, except, as the President of Standing Committee for Finance, Audit and Planning.

The elections of the members of the Standing Committees and their respective Chairmans and Vice Chairman's are to be held after every 2 years for Panchayat Samiti and 5 years for Zilla Parishad. Project Director DRDA, District Panchayat Officer, District Planning Officer, Deputy registrar of Cooperative Societies, Development Officer Institutional Finance, District Statistical Officer, Lead Bank officer, Senior Deputy Collector looking after Revenue Section of the Office of the DM & Collector and a nominated Professor/ Assistant Professor of Economics are the Official Members of the Finance Standing Committee.

The Official Members of Education and Health Standing Committee comprises of Chief Medical Officer, Deputy Director of Education, District Level Officer from Science and Technology Department, Assistant Director of ICAT Department, Deputy Director of Physical Education, District Inspector of Social Education, one nominated Headmaster and Representative of the Ramkrishna Mission.

The Official Members of Works Standing Committee comprises of Superintending Engineer (PWD), Superintending Engineer (Electrical), District Level Officer of the Science and Technology Department, Executive Engineer RD Department, Senior Deputy Collector looking after Development Section of the office of the DM & Collector and the Executive Engineer (PWD) from different Divisions of the district.

Project Director DRDA, General Manager District Industries Centre, Officer-in-Charge of the Cluster Constituted for development of Sericulture and Handloom of the District, Representative of KVIC and the Assistant Marketing Officer / Assistant Development Officer of THHDC LTD constitutes the Official Members in Industry Standing Committee.

District Tribal Welfare Officer, any Member of the Mahila Commission, District Inspector of Social Education, Representative of State Social Welfare Board for the district and representative of the Ramkrishna Mission constitutes the Official Members in Social Justice Standing Committee.

The Official Members of Agriculture Standing Committee comprises of Senior Collector looking after the Food and Civil Supplies in the office of the DM & Collector, Executive Engineer of concerned MIFC Division, Deputy Registrar Cooperative Societies Deputy Director of Agriculture, Horticulturist, Deputy Project Officer (Soil Conservation), Deputy Director of Fisheries and the Deputy Director of Animal Resources Development.

The Official Members of Poverty Alleviation Standing Committee is constituted of the Conservator of Forest, Additional District Magistrate & Collector, Project Director DRDA, Executive Engineer RD Division, Deputy Director of Fisheries, Horticulturist and the Executive Engineer PHE. The Gram Panchayats in the non-tribal areas and the ADC villages in the tribal areas are directly responsible to the villagers for all the development activities of their electoral constituency. The Gram Panchayat is regularly conducting Gram Sabha, a forum of active participation by the electorates in the constituency. The following agendas are being normally laid down and discussed in the Gram Sabha:

(a) Accounts of income & expenditure of the Gram Panchayat.

(b) Annual Administrative Report for the last financial year.

(c) Last Audit Note and resolutions regarding rectification.

(d) Budget of the Gram Panchayat for the current financial year.

(e) Details of the receipt of fund and developmental activities taken up and completed during the last financial year.

(f) Likely receipt of fund and proposed developmental activities to be taken up during the current financial year.

As per the provisions of Panchayat Act, Gram Sansad has also been constituted at the Gram Panchayat Constituency level (Wards) to involve citizens more in the development aspects of the Gram Panchayat.

Politics of Constitutional Amendments in India

A Constitution is a dynamic document. It should grow with a growing' nation and should suit the changing needs and circumstances of a growing a changing people. Sometimes under the impact of new powerful social and economic forces, the pattern of government will require major changes. If the Constitution stands as a stumbling block to such desirable changes, it may under extreme pressure, be destroyed. A Constitution, as such, cannot have an: claim to permanence; nor should it, because it has been adopted and has been working ever since, claim absolute sanctity. Mulford has rightly said: ", unamendable constitution is the worst tyranny of time or rather the very tyranny of time.".

Herman Finer defined constitution as the process of amendment, for in his view, to amend is to deconstitute or reconstitute. W. Munro has rightly observed: "....... it is impossible to conceive of an unamendable constitution as any thing but a contradiction in terms."

A Constitution is a fundamental document of the land. It is a document which defines the position and power of the three organs of the State--the Executive, the Legislature and the Judiciary. It also defines the powers of the Executive and the Legislature as against the citizens.

In fact, the purpose of a Constitution is not merely to create the organs of the state but also to limit their authority, because if no limitation is imposed upon the authority of the organs, there will be tyranny and oppression. Naturally, such a fundamental document as a constitution should not undergo too frequent and easy changes as that would undermine the confidence of the citizens in the abiding nature of the Constitution.

Jawahar Lal Nehru has rightly said, "......The Constitution cannot and should not be changed frequently. Obviously also, it can and must be changed when the situation requires it to be changed." A Constitution to be living must be growing; must be adaptable; must be flexible, must be changeable. Indeed, any amendment of the constitution should be justified by compelling reasons and circumstances.

Amendment Process in the Indian Constitution

Federal Constitutions as a rule are rigid as most of them have extremely difficult and even complicated procedures of amendment. Amending a federal constitution like that of the U.S.A. and Australia is perhaps the most difficult.

In contrast, the Constitution of India presents a much simpler process. As Ambedkar pointed out in the Constituent Assembly, "The provisions for amendment while they embodied in certain measure of rigidity with regard to some parts of the Constitution, were flexible and afforded facilities for a simple process of amendment with regard to others." Pointing out the details of the scheme he stated: 'We propose to divide the various articles of the Constitution into three categories.

In First category we have placed certain articles which would be open to amendment by Parliament by simple majority. The Second set of articles requires a two-thirds majority of Parliament. The Third category requires a two-thirds majority of Parliament plus ratification by the States. The States are given an important voice in the amendment of these matters. These are fundamental matters where States have important powers under the Constitution and any unilateral amendment by Parliament may vitally affect the fundamental basis of the system built up by the Constitution."

The procedure for amendment is detailed under Article 368 of the Constitution. According to this, there are three ways of amending the Constitution:

Amendment by Simple Majority: There are a good number of Articles in Constitution which are of transitory nature. Though they can be changed by Parliament by passing a law by simple majority technically speaking changes made therein, are not to be considered as amendment of the Constitution. By simple majority is meant, simple majority of the members present and voting. For example, changes in the names and boundaries of the States, creation or abolition of the Legislative Councils in the States, salaries and allowances of the President, Governors and Judges of the Supreme Court and High Courts, etc., can be made by Parliament by passing a law by simple majority.

The following provisions of the Constitution also fall under this category:

1. Second Schedule of the Constitution.
2. Article 100(3) of the Constitution which fixes quorum of the transaction of business in the Parliament.
3. Article 105 of the Constitution which deals with powers, privileges and immunities of Members of Parliament.
4. Article 11 regarding acquisition and termination of citizenship.
5. Article 124 which deals with the appointment of Judges in the Supreme Court.
6. Article 135 which deals with conferring more jurisdictions on the Supreme Court.
7. Article 81 relating to the delimitation of Constituencies.
8. Article 137 of the Constitution which deals with Supreme Court's powers to review its own judgment.

Amendment by Special Majority: An amendment of the Constitution may be initiated only by the introduction of a Bill for the purpose in either House of Parliament. When the Bill is passed in each House by a majority of the total membership of that House and by a majority of not less than two-thirds of the members of that House present and voting, it shall be presented to the President for his assent. When the President gives his assent, the Constitution stands amended in accordance with the terms of the Bill.

Ratification by the State Legislatures: For the amendment of certain other provisions of the Constitution, a Bill has to be passed by each House of Parliament by a majority of the total membership of that House and by a majority of not less than two-thirds of the members present and voting, then the amendment must be ratified by the Legislatures of not less than one-half of the States by resolutions to that effect is required before the amendment Bill is presented to the President for assent. The following provisions of the' Constitution fall under this category:

1. Election of President (Article 57);

2. Extent of the Executive power of the Union (Article 73);
3. Extent of the Executive power of States (Article 162);
4. Union Judiciary (Chapter IV of Part V);
5. High Courts in the States (Chapter V of Part VI);
6. Any of the Lists in the Seventh Schedule;
7. The representation of States in Parliament; and
8. Provisions dealing with amendment of the Constitution.

Salient Features of the Amendment Process

The salient features of the Amendment Process are:

1. *Introduction only in either House of Parliament*: The Bill for the amendment of the Constitution can be introduced in either House of parliament and not in any State Assembly.
2. *Both Houses of Parliament must pass it separately*: An Amendment Bill should be passed by both the Houses of Parliament separately. The Constitution cannot be amended in case of a deadlock between the two. Houses. There is no provision for a joint sitting if both Houses differ. For example, in 1970, the Rajya Sabha rejected the 24th Constitutional Amendment Bill which provided for the derecognition of the Princes and again in 1978, as many as five out of forty-nine clauses of the 45th Constitution Amendment Bill were rejected by the Rajya Sabha and as a result there of, the Lok Sabha had no alternative but to dele these five clauses.
3. *Meaning of majority of total membership*: The expression 'majority Of total membership' means that it is not the majority of the actual membership of the House but the majority of the total prescribed strength of the House notwithstanding the vacancies therein.
4. *Special majority at every stage of the passing of the Bill*: Whether this 'special majority' mentioned above is needed at the time of final voting on the Bill or even on the earlier stages of the Bill. The Constitution Amendment Bill even at its introduction stage must be supported by a two-thirds majority of members present and voting which should not

be less than 50 per cent of the total strength. In 1969, the 24th Constitution Amendment Bill regarding abolition of Privy Purses could not be introduced because the requisite majority did not support it. It means special majority is needed at the passing of every stage of the Bill.

5. *Ratification by the Legislatures of not less than one-half of the States.* The amendment of the articles mentioned in the provision of Article 368, must be ratified by one-half of the State Legislatures by passing resolutions in that of, respect. The expression 'State Legislature' does not include the legislatures of the Union Territories. Wherever the State Legislature is bicameral, the resolutions must be passed by both Houses separately and the resolutions so passed do not require the signature or the assent of the Governor.
6. *Presidential assent.* In the final stage, the Constitution Amendment Bill is presented to the President for his assent which the President cannot refuse. But there is no time limit within which the President must give his assent. He can keep it pending for some time in the first instance, though ordinarily it is expected that he would give his assent as soon as possible.

Thus, the Constitution is partly rigid and partly flexible document. "There; is hardly another federal constitution which provides a comparable example, winning rigidity and flexibility. In the words of Jawahar Lal Nehru: "While 'we want this Constitution to be as solid and as permanent a structure as we make it, nevertheless there is no permanence in constitutions. There should be a certain flexibility. If you make anything rigid and permanent, you stop a nation's growth, the growth of a living vital organic people. Therefore, it has to, be flexible." K.C. Where are, keeping in view the 'wide variety of the amending, process, has commented that it strikes a good balance by protecting the rights of the States while leaving the remainder of the Constitution easy to amend. But-we must bear the testimony of the fact that this 'ease' in amending process of the Indian Constitution was due to the one-party dominance both at the centre and in the State for nearly thirty years.

The practical limitations of ending process are for the first time being experienced by the Janata Government at the Centre, where it was lacking a two-thirds majority in Rajya Sabha. Under such situation, the Janata Government was unable to remove the controversial clauses of the 42nd amendment without seeking, the cooperation of the Congress Party. The '64th Constitutional Amendment Bill also had fallen through on March 30, 1990 in, the Lok Sabha for want of the requisite two-thirds majority, even though all parties had declared their support for the measure. The bill was related to extend President's rule in Punjab for six months. The 75th amendment bill, for the same purpose, also fell through (in October 1990) because the Congress (I) declined to back it. At the same time, another feature which strikes the minds of critics, is that the units or States, like those of the American States, have no Jurisdiction to Initiate any formal constitutional amendment neither there is any provision for referendum as 'such. It should appear, thus, that although the States say in the formal amendment of the Constitution is not considerable, their vital interests have been shielded by the Constitution.

The Amending Power and the Doctrine of Basic Structure

The Golak Nath case judgment and the amendments which sought to nullify its effect, when came up for the Supreme Court's scrutiny in the case of Kesavananda Bharti against the State of Kerala and other allied petitions In 1973, it propounded the doctrine of implied powers and the doctrine of basic structure, which were hitherto unknown in India. In Kesavananda Bharti vs. State of Kerala, the Supreme Court reasonably upheld the validity of the 24th Amendment. It was, however, held by the majority that Parliament's power of Amendment was subject to implied limitation, namely, Parliament could not amend the Constitution to bring about change in the basic features of the Constitution.

In this case the Supreme Court invalidated the following portion of Article 31(c) which was inserted through 25th Amendment Act. ".....and now law containing a declaration that it is for giving effect to such policy be called in question in any court on the ground that it does not give effect to such policy." The Court through its decision in Kesavananda's case tried to protect its right of judicial review and exposed the nefarious intention of the government in " excluding judicial review, when the law did not give effect to the policy involving Articles 39(b) and (c).

In the Kesavananda Bharti's case, the majority of judges held that the amending power was a limited one even though they knew that the legislature was bent upon giving unlimited amending power to itself. This courageous and independent stand was taken on the basis of the principle called 'inherent and implied limitation'. No doubt, the Constitution does not have any provision for drafting a new_ Constitution but that does not mean that the legislature can destroy, reshape of" or restructure the Constitution. It is, therefore, logical to assume that the implied limitation restricts the legislature in changing the Constitution unidentifiably. An argument stating that Parliament's will is people's will and therefore, Parliament still have an unlimited amending power, is preposterous because the electorate does not take into account the constitutional amendments while voting in the Parliamentary elections. Had people's will been Parliament's will, the Australian electorate would not have approved only five out of thirty-two changes in the Constitution proposed by Parliament in 74 years.

So, what has to be understood clearly is that Article 368 allows the legislature to make amendments only to the extent that the Constitution does not lose its identity. Parliament by passing the 24th amendment, altered Article, 368 to' enlarge the ambit of its amending power under that very article. This is a clear violation of the principle of implied limitation. A creature of the Constitution, however, vast its power, cannot regard itself superior to the Constitution. N.A. Palkhivala is very right when he says that "It cannot itself as the master and make the Constitution subservient; it cannot convert con_ trolled constitution into an uncontrolled one.

In Kesvananda Bharti's case" six senior judges of the Supreme Court an C.J., S.M. Sikri held as follows:

(i) *Parliament's amending power is limited*. While Parliament is entitled' to a bridge any Fundamental Right or amend any provision of the Constitution, the amending power does not extend to damaging or destroying any of the essential features of the Constitution fundamental Rights are among the essential features of the Constitution; therefore, while they may be abridged. The abridgement cannot attend to the limit of damage to or destruction of their core.

(ii) Article 31C is void since it takes many invaluable Fundamental Rights even those unconnected with property.

To sum, the Supreme Court held that the Constitution is not made to suffer a loss of identity through the amending process. The identity of the Constitution is the sum of its essential features. Article 368 cannot be read as expressing the, death wish of the Constitution or as a provision for its legal suicide.

The Philosophy of the Indian Constitution

The concepts of democracy, representative institutions, limitations on the arbitrary powers of the rulers, and rule of law were not alien to India in the hoary past. The concept of the supremacy of Dharma was hardly different from the rule of law or limited government. The rulers in ancient India were bound by Dharma, no one was above Dharma. Enough evidence has come to light to show that republican forms of government, representative deliberative bodies and local self-government institutions existed in many parts of ancient India and democratic thinking and practices permeated different aspects of the life of the people right from the Vedic age (circa 3000-1000 B.C.).

The Rigveda and the Atharvaveda mention the Sabha (General Assembly) and the Samiti (House of Elders). The Aitareya Brahmana, Panini's Ashtadhyayi, Kautilya's Arthashastra, the Mahabharata, inscriptions on Ashoka's pillars, the Budhhist and Jain texts of the period and the Manusmriti all bear witness to the existence of several functioning republics during the post-Vedic period of Indian history. After the Mahabharata particularly, large empires gave way to a number of small republican states. Jatakas make many references to how these republics functioned. The members met in Santhagar. Representatives were elected in open assembly. They selected their gopa who became King and ruled with the help of a Council of Ministers.

In the 4th century B.C. the republican federation known as the Kshudrak MalIa Sangha offered strong resistance to Alexander. Near Patliputra (Patna), there, was Vaishali, the Capital of Lichchavis. The state was a republic governed by an assembly with an elected President called Nayak. Unfortunately, we know little of the details of the constitution of these republics. The Greek scholar Megasthenes has left records of popular assemblies that were preserved in the South and which restrained the power of Kings.

Kautilya's Arthashastra also records that autocracy or the Divine Right of Kings had no place in ancient Indian polity. The power of the Indian King was hedged in by safeguards against abuse and limited by liberties and powers of other public authorities and interests. He was, in fact, a limited or a constitutional monarch. Manu and the Mahabharata say that an unjust and oppressive ruler should be killed by his own subjects like a street dog gone mad. Nitisara (Science of Polity) of Shukracharya written in the tenth century is a book on constitution. It deals with the organization of the central government as well as village and town life, of the King's Council and of various departments of government. The King was to act on the opinion of the majority of the people. Independent Sovereign Republic and to draw up for her future governance a Constitution:

WHEREIN the territories that now comprise British India, the territories that now form the Indian States, and such other parts of India as are outside British India and the States as well as such other territories as are willing to be constituted into the Independent Sovereign India, shall be a Union of them all; and

WHEREIN the said territories, whether with their present boundaries or with such others as may be determined by the Constituent Assembly and thereafter according to the law of the constitution, shah possess and retain the status of autonomous units, together with residuary powers, and exercise all powers and functions of Government and administration, save and except such powers and functions as are vested in or assigned to the Union, or as are inherent or implied in the Union or resulting therefrom; and

WHEREIN all power and authority of the Sovereign Independent India, its constituent parts and organs of Governments are derived from the people; and

WHEREIN shall be guaranteed and secured to all the people of India justice, social, economic and political; equality of status, of opportunity, and before the law; freedom of thought, expression, belief, faith, worship, vocation, association and action, subject to law and public morality; and

WHEREIN adequate safeguards shall be provided for minorities, backward and tribal areas, and depressed and other backward classes; and

WHEREIN shall be maintained the integrity of the territory of the Republic and its sovereign rights' on land, sea, and air according to justice and the law of civilisea, nations; and

The ancient land attain its rightful and honoured place in the world and make its full and fulfilling contribution to the promotion of world peace and the welfare of mankind."

In the words of Pandit Nehru, the aforesaid Resolution was "something more than a resolution. It is a declaration, a firm resolve, a pledge, an undertaking and for all of us a dedication".

3

Party System and Elections

Nature of Party System in India

Political parties are indispensable for the successful functioning of democracy. Modern democracies are representative or indirect democracies. The citizens of a state elect the representatives periodically at election. Political parties put up the candidates and present their programmes and appeal to' the electors to vote for their candidates. The party, which secures the majority at election, forms the government and implements the programmes, which they had put before the electorate and are approved by them. The political parties have come to occupy the most influential and dominating position in the process of democratic government. Yet they are an extra-legal growth. No democratic constitution mentions the existence of a political party.

There were no political parties during the initial stages of some of the major democracies of today. Unlike other political institutions, it is not created by or not even referred to in any constitution. But later it has become as indispensable as the constitution itself. In Britain where the party system 6riginated, it is still outside the legal framework of the state. But without political parties the British constitution, which is mainly based on conventions is unworkable. Similarly the makers of the constitutions of USA abhorred political parties, because they thought, it would encourage division, strife, and manipulation. But within a few years the party system became the mainstay of American democratic system. Presently Political parties influence, control and dominate almost the entire game of politics in almost every country. They exist not only in the democratic countries but also in totalitarian states, though they differ in their purposes and functions.

Definition

There are various definitions offered by different writers on political party. Gettle defines 'political party as a group of citizens, more or less organised, who act as a political unit and who by the use of their voting power aim to control the government and carry out their general policy.' Ranny and Kendall define a political party 'as an autonomous organised group that makes nominations and contest election in the hope of eventually gaining and exercising control of the personnel and policies of government.' Prof. R.N.Gilchrist defines a political party 'as an organised group of citizens who profess to share the same political views and who by acting as a political unit, try to control the government. Politics is a contest among different interests and groups organised or unorganized for influence over the politics of the government.

Four elements are necessary to constitute a group of persons into a political party 1) People must be organised. Without organisation it is difficult to carry out. The plan of the lesson is to teach you the different types of party systems in the world and their functions common programmes. 2) What binds the people together is a common belief in certain principles. There may be differences in detail, but all of them must agree in fundamentals 3) A political party seeks to carryout its policies by constitutional means and by capturing the government. It is the ballot box, which gives them power 4) political party, exists to promote the national interests as distinguished from the sectarian or Communal interests.

Sir Edmund Bruke defines a political party "as a body of men united for promoting by their joint endeavours the national interests upon some particular principles in which they are all agreed." The political parties in the present form came to existence only a couple of centuries ago. Before that as Maciver says, there were only 'trends of opinion, popular clubs, philosophical societies and parliamentary groups, but no real political parties.' Political parties have become indispensable only after the introduction of universal suffrage. When the voting right has passed on to the masses, it became necessary to organize, educate, and canalize the voters to gain control of the government and this led to the formation of political parties.

Classification of Political Parties

Party system is a term used by political scientists to identify certain general characteristics of political parties in a country. The most common criterion used is the number of parties. It does not account all the parties in existence but only those which have been strong enough and able to secure a substantial amount of votes and form the government or to form a recognized opposition in the near future. On this basis we may classify the party into 'single party', 'bi-party' and 'multi-party' systems.

Single Party System

Single party system is referred to a party system where only 'one party' dominates in the politics of that country. There may be other parties, but they are not popular, influential and strong enough to secure substantial amount of votes to form government or an effective opposition. However now a days the term single party system is referred to denote the single party dominance in totalitarian states. The Nazi party of Germany during the dictatorship of Hitler, the Fascist party of Italy during the dictatorship of Mussolini and the Communist party of China are examples of single party system. In a single party system the authority of the party is totalitarian. They are organised like well disciplined armies, they have an ideology and the faith in it is unflinching and dogmatic like a religious order. Single party system aims to canalize the political life of the country in a single way. The life of the nation is regimented to the pattern of that party and opposing parties are liquidated either as a consequence of the positive law or by force. The Single party thus, becomes the engine of the whole life of the nation. Party instead of remaining a means to democracy becomes the end.

A single party system is, therefore, totalitarian. All the authority of the state is concentrated in a, single integrated political party. It even absorbs the state instead of merely acting on its behalf. Any single authority by its nature is total. It has no other authority at its side with which it must divide the exercise of power. Its authority, accordingly, embraces all aspects of human life and every form and phase of community's life. It was national unity for the Nazis and fascist and it is social unity with in communists

Merits of Single Party System

1) Single party system can provide a stable government, since it has monopoly over the government and politics and there is no opposition to dislodge it from Power 2) It is suited for undeveloped states which cannot afford the wasteful luxury of frequent elections and expensive election campaigns 3) It can provide an efficient government and can bring rapid prosperity to the country 4) There will be no conflict between the party and the government, since members of one are also members of the other. This provides for smooth functioning of the government 5) A single party system is able to achieve national and social unity 6) It helps to avoid classes and cleavages and clashes of interests in society.

Demerits

1) The main defect of one party system is that, since the party has a monopoly over the government and politics of the nation, it would tend to become tyrannical and irresponsible. It ruthlessly suppresses and eliminates all oppositions 2) There is no alternate government that can be formed and no genuine option for the people at the election 3) One party system leads to totalitarian rule where the political and social get identified with each other 4) It leads to the rule of the elite and the supreme leader becomes unrestrained 5) It is prone to commit mistakes and repeat them since there is no opposition to criticize them.

Bi-party System

A Bi-party system is that in which only two parties regularly secure substantial portion of the votes and public offices and in which the two major parties alternate in the exercise of power.

Such system might also contain many other minor parties, which will nominate the candidates for election, but rarely win more than a fraction of the votes or elect any candidate. In a two party system the political opinion is polarized into two major parties. In the election, the party, which secures a majority in the legislature, forms the government and the other forms the opposition. In the presidential form, the candidate of one of the parties is elected as the president and the same party or the other will have majority in legislature m-party system is prevalent in countries such as USA, UK, Canada, Australia, New Zealand and South Africa. In a BI-party system, the parties are moderate and are normally of broker type rather than of missionary type. Their views are usually identical.

Merits of Bi-party System

(1) A two party system ensures stability. A majority in the legislature in such a context will be a decisive majority and-not a relative majority. A cabinet supported by such a majority can be strong and masterful. It can effectively implement its programmes and can give forceful leadership in the legislature.

(2) In a Bi-Party system the election is simple. It presents just two alternatives to the electorates, making it easy for them to choose. Besides a two party system provides an alternate government, an alternate policy and an alternate leadership.

(3) There is less chances of corruption in this system because the ruling party is not obliged to satisfy any other party by allowing or ignoring or defending some political corruption for their support to retain the ministry.

(4) In a two party system the responsibilities are easily identified. One party rules and the other forms the opposition. The leaders of both the parties and the people know the responsibilities of each.

Demerits

(1) A two party system can lead to a very strong executive. Supported by a majority in the legislature, the cabinet can establish its dictatorship.

(2) In this system the choice of the voters is limited to only two alternative policies and programmes. It helps to create polarization of vested interests and party prejudices. It may ignore minority interests.

(3) In a bi-party system the ruling party might ignore the opposition or even public opinion because it is secure by virtue of its majority. It can be removed from power only through a general election. Similarly if the opposition is too strong the work of the government is hampered by too much of criticism.

(4) A two party system implies that both the parties must be well disciplined and the rigidity of the party discipline nullifies the freedom of the party members to make their own decisions.

Multi Party System

A multi party system is that in which at least three or more parties regularly secure a substantial number of votes and public offices and usually a single party is not able to secure an absolute majority to form the government. The result of such a situation is coalition government.

In a multiparty system, there are number of major parties, each well organised on an ideology of its own and has considerable influence over the national politics. In a general election., It is very rare for one single party to win a majority of votes or seats in the legislature to form the government. Multiparty system prevails in many countries of Europe. Presently India also can be included in this category. Most of the parties differ in name in different countries but closely resemble in their ideology, organisation, policies and programmes.

Merits

(1) It is more democratic than any other system. Since various parties represent various ideologies, interests and shades of opinion, a combination of these parties in a coalition government naturally reflect various shades of public opinion, hence more democratic.

(2) In a multiparty system the government is more sensitive and responsive to public opinion. It cannot ignore any section of interest or opinion as it would sometimes lead to the downfall of the ministry.

(3) In a multiparty system people have enough choice. People can vote for a party, which they think, represent and would work for their interests.

Demerits

(1) The main drawback of multiparty system is the instability of the government. Since it is almost always a coalition of heterogeneous political parties, it is very likely to collapse on simple reasons.

(2) The legislature becomes a hotbed of intrigues and 'horse trading'. Alliances and counter-alliances are formed among the parties adversely affecting the efficiency and stability of the government.

(3) There is no continuity of policy or programmes for the government. Each party puts forward its own ideology, policy and plans to the electorate. They might even be mutually opposing. After the election, a coalition is formed on a common minimum programme. But each party is enthusiastic to give more consideration to its own policies and plans.

(4) The government is compelled to make any political compromise and grant concessions to the constituent parties in order to remain in power. This leads to political corruption.

(5) Multiparty system confuses the voters. In this system the choice becomes very wide and hence confusing. Out of the welter of manifestoes and programmes the elector has to choose only one. The general masses of electors are bewildered by the complexity of choice.

(6) Finally in this system the community is divided into mutually opposing political groups.

Functions of Political Parties

Democracy and Political parties go hand in hand. Parties can exist under other conditions too, but can flourish most in a democratic state, as the representative government is the best medium for the expression of public opinion. Political parties, accordingly, perform certain indispensable functions.

(1) Political parties organize and fight elections on a determined program, which is put before the electorate. They choose the most capable and popular persons who have a chance of winning the election, as their candidate.

(2) Political parties assist in the formulation and expression of the general will by organizing and winning the election. They bring order out of chaos of multitude of voters by putting the programmes of the party before them and secure their approval or disapproval.

(3) Political parties educate the people and mould public opinion. They use all available media like press, platform and various other vehicles of propaganda. Political parties act as 'brokers of ideas.

(4) Political parties put into practice the public opinion which they have been instrumental in molding. Control over the governmental machinery gives the party adequate opportunity to fulfil its promises. While the majority party forms the government, the minority parties subject the party in power to a searching criticism.

(5) Political parties secure harmony of action among the various departments of government. 'It is the work of the parties to find these disconnected organs into a unity and secure the harmonious cooperation of the entire government' It is a unifying agency which makes democracy workable.

(6) Political parties also coordinate the members of the legislature. It keeps them under some sort of discipline. The legislative chambers cannot function smoothly without party whip. In its absence the legislature would be a babel of tongue.

(7) Political parties 'Canalize politics and keep the nation politically alive, They are links which keep the individual in touch with the government.'

Apart from these main functions enumerated above, the political parties perform many other functions. It coordinate the functions of the executive and legislative branches of government especially in a presidential form of government. It helps to maintain discipline in legislature. Some parties establish youth organisation to mobilize young electorates, conduct study classes establish libraries and run charitable institutions.

National Parties

National parties are political parties which participate in different elections held all over India. Some of the national parties have their origin even before India's independence. The oldest national party in India is the Indian National Congress (INC). In was established in 1885 as a pro-British Indian organization. Later on it became the main voice of India's freedom struggle. After India's independence, the British passed the administration of India to the leaders of the Indian National Congress.

Until 1966 the Congress was a stable party. In 1966 Indira Gandhi became the leader of the Congress and Prime Minister of India. From this period the Congress lost its stability. Some of the veteran members of the Congress did not accept her leadership and they tried to dispose her. In 1969 the Congress split and her opponents established a new Congress part. But still INC was the largest and ruling party of India.

Indira Gandhi's Congress lost the 1977 elections to the Janata Party. A few months after the defeat, another split happened in the Congress party. The party of Indira Gandhi was called Congress (I), the initial denoting of her name. During this period many more splits and coalitions occurred within the different Congress parties. Some of these new party members including its founders returned later on to the Congress (I) party and the party was renamed Indian National Congress. But there are others who left the INC at different periods and established parties outside the fold of Congress and have a name Congress in their party name. Before the 1999 elections some senior members of the INC were forced to resign because they questioned the leadership of Sonia Gandhi. These people have created the National Congress Party to participate in 1999 elections.

The INC is in the Indian political arena prior to India's independence. There were other parties, which were established after independence, and, for some period, were challenging the continuous rule of the Congress, some of them were almost vanished from the political arena.

The first political party which, was seen as challenging the Congress continuous rule was Swatantra Party. It was established in 1959 and was supported by some big businessmen. It opposed the socialism policy of the Congress It had members in the Lok Sabha until 1977. Another party, which challenged the Congress party but later on almost vanished from the political arena, was Janata Party. Janata Party was the first political party in India to establish a non-Congress government when it won the 1977 elections. Janata Party was established before the 1977 elections. The person responsible for the formation of Janata Party was Jayaprakash Narayan, called in short JP. JP was a freedom fighter and a social activist. Many in India respected him and saw in him a moral figure.

In the early 1970s the reign of Indira Gandhi began to show signs of corruption and dictatorship and there was a general feeling that liberal democracy is coming to an end. JP openly attacked Indira Gandhi's policy and asked other leaders to express their views about the dangers. Between 1975-77 emergency rule was declared. During this period many of Gandhi's political rivals were arrested and put behind the bars. Censorship was enforced on Indian press.

The justice system was restricted and turned into 'puppet show' of the government. The people also suffered a lot from this emergency rule. Under the birth control policy many people were forced to have sterilization. Even so Indira Gandhi was sure that the Indian people would support her because her general intention was to make India a better place and so she declared elections in 1977.

To prevent her victory different political parties organized as one party. This party was called Janata Party. The main factions of this party were, Congress (O), Lok Dal, Jan Sangh, and other parties. This party won the 1977 elections and Morarji Desai became the Prime Minister of India. But this party as it was formed did not survive for a long time. This party which was actually a group of factions with one desire to defeat Indira Gandhi, did not find any thing common among its members after they defeated Gandhi. As long as JP was alive, the different factions still stayed together. But after his death in 1978 a clear split occurred in the Janata Party between Morarji Desai's supporters and Charan Singh's supporters. In 1979 Morarji Desai resigned as Prime Minister and other members tried to replace Prime Minister. During this period Jagjivan Ram, an untouchable according to strict Hindu society, was very near to become a Prime Minister. But finally Charan Singh of the Lok Dal faction was proclaimed the new Prime Minister. A few weeks after Charan Singh became the Prime Minister, because of the instability in the coalition, the president declared on new elections.

In 1980 new national elections took place in which Indira Gandhi's Congress again won the elections. Later on after these elections, different factions of the Janata Party broke up from the Janata Party and established their own parties. Among these parties were Jan Sangh which later on was renamed Bhartiya Janata Party (BJP) and is today the largest party in India. Janata Party continues to survive, but is very small. In the 1996 elections it did not win any seat in the national elections and in the 1998 elections it won only one seat.

Another political party which, was actually a political bloc of different factions and managed to form a government was Janata Dal. This party was established because of the claim that there was corruption in the Congress government. In 1984 Rajiv Gandhi formed the Congress government. The finance minister of his government was VP Singh. VP Singh found out that a Swedish company, Bofors, was bribing some senior members of the Congress. Singh tried to investigate this affair. Gandhi moved him from the office and made him Defence Minister, but Singh resigned from the government and started a new party called Janata Dal. This party was made up of former Janata Party, Lok Dal and some INC members. In the 1989 elections this party came second after INC but it managed to establish a coalition government with other parties. This coalition was called National Front. This front also broke up after two years.

The largest party today is the Bhartiya Janata Party. The BJP began its political career after India's independence with only three members in the first elections held in 1952. The BJP is a Hindu nationalist party, which draws its inspiration from Hinduism. This party sees in India a Hindu state and it emphasizes Hindu pride and Hindu past of India.

This party was established after India's independence, but its origin is also pre-independence. In the 19th century a Hindu nationalist organization, Arya Samaj, was established. The ideas of this organization influenced another Hindu organization established later in British India, the Hindu Mahasabha. Hindu Mahasabha opposed the secular Congress philosophy and wanted to establish a Hindu state in British India. Another Hindu organization in British India was Rashtriya Swayamsevak Sangh (RSS), meaning national volunteers organization. One person who belonged in different stages of his life to these two organizations assassinated Mahatma Gandhi in 1948. After his assassination these two organizations were outlawed for sometime.

The leader of the Hindu Mahasabha, Shyam Mookherji resigned from the party and established with the members of RSS a new Hindu nationalist party, which was named Jana Sangh. This party had moderate ideas than the its former components. In its first two decades the party's major holds were in north India's Hindi speaking regions, because this party supported turning Hindi into the national language of India. In 1977 this party was an important faction of the Janata Party. In the 1980s it broke from the Janata Party and changed its name to Bhartiya Jana Sangh. Later on it renamed itself as Bhartiya Janata Party.

There are also other national parties, which were established in India. The Bahujan Samajwadi Party was established in the 1980s. But even though this party is a national party, its represents only the oppressed classes of India. Samajwadi Party was established in 1992. Two communist parties, Communist Party of India (CPI) and Communist party of India-Marxist (CPM) are also national parties. There are some parties who have national agendas but participate only in certain regions of India and not all over India. For example Forward Bloc which participates in elections only in West Bengal and neighboring Bihar.

Regional Parties

Regional parties are parties whose main holds are in one certain state and mostly they participate in the elections only within that state. Most of these regional parties have agenda fitting certain culture dominant within that state. Some of these regional parties also participate in neighboring states, which have constituencies with culture similar to the first state. Different state parties were established at different periods because of different reasons. Some even have origins prior to India's independence.

In Tamil Nadu in south India, two main state parties are All India Anna Dravida Munnetra Kazagham (AIADMK) and Dravida Munnetra Kazagham (DMK). Of these two parties the DMK is the veteran party. The origins of these parties are prior to India's independence. The main ideology of this party is Tamil national pride. Before India's independence there were two Dravidian parties. One was Independent Party, which demand an independent Dravidstan in south India. Other was Justice Party, which had a Dravidian pride ideology. After India's independence, the Dravida Munnetra Kazagham (DMK) was established from the merger of these two parties in the former state of Madras, in south India. This party first demanded an independent Dravidstan for all of south India. Later on the demand was changed to independent Tamil state. Finally this party compromised on a Tamil Nadu state within the Indian Union.

In the beginning this party was anti-north Indian. They opposed to any entrance of any kind of cultures of north India. They specially attacked the attempt to introduce Hindi language in Tamil Nadu. This party members also saw in the Tamili Brahmans agents of north India who immigrated to south India to enforce to north Indian Aryan culture on the south Indians. The party demanded to reserve the government jobs for Dravidians and not to 'immigrant' Brahmans. In 1972 this party split and a new party was founded by MC Ramachandaran and it was named All India Anna Dravida Munnetra Kazagham (AIADMK). In 1987 Ramachandaran died and Jayalalita inherited him. In the last few years these Tamilian pride parties have moderated their ideologies and before the 1998 elections the AIADMK even cooperated with BJP, which is considered as a north Indian party.

In Andra Pradesh, also in south India, Telegu Desam was founded in 1982 by Telegu film actor, NT Rao. The ideology of the party is similar to the ideology of the AIADMK, which is local cultural pride. In the Telugu Desam case, the local cultural pride is of Telugu culture.

Another one state party is Akali Dal and its main hold is in Punjab, north India. This party is considered a state party, but actually it is a religion oriented party whose followers are the Sikhs. This party also has its origin prior to India's independence. Before independence this party demanded from the British a separate entity for the Sikhs in Punjab. During the independence period these demands were delayed for a while. After independence this party began demanding special status for the Sikh culture and the Punjabi language. They struggled for a Punjabi state with a Sikh majority within the Indian Union and recognition of Punjabi as a distinct language. They succeeded in forming the establishment of Punjab in 1966, but it had a very small majority of the Sikhs. But they also succeeded in obtaining the recognition of Punjabi as a distinct language and not as a dialect of Hindi. Later on the Akali Dal broke up into some factions. Some of the militant factions of the Akali Dal demanded an independent Sikh state to be called Khalistan. But the dominant Akali Dal faction in Punjab wants Punjab to be a part of Indian Union. In Assam in east India and in Maharashtra in west India there are political parties which came into existence because of the discriminatory feelings of the local 'sons of soil' population.

In British India, Assam was a British province. For some period the British attached Assam to the neighboring Bengal province.

During this period the Bengalis held many senior government posts. Later on Assam again became a separate province, but the government posts were still hold by the Bengalis. In the 1960s and the 1970s many Bengali oriented people immigrated to Assam. In the 1980s the Asom Gana Parishad was founded with an agenda to give back Assam to the Assamese people.

In Maharashtra, in west India, the local population is known as Maharashtrians. Their language is known as Marathi. Sometimes the Maharashtrians are also known as Marathi. The capital of Maharashtra is Mumbai, formerly Bombay. During the British rule, the city of Bombay was the capital of Bombay State. The Bombay State included in it regions of present day Maharashtra and present day Gujarat.

The main language of Gujarat is Gujarati. The Gujaratis are the business communities of India. The city of Bombay was the business center of India. Many business communities from Gujarat settled in Bombay and were the important business community of Bombay. But the majority of the population of Bombay was Marathi and they were the working classes of the city. Many Indians from all around India also immigrated to Bombay to find a better future. This made Bombay the largest Indian cosmopolitan.

In 1960 Bombay State was divided into Maharashtra and Gujarat. Bombay the cultural capital of the Marathis and the Gujaratis was made capital of Maharashtra. After Maharashtra was established, a general feeling among many Marathis, was that Bombay is ruled and governed by 'foreigners'. Their main targets were not the Gujarati business communities, but immigrants who arrived from all over India and settled in Bombay. So these people established the Shiv Sena party. This party which began as a protest movement of the Marathis in Bombay, slowly became popular all around Maharashtra. This party ideology was spiced with Hindu-Marathi nationalist pride. Its rivals consider this party as a fanatic and anti-Muslim party. According to the party policy, many places in Maharashtra were renamed with Marathi oriented names. For example Bombay was renamed back to its original name Mumbai.

There are other state parties in India. To name a few there are, National Conference in Kashmir, Haryana Vikas Party in Haryana, Manipur People's Party in Manipur, Maharashtrawadi Gomantak in Goa, Sikkim Democratic Front in Sikkim and many other parties. People who broke away from larger national parties, like the Congress founded some state parties. For example the West Bengal Trinamul Congress, Tamil Manila Congress, Kerala Congress. There are also communist state parties.

Congress Parties

The oldest national party in India is the Indian National Congress (INC). In was established in 1885 as a pro-British Indian organization. The real purpose of the British in establishing this organization was to continue to rule India with the help of liberal and pro-British Indians. Later on this organization became the main voice of India's freedom struggle. Among its founders were Surendranath Benarjee, Dadabhai Naoroji and Justice M. G. Ranade. Before founding of the Congress, Justice M. G. Ranade had established an organization based on the ideas of the 'Brahmo Samaj' with the aim of social and religious reforms in India. One of Ranade's disciple, G. K. Gokhale, became the leader of Indian National Congress till 1915. Gokhale was considered by Mahatma Gandhi as his political guru. Mahatma Gandhi, more than any other Indian, is identified with modern India's creation.

After India's independence, the British passed the administration of India to the leaders of the Indian National Congress. Mahatma Gandhi who was the father figure of the Congress party, suggested to transform the Indian National Congress into a charity organization, because the main cause of the Congress party was achieved. But the other leaders of the Congress did not accept his proposal and the Indian National Congress became a political party with a secular, socialist and democratic tendency.

During its independence, two Congress leaders Jawarharlal Nehru and Vallabbhai Patel wanted to be the first Prime Minister of India. Nehru, who was younger, was secular and socialist oriented, while Patel was more Hindu nationalist oriented.

Mahatma Gandhi wanted the young Jawarharlal Nehru to be India's first Prime Minister and therefore Patel withdrew his candidacy. Before independence the Congress was a roof organization and it included many factions. After independence the Congress leaders changed the structure of the party and established a new political agenda. The different factions in the Congress could either join the new agenda or leave the Congress. Some left the Congress and established other political parties outside the Congress. And so some new political parties were established among them the Socialist Party of India and Forward Bloc

Until 1950 the Congress was under the influence of these two leaders. After Patel's death in 1950, Congress came under full influence of Jawarharlal Nehru. Nehru died in 1964, without appointing an heir. The party chose Lal Bahadur Shastri as the new leader. In 1966 Shastri arrived in Tashkent, in former Soviet Union to sign a cease-fire agreement with Pakistan. Shastri died in his sleep in Tashkent. After Shastri's death, some Congress leaders competed for the leadership of the party. Surprisingly the inter party election was won by the less favourite candidate, Indira Gandhi. Indira Gandhi was Jawarharlal Nehru's daughter (and had no family relations with Mahatma Gandhi). Some of the veteran members of the Congress did not accept her leadership and they tried to dispose her of. In 1969 the Congress split up into two parties.

The veteran members of the Congress established the Congress (O) party, while Indian National Congress was recognised as Congress (R). Of these two parties the INC was the larger and dominant party. The Congress (O) was no threat to Indira Gandhi's Congress.

Indira Gandhi was a very centralist leader. She pulled all the strings in the party and was seen as the dictator of her party. She planned to inherit her party to her younger son, Sanjay Gandhi. Between the years 1975-77 Indira Gandhi proclaimed emergency rule. During this period many of Gandhi's political rivals were arrested and put behind the bars. Censorship was enforced on Indian press. The justice system was restricted and turned into 'puppet show' of the government. The people also suffered a lot from this emergency rule. Under the birth control policy many people were forced to have sterilisation. Even so Indira Gandhi was sure that the Indian people supported her because her general intention of making India a better place and so she declared elections in 1977.

Her party lost the 1977 elections to the Janata Party. A few months after the Congress defeat in the elections, another split occurred in the Congress party. The party of Indira Gandhi was called Congress (I), because of the initial of her name. During this period many more splits and coalitions occurred within the different Congress parties. Former Congress member Sharad Pawar established one such party of the Congress during this period. He even established a government in the state of Maharashtra with this party which later on was known as Congress (S). Another party was established in Uttar Pradesh. Some of these new party members including it establishers like Sharad Pawar returned later on to the Congress (I) party and the party was renamed Indian National Congress. But there are others who left the INC at different periods and established parties outside the Congress and have a name Congress in their party name. For example Mumta Benarjee established West Bengal Trinamool Congress in West Bengal before the 1998 elections.

Moopanar established Tamil Maanila Congress in Tamil Nadu. And there are more other such parties. There were some Congress members who resigned from the Congress and established parties without having the name Congress in their party name. For example Lok Dal that was established in the 1960s by Charan Singh and Janata Dal, which was established by VP Singh after resigning from the INC in the late 1980s. Before the 1999 elections some senior members of the INC were forced to resign because they questioned the leadership of Sonia Gandhi. These people have created the National Congress Party to participate in 1999 elections.

Sonia Gandhi who lead the INC in the 1999 elections is the widow of Rajiv Gandhi, the elder son of Indira Gandhi. She was born in Italy to a European Christian family. She met Rajiv Gandhi in England and married him. Indira Gandhi intended to inherit her party to her younger son Sanjay. But Sanjay died in a plane crash in 1980. So Indira Gandhi forced her elder son, who had no interest in politics, to resign from his job as a pilot and join politics. In 1984, her Sikh bodyguards assassinated Indira Gandhi. Rajiv Gandhi was proclaimed her heir. He was Prime Minister of India until 1989. In the 1991 election campaign a suicide bomber assassinated him. The Congress appointed Narsimha Rao as its new leader. After losing the 1996 elections Rao resigned. For sometime Sitaram Kesari was the leader, but many Congress members saw in Sonia Gandhi as the new leader and gave her lot of respect. They thought that the Congress needs a 'Gandhi' as its leader to attract votes.

Communist Parties in India

In the early 19th century a new philosophy in political world emerged and it was Marxism. Many people in India were impressed by Marxist ideas and many communists from around the world arrived in India to teach and preach the communist philosophy. After the communist revolution, which occurred in Russia in 1917, many in India wished to cause same kind of revolution in India against the British. Under inspiration from Moscow the Communist Party of India (CPI) was established. Like other communist parties in the world, this party's members also had strong relations with Moscow and Moscow dictated its actions. This party did not support the freedom struggle, which was organized by the Indian National Congress and saw it as a struggle organized by rich businessmen.

After India's independence, many Indian leaders blamed the Communist party as a Russian agent and as a party acting according to orders from Moscow. In 1957 this party won the state elections held in Keralla, in south India, and so gave the world a precedent in which people democratically elected a communist regime.

In 1964 the Communist Party of India split into two parties. The new party added the word Marxist to the party name and is called in short, CPM. The CPI, between these two parties was considered as a Russian agent in India until the emergence of Prestroika in Russia. Of these two parties the CPM is the stronger party. Their main strength was in West Bengal in east India and in Keralla, south India.

Along with these two national level communist parties, there are also communist parties who act only within one state. Such parties exist in West Bengal, Tripura and Keralla. There are also some communist oriented violent local organisations that tried to fulfil the communist ideology with violent methods. These groups attacked big landlords, government representatives and government property. These groups are sometimes called Maoist groups or Naxalite groups, because of the place named Naxalbari where first such violent attempt took place

Elections

324. Superintendence, direction and control of elections to be vested in an Election Commission.-

(1) The superintendence, direction and control of the preparation of the electoral rolls for, and the conduct of, all elections to Parliament and to the Legislature of every State and of elections to the offices of President and Vice-President held under this Constitution shall be vested in a Commission (referred to in this Constitution as the Election Commission).

(2) The Election Commission shall consist of the Chief Election Commissioner and such number of other Election Commissioners, if any, as the President may from time to time fix and the appointment of the Chief Election Commissioner and other Election Commissioners shall, subject to the provisions of any law made in that behalf by Parliament, be made by the President.

(3) When any other Election Commissioner is so appointed the Chief Election Commissioner shall act as the Chairman of the Election Commission.

(4) Before each general election to the House of the People and to the Legislative Assembly of each State, and before the first general election and thereafter before each biennial election to the Legislative Council of each State having such Council, the President may also appoint after

consultation with the Election Commission such Regional Commissioners as he may consider necessary to assist the Election Commission in the performance of the functions conferred on the Commission by clause (1).

(5) Subject to the provisions of any law made by Parliament, the conditions of service and tenure of office of the Election Commissioners and the Regional Commissioners shall be such as the President may by rule determine:

Provided that the Chief Election Commissioner shall not be removed from his office except in like manner and on the like grounds as a Judge of the Supreme Court and the conditions of service of the Chief Election Commissioner shall not be varied to his disadvantage after his appointment:

Provided further that any other Election Commissioner or a Regional Commissioner shall not be removed from office except on the recommendation of the Chief Election Commissioner.

(6) The President, or the Governor of a State, shall, when so requested by the Election Commission, make available to the Election Commission or to a Regional Commissioner such staff as may be necessary for the discharge of the functions conferred on the Election Commission by clause (1).

325. No person to be ineligible for inclusion in, or to claim to be included in a special, electoral roll on grounds of religion, race, caste or sex.- There shall be one general electoral roll for every territorial constituency for election to either House of Parliament or to the House or either House of the Legislature of a State and no person shall be ineligible for inclusion in any such roll or claim to be included in any special electoral roll for any such constituency on grounds only of religion, race, caste, sex or any of them.

326. Elections to the House of the People and to the Legislative Assemblies of States to be on the basis of adult suffrage.- The elections to the House of the People and to the Legislative Assembly of every State shall be on the basis of adult suffrage; that is to say,

every person who is a citizen of India and who is not less than eighteen years of age on such date as may be fixed in that behalf by or under any law made by the appropriate Legislature and is not otherwise disqualified under this Constitution or any law made by the appropriate Legislature on the ground of non-residence, unsoundness of mind, crime or corrupt or illegal practice, shall be entitled to be registered as a voter at any such election.

327. Power of Parliament to make provision with respect to elections to Legislatures.- Subject to the provisions of this Constitution, Parliament may from time to time by law make provision with respect to all matters relating to, or in connection with, elections to either House of Parliament or to the House or either House of the Legislature of a State including the preparation of electoral rolls, the delimitation of constituencies and all other matters necessary for securing the due constitution of such House or Houses.

328. Power of Legislature of a State to make provision with respect to elections to such Legislature.- Subject to the provisions of this Constitution and in so far as provision in that behalf is not made by Parliament, the Legislature of a State may from time to time by law make provision with respect to all matters relating to, or in connection with, the elections to the House or either House of the Legislature of the State including the preparation of electoral rolls and all other matters necessary for securing the due constitution of such House or Houses.

329. Bar to interference by courts in electoral matters.- Notwithstanding anything in this Constitution-

(a) the validity of any law relating to the delimitation of constituencies or the allotment of seats to such constituencies, made or purporting to be made under article 327 or article 328, shall not be called in question in any court;

(b) no election to either House of Parliament or to the House or either House of the Legislature of a State shall be called in question except by an election petition presented to such authority and in such manner as may be provided for by or under any law made by the appropriate Legislature.

329A. [Special provision as to elections to Parliament in the case of Prime Minister and Speaker.] Rep. by the Constitution (Forty-fourth Amendment) Act, 1978, s. 36 (w.e.f. 20-6-1979).

Electoral Laws and System

Elections are conducted according to the constitutional provisions, supplemented by laws made by Parliament. The major laws are Representation of the People Act, 1950, which mainly deals with the preparation and revision of electoral rolls, the Representation of the People Act, 1951 which deals, in detail, with all aspects of conduct of elections and post election disputes. The Supreme Court of India has held that where the enacted laws are silent or make insufficient provision to deal with a given situation in the conduct of elections, the Election Commission has the residuary powers under the Constitution to act in an appropriate manner.

A Constitutional Body

Election Commission of India is a permanent Constitutional Body. The Election Commission was established in accordance with the Constitution on 25th January 1950. The Commission celebrated its Golden Jubilee in 2001. Originally the commission had only a Chief Election Commissioner. It currently consists of Chief Election Commissioner and two Election Commissioners, for a long time, though, it had only the Chief Election Commissioner. For the first time two additional Commissioners were appointed on 16th October 1989 but they had a very short tenure till 1st January 1990. Later on 1st October 1993 two additional Election Commissioners were appointed. The concept of multi-member Commission has been in operation since then, with decision making power by majority vote.

Appointment and Tenure of Commissioners

The President appoints Chief Election Commissioner and Election Commissioners. They have tenure of six years, or up to the age of 65 years, whichever is earlier. They enjoy the same status and receive salary and perks as available to Judges of the Supreme Court of India. The Chief Election Commissioner can be removed from office only through impeachment by Parliament.

Transaction of Business

The Commission transacts its business by holding regular meetings and also by circulation of papers. All Election Commissioners have equal say in the decision making of the Commission. The Commission, from time to time, delegates some of its executive functions to its officers in its Secretariat.

Election Machinery

The Commission has a separate Secretariat at New Delhi, consisting of about 300 officials, in a hierarchical set up.

Two Deputy Election Commissioners who are the senior most officers in the Secretariat assist the Commission. They are generally appointed from the national civil service of the country and are selected and appointed by the Commission with tenure. Directors, Principal Secretaries, and Secretaries, Under Secretaries and Deputy Directors support the Deputy Election Commissioners in turn. There is functional and territorial distribution of work in the Commission. The work is organised in Divisions, Branches and sections; each of the last mentioned units is in charge of a Section Officer. The main functional divisions are Planning, Judicial, Administration, Information Systems, Media and Secretariat Co-ordination. The territorial work is distributed among separate units responsible for different Zones into which the 35 constituent States and Union Territories of the country are grouped for convenience of management. At the state level, the election work is supervised, subject to overall superintendence, direction and control of the Commission, by the Chief Electoral Officer of the State, who is appointed by the Commission from amongst senior civil servants proposed by the concerned state government. He is, in most of the States, a full time officer and has a team of supporting staff.

At the district and constituency levels, the District Election Officers, Electoral Registration Officers and Returning Officers, who are assisted by a large number of junior functionaries, perform election work. They all perform their functions relating to elections in addition to their other responsibilities. During election time, however, they are available to the Commission, more or less, on a full time basis.

The gigantic task force for conducting a countrywide general election consists of nearly five million polling personnel and civil police forces. This huge election machinery is deemed to be on deputation to the Election Commission and is subject to its control, superintendence and discipline during the election period, extending over a period of one and half to two months.

Budget and Expenditure

The Secretariat of the Commission has an independent budget, which is finalised directly in consultation between the Commission and the Finance Ministry of the Union Government. The latter generally accepts the recommendations of the Commission for its budgets. The major expenditure on actual conduct of elections is, however, reflected in the budgets of the concerned constituent unit of the Union-State and Union Territory. If elections are being held only for the Parliament, the expenditure is borne entirely by the Union Government while for the elections being held only for the State Legislature, the expenditure is borne entirely by the concerned State. In case of simultaneous elections to the Parliament and State Legislature, the expenditure is shared equally between the Union and the State Governments. For Capital Equipment, expenditure related to preparation for electoral rolls and the scheme for Electors' Identity

Executive Interference Barred

In the performance of its functions, Election Commission is insulated from executive interference. It is the Commission which decides the election schedules for the conduct of elections, whether general elections or bye-elections. Again, it is the Commission, which decides on the location polling stations, assignment of voters to the polling stations, location of counting centres, arrangements to be made in and around polling stations and counting centres and all allied matters.

Election Schedule

The Commission normally announces the schedule of elections in a major Press Conference a few weeks before the formal process is set in motion. The Model Code of Conduct for guidance of candidates and Political Parties immediately comes into effect after such announcement. The formal process for the elections starts with the Notification or Notifications calling upon the electorate to elect Members of a House. As soon as Notifications are issued, Candidates can start filing their nominations in the constituencies from where they wish to contest. These are scrutinised by the Returning Officer of the constituency concerned after the last date for the same is over after about a week. The validly nominated candidates can withdraw from the contest within two days from the date of scrutiny.

Contesting candidates get at least two weeks for political campaign before the actual date of poll. On account of the vast magnitude of operations and the massive size of the electorate, polling is held at least on three days for the national elections. A separate date for counting is fixed and the results declared for each constituency by the concerned Returning Officer. The Commission compiles the complete list of Members elected and issues an appropriate Notification for the due Constitution of the House. With this, the process of elections is complete and the President, in case of the Lok Sabha, and the Governors of the concerned States, in case of Vidhan Sabhas, can then convene their respective Houses to hold their sessions. The entire process takes between 5 to 8 weeks for the national elections, 4 to 5 weeks for separate elections only for Legislative Assemblies.

Indian Elections, the Largest Event in the World

Conduct of General Elections in India for electing a new Lower House of Parliament (Lok Sabha) involves management of the largest event in the world. The electorate exceeds 668 million voting in 800,000 polling stations spread across widely varying geographic and climatic zones. Polling stations are located in the snow-clad mountains in the Himalayas, the deserts of the Rajasthan and in sparsely populated islands in the Indian Ocean.

Social Movement in India

From the early 1970s new forms of social mobilisation began in India. They gained a variety of names like social movement- people's movement- popular movements etc. These movements emerged and highlighted some of the major issues as gender and environment.

One of the leading analyst and participant in social movements in India, Sanajay Sangvi, identified the major agendas of them as "Movements of landless, unorganised labour in rural and urban areas, adivasis, dalits, displaced people, peasants, urban poor, small entrepreneurs and unemployed youth took up the issues of livelihood, opportunities, dignity and development."

Most well known movements in the country are Chipko movement, Save Silent Valley, Narmada Bachao Andolen, Koel Karo, Chhattisgarh Mukti Morcha, These movements largely distanced themselves from political parties, or tried to cut across the ideologies of the political parties. Yet many of them rooted themselves or drew from ideologies of the Mahatma Gandhi, various shades environmentalisms or gender politics, or socialism. Some of the popular leaders of such movements are Sunderlal Bahuguna, Medha Patkar, Baba Amte, Vandana Shiva, etc.

Social Movements Types

Reform Movements: Reform movements are organized to carry out reforms in some specific areas. The reformers endeavor to change elements of the system for better. For example: Civil Rights Movement, Women's Liberation Movement, Arya Samaj Movement, Brahmo Samaj Movement etc.

Revolutionary Movements: The revolutionary movements deny that the system will even work. These movements are deeply dissatisfied with the social order and work for radical change. They advocate replacing the entire existing structure. Their objective is the reorganization of society in accordance with their own ideological blueprint. Revolutionary movements generally become violent as they progress. Example: The Protestant Reformation Movement, the Socialist Movement, the Communist Revolution of China.

Reactionary or Revivalist Movement: Some movements are known as reactionary or regressive movements. These aims to reverse the social change.They highlight the importance and greatness of traditional values, ideologies and institutional arrangements. They strongly criticize the fast moving changes of the present.

Resistance Movement: These movements are formed to resist a change that is already taking place in society. These can be directed against social and cultural changes which are already happening in the country.

Utopian Movement: These are attempts to take the society or a section of it towards a state of perfection. These are loosely structured collectivities that envision a radically changed and blissful state, either on a large scale at some time in the future or on a smaller scale in the present. The Utopian ideal and the means of it are often vague, but many utopian movements have quite specific programmes for social change. The Hare Krishna Movement of the seventies, the movement towards the establishment of Ram Rajya and the Sangh Parivar, the Communists and Socialists pronouncement of a movement towards the classless, casteless society free from all kinds of exploitation etc.

Peasant Movement: Peasant movement is defined by Kathleen Gough as an attempt of a group to effect change in the face of resistance and the peasant are people who are engaged in an agricultural or related production with primitive means who surrender part of their or its equivalent to landlords or to agents of change. The history of peasant movements can be traced to colonial period when repressive economic policies, the new land revenue system, the colonial administrative and judicial system and the ruin of handicrafts leading to the overcrowding of land transformed the agrarian structure and impoverished the peasantry. In the zamindari system peasants were left to the mercies of the Zamindars who exploited them in form of illegal dues. The British government levied heavy land revenue in the Ryotwari areas. Peasants were forced to borrow money from the moneylenders and they were reduced to the status of tenants at will, share croppers and landless laborers while their lands, crops and cattle passed into the hands to landlords, trader moneylenders and such peasants. When the peasants could take it no longer they resisted against the oppression and exploitation through uprisings. Peasant Movements occupy an important place in the history of social unrest in India though the aims and objectives of these movements differ in nature and degree from region to region. It is in this sense that these movements also aimed at the unification of the peasants of a region, development of leadership, ideology and a peasant elite. Through these movements emerged a new power structure and peasant alliance. The genesis of peasant movements rest in the relationship patterns of different social categories existing within the framework of feudal and semi feudal structure of our society. In the post Independence period the nature and objectives of the peasant movement have changed to getting remunerative prices for agricultural produce, to increase agricultural production, to establish parity between prices of agricultural produce and industrial goods and to get minimum wages for the agricultural laborers.

Women's Movement: The women's movement in India is a rich and vibrant movement which has taken different forms in different parts of the country. Fifty years ago when India became independent, it was widely acknowledged that the battle for freedom had been fought as much by women as by men. One of the methods M K Gandhi chose to undermine the authority of the British was for Indians to defy the law which made it illegal for them to make salt. At the time, salt-making was a monopoly and earned considerable revenues for the British. Gandhi began his campaign by going on a march- the salt march- through many villages, leading finally to the sea, where he and others broke the law by making salt. No woman had been included by Gandhi in his chosen number of marchers. But nationalist women protested, and they forced him to allow them to participate. The first to join was Sarojini Naidu, who went on to become the first woman President of the Indian National Congress in 1925. Her presence was a signal for hundreds of other women to join, and eventually the salt protest was made successful by the many women who not only made salt, but also sat openly in marketplaces selling, and indeed, buying it. The trajectory of this movement is usually traced from the social reform movements of the 19th century when campaigns for the betterment of the conditions of women's lives were taken up, initially by men.

By the end of the century women had begun to organize themselves and gradually they took up a number of causes such as education, the conditions of women's work and so on. It was in the early part of the 20th century that women's organizations were set up, and many of the women who were active in these later became involved in the freedom movement. Independence brought many promises and dreams for women in India- the dream of an egalitarian, just, democratic society in which both men and women would have a voice.

The reality was, however, somewhat different. For all that had happened was that, despite some improvements in the status of women, patriarchy had simply taken on new and different forms. By the 1960s it was clear that many of the promises of Independence were still unfulfilled. It was thus that the 1960s and 1970s saw a spate of movements in which women took part: campaigns against rising prices, movements for land rights, peasant movements. Women from different parts of the country came together to form groups both inside and outside political parties.

Everywhere, in the different movements that were sweeping the country, women participated in large numbers. Everywhere, their participation resulted in transforming the movements from within. One of the first issues to receive countrywide attention from women's groups was violence against women, specifically in the form of rape, and 'dowry deaths'. This was also the beginning of a process of learning for women: most protests were directed at the State.

Because women were able to mobilize support, the State responded, seemingly positively, by changing the law on rape and dowry, making both more stringent. In the early campaigns, groups learnt from day to day that targeting the State was not enough and that victims also needed support. So a further level of work was needed: awareness raising so that violence against women could be prevented, rather than only dealt with after it had happened. Legal aid and counseling centres were set up, and attempts were made to establish women's shelters. Knowledge was also recognized as an important need.

The women's activity was geared towards improving the conditions of women's lives. In recent years, the euphoria of the 1970s and early 1980s, symbolized by street-level protests, campaigns in which groups mobilized at a national level, has been replaced by a more considered and complex response to issues. In many parts of India, women are no longer to be seen out on the streets protesting about this or that form of injustice.

This apparent lack of a visible movement has led to the accusation that the women's movement is dead or dying. While the participation of urban, middle class women is undeniable, it is not they who make up the backbone of the movement, or of the many, different campaigns that are generally seen as comprising the movement. The anti-alcohol agitation in Andhra Pradesh and similar campaigns in other parts of India were started and sustained by poor, low-caste, often working-class women. The movement to protect the environment was begun by poor women in a village called Reni in the northern hill regions of India, and only after that did it spread to other parts of the country.

One of the biggest challenges women have had to face in recent years is the growing influence of the religious right in India. Right-wing groups have built much of their support on the involvement of women: offering to help them with domestic problems, enabling them to enter the public space in a limited way, and all the while ensuring that the overall ideology within which they operate remains firmly patriarchal.

For activists too, this has posed major problems. It has forced them to confront the fact that they cannot assume solidarity as women that cuts across class, religion, caste, ethnic difference. It is important to recognize that for a country of India's magnitude, change in male-female relations and the kinds of issues the women's movement is focusing on will not come easy. For every step the movement takes forward, there will be a possible backlash, a possible regression. And it is this that makes for the contradictions, this that makes it possible for there to be women who can aspire to, and attain, the highest political office in the country, and for women to continue to have to confront patriarchy within the home, in the workplace, throughout their lives.

Backward Caste Movement: The Backward castes have been deprived of many social, economic, political and religious privileges. These people provided manual labor and the untouchables occupied the lowest position among the caste hierarchy. They were subjected to extreme form of exploitation. The colonial power accentuated the disparities in the distribution of economic power. The atrocities united the lower castes against the upper castes. Some of the important backward caste movement which came up was Satyashodak Samaj and Nadar Movement which consolidated the masses along the castelines. E.V Ramaswamy started Self-Respect movement against the Brahmins in South India. The SNDP movement in Kerala was more of a reformist movement. In 1950s there was a widespread desire among the non-Brahmin castes to be categorized as Backward. Subsequently Backward Class commission was set up to look into the conditions and requirements of these classes. Mandal Commission submitted its report in 1980 recommending reservations for backward castes in educational institutions and government offices. However this move resulted in anti- Mandal Commission movement which resulted in large scale violence and many students lost their lives.

Dalit Movement: Dalits are the suppressed people at the lost rung of the cast-based hierarchy. Their inferior occupations and low levels of ascriptive status make them vulnerable for attacks at the hands of upper-caste people. The organizational efforts made by Dalit leadership for uplifting their status are known as Dalit movement. It is a protest against untouchability, casteism and discrimination faced by the dalits. Dalit movement indicates some trends of protest ideologies which entail the following- withdrawal and self organization, high varna status and extolling of non-Aryan culture's virtues, abandoning of Hinduism and embracing other religions like Buddhism and Islam. Mahatma Gandhi in 1923 founded the All India Harijan Sevak Sangh to start education and schools for the dalits. Another most important dalit leader Dr.Ambedkar struggled to secure the basic human dignity to the dalits. The Mahad Satyagarh for the right of water led by him was one of the outstanding movements of the dalits to win equal social rights. The role of All India Depressed Classes Association and All India Depressed Classes Federation were the principal organizations which initiated a movement to improve the conditions of the dalits.These organizations aimed at improving their miserable conditions and to spread education among them. They worked to secure rights of admission to school, drawing water from the public wells, entering the temples and to use the roads.

Narmada Bachao Andolan

Narmada Bachao Andolan (NBA) is a non-governmental organisation (NGO) that mobilised tribal people, *adivasis*, farmers, environmentalists and human rights activists against the Sardar Sarovar Dam being built across the Narmada river, Gujarat, India. Their mode of campaign includes hunger strikes, mass media publicities, garnering support from noted film and art personalities [aamir khan] etc. Narmada Bachao Andolan, together with its leading spokespersons Medha Patkar and Baba Amte, were the 1991 recipient of the Right Livelihood Award.

Background

Post-1947, investigations were carried out to evaluate mechanisms in utilizing water from the Narmada river, which flows into the Arabian Sea after passing through the states of Madhya Pradesh, Gujarat and Maharashtra. Due to inter-state differences in implementing schemes and sharing of water, the Narmada Water Disputes Tribunal was constituted by the Government of India on October 6, 1969 to adjudicate over the water disputes. This Tribunal investigated the matters referred to it and responded after more than 10 years. On December 12, 1979, the decision as given by the Tribunal, with all the parties at dispute binding to it, was released by the Indian Government.

As per the Tribunal's decision, 30 major, 135 medium, and 3000 small dams, were granted approval for construction including raising the height of the Sardar Sarovar dam.

In 1985, after hearing about the Sardar Sarovar dam, Medha Patkar and her colleagues visited the project site and noticed the project work being shelved due to an order by the Ministry of Environment and Forests, Government of India.

The reasons for this was cited as "non-fulfillment of basic environmental conditions and the lack of completion of crucial studies and plans". What she noticed was that the people who were going to be affected were given no information, but for the offer for rehabilitation.

Due to this, the villagers had many questions right from why their permission was not taken to whether a good assessment on the ensuing destruction was taken. Furthermore, the officials related to the project had no answers to their questions. While World Bank, the financing agency for this project, came into the picture, Patkar approached the Ministry of Environment to seek clarifications. She realized, after seeking answers from the ministry, that the project was not sanctioned at all, and wondered as to how funds were even sanctioned by the World Bank. After several studies, they realized that the officials had overlooked the post-project problems.

Through Patkar's channel of communication between the government and the residents, she provided critiques to the project authorities and the governments involved. At the same time, her group realized that all those displaced were only given compensation for the immediate standing crop and not for displacement and rehabilitation.

As Patkar remained immersed in the Narmada struggle, she chose to quit her Ph. D. studies and focus entirely on the Narmada activity.

Thereafter, she organized a 36-day long, solidarity march among the neighboring states of the Narmada valley from Madhya Pradesh to the Sardar Sarovar dam site. She said that the march was "a path symbolizing the long path of struggle (both immediate and long-term) that [they] really had". This march was resisted by the police, who according to Patkar were "caning the marchers and arresting them and tearing the clothes off women activists".

Formation

There were groups such as Gujarat-based Arch-Vahini (Action Research in Community Health and Development) and Narmada Asargrastha Samiti (Committee for people affected by the Narmada dam), Madhya Pradesh-based Narmada Ghati Nav Nirman Samiti (Committee for a new life in the Narmada Valley) and Maharashtra-based Narmada Dharangrastha Samiti (Committee for Narmada dam-affected people) who either believed in the need for fair rehabilitation plans for the people or who vehemently opposed dam construction despite a resettlement policy.

While Patkar established Narmada Bachao Andolan in 1989, all these groups joined this national coalition of environmental and human rights activists, scientists, academics and project-affected people with a nonviolent approach.

Aftermath

Within the focus of Narmada Bachao Andolan towards the stoppage of the Sardar Sarovar dam, she advised addition of World Bank to their propaganda. Using the right to fasting, she undertook a 22 day fast that almost took her life. In 1991, her actions led to an unprecedented independent review by the World Bank. The Morse Commission, appointed in June 1991 at the recommendation of The World Bank President Barber Coinable, conducted its first independent review of a World Bank project. This independent review stated that "performance under these projects has fallen short of what is called for under Bank policies and guidelines and the policies of the Government of India." This resulted in the Indian Government pulling out of its loan agreement with the World Bank. In response, Patkar said "It is very clear and obvious that they used this as a face-saving device", suggesting that if this were not to happen, the World Bank would eventually would have withdrawn the loan. The World Bank's participation in these projects was eventually cancelled in 1995.

She further undertook a similar fast in 1993 and resisted evacuation from the dam site. In 1994, the Bachao Andolan office was attacked reportedly by a couple of political parties, where Patkar and other activists were physically assaulted and verbally abused. In protest, a few NBA activists and she began a fast and 20 days later, they were arrested and forcibly fed intravenously.

Supreme Court's Decision

Patkar led Narmada Bachao Andolan had filed a written petition with the Supreme Court of India [the nation's apex court] seeking stoppage of construction on the Sardar Sarovar dam. The court initially ruled the decision in the Andolan's favour thereby effecting an immediate stoppage of work at the dam and directing the concerned states to first complete the rehabilitation and replacement process.

The Supreme Court also deliberated on this issue further for several years but finally upheld the Tribunal Award and allowed the construction to proceed, subject to conditions. The court introduced a mechanism to monitor the progress of resettlement pari passu with the raising of the height of the dam through the Grievance Redressal Authorities (GRA) in each of the party states. The court's decision referred in this document, given in the year 2000 after seven years of deliberations, has paved the way for completing the project to attain full envisaged benefits. The court's final line of the order states, "Every endeavour shall be made to see that the project is completed as expeditiously as possible".

Subsequent to the court's verdict, Press Information Bureau (PIB) featured an article which states that:

"The Narmada Bachao Andolan has rendered a yeoman`s service to the country by creating a high-level of awareness about the environmental and rehabilitation and relief aspects of Sardar Sarovar and other projects on the Narmada. But, after the court verdict it is incumbent on it to adopt a new role. Instead of `damning the dam` any longer, it could assume the role of vigilant observer to see that the resettlement work is as humane and painless as possible and that the environmental aspects are taken due care of".

People Involved

Amongst the major celebrities who have shown their support for Narmada Bachao Andolan are Booker Prize winner,

Arundhati Roy and Aamir Khan in 1994, saw the launch of *Narmada : A valley Rises*, by filmmaker Ali Kazimi.This film documents the five week long Sangharsh Yatra of 1991. The film went on to win several awards and is considered by many to be a classic film on the issue. In 1996, veteran documentary filmmaker, Anand Patwardhan, made an award-winning documentary on this issue, titled: 'A Narmada Diary'.

Criticism

The Narmada dam's benefits include provision drinking water, power generation and irrigation facilities. However, the campaign led by the NBA activists has held up the project's completion, and the NBA supporters have indulged in physical attacks on local people who accepted compensation for moving.

Chipko Movement

The Chipko movement or Chipko Andolan is a socio-ecological movement that practised the Gandhian methods of satyagraha and nonviolent resistance, through the act of hugging trees to protect them from being felled. The modern Chipko movement started in the early 1970s in the Garhwal Himalayas of Uttarakhand, with growing awareness towards rapid deforestation. The landmark event in this struggle took place on March 26, 1974, when a group of female peasants in Reni village, Hemwalghati, in Chamoli district, Uttarakhand, India, acted to prevent the cutting of trees and reclaim their traditional forest rights that were threatened by the contractor system of the state Forest Department, and transpired hundreds of such grassroot level actions, throughout the region. By the 80s, the movement spread throughout India, and led to formulation of people sensitive forest policies and stopping of open felling of trees in regions as far reaching as Vindhyas and the Western Ghats.

The first recorded event of *Chipko* however, took place in village Khejarli, Jodhpur district, in 1730 AD, when 363 Bishnois, led by Amrita Devi sacrificed their lives while protecting green Khejri trees, considered sacred by the community, by hugging them, and braved the axes of loggers sent by the local ruler, today it is seen an inspiration and a precursor for Chipko movement of Garhwal.

The Chipko movement, though primarily a livelihood movement rather than a forest conservation movement, went on to become a rallying point for many future environmentalists, environmental protests and movements the world over and created a precedent for nonviolent protest. It occurred at a time when there was hardly any environmental movement in the developing world, and its success meant that the world immediately took notice of this nonviolent Tree hugging movement, which was to inspire in time, many such eco-groups, helped in slowing down the rapid deforestation, exposed vested interests, increased ecological awareness, and demonstrate the viability of people power. Above all, it stirred up existing civil society in India like never before, which started looking towards tribal, and marginalized people and their issues like never before. So much so that, quarter a century later, *India Today* mentioned, the people behind the "forest satyagraha" of the Chipko movement, as amongst "100 people who shaped India". Today, beyond the eco-socialism hue, it is being seen increasingly as an ecofeminism movement, as though many of its leaders were men, women were not just its backbone, but also its mainstay, because they were the ones most affected by the rampant deforestation, leading to lack of firewood and fodder as well as water of drinking and irrigation. Over the years they also became primary stakeholders in majority of the afforestation work that happened under the Chipko movement.

History

The Himalayan region had always been exploited for its natural wealth, be it minerals or timber, including by the British. The end of the nineteenth century saw implementation of new approaches in forestry, coupled with reservation of forests for commercial forestry, causing disruption in the age-old symbiotic relationship between the natural environment and the rural peasant, both in Kumaon and Garhwal. The few peasant protests that arose during this period were crushed severely. Notable protests in 20th century, were that of 1906, followed by the 1921 protest which was linked with then independence movement imbued with Gandhian ideologies, the 1940s was again marked with a series of protests in Tehri Garhwal region.

Post-independence period, when waves of a resurgent India were hitting even the far reaches of India, the landscape of upper Himalayan region was only slowly changing, and largely remained inaccessible. But all this was to change soon, when an important event in the environmental history of the Garhwal region occurred in the India-China War of 1962, in which India faced heavy losses. Though, the region was not involved in the war directly, the government wisened by its losses and war casualties, took rapid initiatives to secure its borders, set up army bases, build road network, deep into the upper reaches of Garhwal, on India's border with Chinese-ruled Tibet, an area which was till now all but cut off from the rest of nation. However with construction of roads, and subsequent developments also came mining projects for limestone, magnesium, and potassium, timber merchants and commercial forestry which now had access to forests inaccessible till now.

Soon, the forest cover started deteriorating at an alarming rate, resulting in hardships in labour intensive fodder and firewood collection. This also led to a deterioration in the soil conditions, and soil erosion in the area as the water sources dried up in the hills, and water shortages became rampant. Subsequently, communities gave up the raising livestock, adding to the problems of malnutrition in the region. This crisis was heightened by the fact that Forest conservation policies, like Indian Forest Act, 1927, traditionally restricted the access of local communities to the forests, resulting in scarce farmlands, in an over populated and extremely poor area, despite all its natural wealth. Thus the sharp decline in the local agrarian economy, lead to migration of people into the plains, looking for jobs, which created several de-populated villages in the 1960s.

Gradually a rising awareness about the ecological crisis, which arose from an immediate loss of livelihood caused by it, resulted in initial activism sparks in the region. Starting in 1964 with the establishment of *Dasholi Gram Swarajya Sangh* (DGSS) ("Dasholi Society for Village Self-Rule"), set up by Gandhian social worker,

Chandi Prasad Bhatt in Gopeshwar, and inspired Jayaprakash Narayan and the Sarvodaya movement, with an aim to set up small industries using the resources of the forests, their first project was a small workshop making farm tools for local use. Its name was later changed to *Dasholi Gram Swarajya Sangh* (DGSS) from original *Dasholi Gram Swarajya Mandal* (DGSM) in the 1980s. Here they had to face the restrictive forest policies, a hangover of colonial era still prevalent and on top of it the "contractor system", in which these pieces of forest land were commodified and auctioned to big contractors, usually from the plains, who brought along their own skilled and semiskilled laborers, leaving only the menial jobs like hauling rocks for the hill people, which paid next meagrely. On the other hand, hill regions saw an influx of new population, which added to already strained ecological balance and cracks started showing everywhere.

Hastened by increasing hardships, the Garhwal Himalayas soon became centre rising social ecological awareness against reckless deforestation which had denuded much of forest cover, which eventually resulted in the devastating Alaknanda River floods, in July 1970, when a major landslide blocked the river, and effected an area starting from Hanumanchatti, near Badrinath to 350 km downstream till Haridwar, further numerous villages, bridges and roads were washed away. Thereafter incidences of landslides and land subsidence became a common feature in an area which was experiencing rapid civil construction.

"Maatu hamru, paani hamru, hamra hi chhan yi baun bhi... Pitron na lagai baun, hamunahi ta bachon bhi"

Soil ours, water ours, ours are these forests. Our forefathers raised them, it's we who must protect them. — *Old Chipko Song* (Garhwali language)

Soon villagers, especially women had started organizing themselves under several smaller groups, taking up local causes with the authorities, and standing up against commercial logging operations that threatened their livelihoods. In October 1971, the Sangh workers held a demonstration in Gopeshwar to protest against the policies of the Forest Department. More rallies and marches were held in late 1972, but to little effect, that is when the decision to take direct action was taken, and first such occasion arrived when the Forest Department turned down the Sangh's annual request for ten ash trees for its farm tools workshop, and instead a awarded contract for 300 trees to Simon Company, a sports good manufacturer in distant Allahabad, to make Tennis rackets. In March 1973, the lumberers arrived at Gopeshwar, and after a couple of weeks, they were confronted at village Mandal on April 24, 1973, where about hundred villagers and DGSS workers beating drums and shouting slogans, forced the contractors and their lumberers to retreat. This was the first confrontation of the movement, and finally the contract was cancelled and awarded to the Sangh instead. Though by now, the issue had enlarged from procuring the annual quota of three ash trees, and encompassed a growing concern over the commercial logging, and forest policy of the government, which the villagers saw as unfavourable towards them. The Sangh also decided to resort to hugging the tree, Chipko as a mechanism of nonviolent protest.

But the struggle was far from over, as the same company was awarded more ash trees, in the Phata forest, 80 km away from Gopeshwar. Here again, due to local opposition, starting 20 June 1973, the contractors retreated after a stand off that lasted a few days. Thereafter the villagers of Phata and Tarsali, formed a vigil group and watched over the trees till December, when they had another successful stand-off, when the activists reached the site in time, and the lumberers retreated leaving behind the five ash trees felled. The final flash point began few months, when the government announced an auction scheduled in January 1974, for 2,500 trees near Reni village, overlooking the Alaknanda River. Bhatt set out for the villages in the Reni area, and enraged the villagers, decided to protested against the move of the government by hugging the trees, over the next few weeks, rallies and meeting continued in the Reni area, and the villagers were prepared for the stand-off.

On March 26, 1974, the day the lumberers were to axe the trees, the men of the Reni village, and DGSS workers, were in Chamoli, diverted by state government and contractors to a fictional compensation payment site, while back home labourers arrived a truckload to the start logging operations. Finally when a girl on seeing them rush to inform Gaura Devi, the head of the village *Mahila Mangal Dal,* at Reni village (Laata was her ancestral home and Reni adopted home). Gaura Devi led 27 women of Reni village, reached the site and confronted the loggers. When all talking failed, and instead loggers started shouting and abusing the women, threatening them with guns, the women resorted to hugging the trees to stop the them from being axed. This went on into late hours, and the women kept a whole night vigil guarding their trees from the cutters, till a few of them relented and left the village. The next day, when with the men and leaders back, the news of the movement spread to the neighbouring Laata and others villages also Henwalghati, and more people joined in. Eventually only after a four-day stand off, the contractors left. The Chipko movement is often called 'the chippy'.

Aftermath

The news reached the state capital, and then state Chief Minister, Hemwati Nandan Bahuguna, set up a committee to look into the issue which eventually, ruled in the favour of the villagers. This then became a turning point in the history of eco-development struggles in the region and also across the world. The struggle soon spread across many parts of the region, and such spontaneous stand-offs between the local community and timber merchants occurred at several locations, with hill women demonstrating their new-found power as nonviolent activists. As the movement gathered shape under its leaders, the name Chipko Movement got attached to their activities. As per Chipko historians, the term originally used by Bhatt was the Garhwali lanaguge word, "angalwaltha", or embrace, which later adapted to Hindi word, *Chipko,* which means to stick.

Subsequently, over the next five years the movement spread to many districts of region, and within a decade throughout the Uttarakhand Himalayas. Larger issues of ecological and economic exploitation of the region were raised. The villagers demanded that no forest-exploiting contracts should be given to outsiders and local communities should have effective control over natural resources like land, water and forests. They wanted the government to provide low cost materials to small industries and ensure development of the region without disturbing the ecological balance. The movement took up economic issues of landless forest workers and asked for guarantees of minimum wage. Globally Chipko demonstrated a clear link between environment concerns till now considered a luxury of the rich, in a new perspective as a matter of life and death for the poor, always the first ones to be devastated by an environmental tragedy, and several scholarly studies were made in the backdrop of the movement. In 1977, in another area, women tied a sacred threads, Rakhi, around trees earmarked for felling, in a Hindu tradition which signifies a bond between brother and sisters.

Women's active participation in the Chipko agitation was a very novel aspect of the movement. The forest contractors of the region usually doubled up as suppliers of alcohol to men. Women held sustained agitations against the habit of alcoholism and broadened the agenda of the movement to cover other social issues. The movement achieved a victory when the government issued a ban on felling of trees in the Himalayan regions for fifteen years in 1980, by then Prime Minister, Indira Gandhi, until the green cover was fully restored. One of the prominent Chipko leaders, Gandhian Sunderlal Bahuguna took a 5,000 kilometre trans-Himalaya footmarch in 1981-83, spreading the Chipko message to a far greater area. Gradually, women set up cooperatives to guard local forests, and also organized fodder production at rates condusive to local environment. Next, they joined in land rotation schemes for fodder collection, helped replant degraded land, and established and ran nurseries stocked with species they select..

Participants

One of Chipko's most salient features was the mass participation of female villagers. As the backbone of Uttarakhand's agrarian economy, women were most directly affected by environmental degradation and deforestation, and thus connected the issues most easily. How much this participation impacted or derived from the ideology of Chipko, has been fiercely debated in academic circles.

Despite this, both female and male activists did play pivotal roles in the movement including Gaura Devi, Sudesha Devi, Bachni Devi, Chandi Prasad Bhatt, Sundarlal Bahuguna, Govind Singh Rawat, Dhoom Singh Negi, Shamsher Singh Bisht and Ghanasyam Raturi, the Chipko poet, whose songs echo throughout the Himalayas. Out of which, Chandi Prasad Bhatt was awarded the Ramon Magsaysay Award in 1982, and Sundarlal Bahuguna was awarded the Right Livelihood Award in 1987, and Padma Vibhushan in 2009.

Legacy

In Tehri district, Chipko activists would go on to protest limestone mining in the Doon Valley (Dehra Dun) in the 1980s, as the spark spread through the Dehradun district, which had earlier seen devastation of its forest cover leading to heavy loss of flora and fauna. Finally quarrying was banned after years of agitation by Chipko activists, and followed it up with vast public drive of afforestation, which turned around the valley, just in time. Also in the 80s, the activists like Bahuguna took on protest against construction of the Tehri dam on the Bhagirathi River, which went on for the next two decades. Before founding the *Beej Bachao Andolan*, Save the Seeds movement that continues to the present day.

Over time, as a United Nations Environment Programme report mentioned, Chipko activists started "working a socioeconomic revolution by winning control of their forest resources from the hands of a distant bureaucracy which is concerned with selling the forest for making urban-oriented products.". It became a benchmark for socio-ecological movements in other forest areas of Himachal Pradesh, Rajasthan and Bihar; in September 1983, Chipko inspired a similar, Appiko movement in Karnataka state of India, tree felling in Western Ghats and Vindhyas was stopped. In Kumaon region, Chipko took on a more radical hue, combining with the general movement for a separate Uttarakhand state, which was eventually achieved in 2000.

In the coming years, the movement not just inspired numerous people to work on practical programmes of water management, energy conservation, afforestation, and recycling, but scholars to start studying issues of environmental degradation and methods of conservation in the Himalayas and throughout India.

On March 26, 2004, Reni and Lata and other villages of the Niti Valley, celebrated the 30th anniversary of the Chipko Movement, where all the surviving original participants united. The celebrations started at Laata, the ancestral home of Gaura Devi, where Pushpa Devi, wife of late Chipko Leader Govind Singh Rawat, Dhoom Singh Negi, Chipko leader of Henwalghati, Tehri Garhwal, and others were felicitated, from here a procession went to Reni, the neighbouring village where the actual Chipko action took place on March 26, 1974..

Appiko Movement

The Appiko movement was a revolutionary movement based on environmental conservation in India. The "Chipko Andolan" (Hug the Trees Movement) in Uttarakhand in the Himalayas inspired the villagers of the Uttara Kannada district of Karnataka Province in southern India to launch a similar movement to save their forests. In September 1983, men, women and children of Salkani "hugged the trees" in Kalase forest. (The local term for "hugging" in Kannada is appiko.) Appiko Andolan gave birth to a new awareness all over southern India.

In 1950, Uttara Kannada district forest covered more than 81 percent of its geographical area. The government, declaring this forest district a "backward" area, then initiated the process of "development". Their major industries- a pulp and paper mill, a plywood factory and a chain of hydroelectric dams constructed to harness the rivers- sprouted in the area. These industries have overexploited the forest resource, and the dams have submerged huge-forest and agricultural areas. The forest had shrunk to nearly 25 percent of the district's area by 1980. The local population, especially the poorest groups, were displaced by the dams. The conversion of the natural mixed forests into teak and eucalyptus plantations dried up the water sources, directly affecting forest dwellers. In a nutshell, the three major p's—paper, plywood and power—which were intended for the development of the people, have resulted in a fourth p: poverty.

Deforestation in the Western Ghats

The Sahyadri Range, or the Western Ghats, in southern India is the home of a tropical forest ecosystem. Although this tropical forest constitutes a potentially renewable resource, it is also a very fragile ecosystem and therefore merits special attention. The past 30 years have seen the onslaught of "development" activities and an increase in population, both of which have exhausted this fragile resource system. In the case of Kerala, which comprises 42 percent of the entire Western Ghat area, the forest cover fell from 44 percent in 1905 to a meager 9 percent in 1984. Such deforestation in the Western Ghats has caused severe problems for all southern India. The recurring drought in the provinces of Karnataka, Maharashtra, Kerala and Tamil Nadu clearly indicates watershed degradation. The power generation, water supply and ultimately the whole economy of southern India is adversely affected. The drought in Karnataka Province indicates the extent of the damage caused by change in Sahyadri's fragile ecosystem. The ongoing "development" policy of exploiting the "resources- mainly forest and mineral resources- in the Western Ghats for the benefit of the elite has deprived the poor of their self-supporting systems.

The Appiko Movement is trying to save the Western Ghats by spreading its roots all over southern India. The movement's objectives can be classified into three major areas. First, the Appiko Movement is struggling to save the remaining tropical forests in the Western Ghats. Second, it is making a modest attempt to restore the greenery to denuded areas. Third, it is striving to propagate the idea of rational utilization in order to reduce the pressure on forest resources. To save, to grow and to use rationally- popularly known in Kannada as Ulisu ("save"), Belesu ("grow") and Balasu ("rational use")- is movement's popular slogan.

As said earlier, the deforestation in the Western Ghats has already affected hydroelectric dams, reservoirs and agriculture. The central government's Planning Commission has recognized the "high depletion" of natural resources in the Western Ghats in its Seventh Five Year Plan document. The first area of priority for the Appiko Movement is the remaining tropical forests of Western Ghats. The area is so sensitive that to remove the forest cover will lead to a laterization process, converting the land into rocky mountains. Thus a renewable resources becomes a nonrenewable one. Once laterization sets in, it will take centuries for trees to grow on that land. Before we reach such an extreme point the Appiko Movement aims to save the remaining forests in the Western Ghats through organizing decentralized groups at the grassroots level to take direct action.

The Movement Methods

The Appiko Movement uses various techniques to raise awareness: foot marches in the interior forests, slide shows, folk dances, street plays and so on. The movement has achieved a fair amount of success: the state government has banned felling of green trees in some forest areas; only dead, dying and dry trees are felled to meet local requirements. The movement has spread to the four hill districts of Karnataka Province, and has the potential to spread to the Eastern Ghats in Tamil Nadu Province and to Goa Province.

The second area of the Appiko Movement's work is to promote afforestation on denuded lands. In the villagers to grow saplings. Individual families as well as village youth clubs have taken an active interest in growing decentralized nurseries. An all-time record of 1.2 million saplings were grown by people in the Sirsi area in 1984-1985. No doubt this was possible due to the cooperation of the forest department, which supplied the plastic bags for growing saplings. In the process of developing the decentralized nursery, the activists realized that forest department makes extra money in raising a nursery. The cost paid for one sapling grown by a villager was 20 paise (US 2c), whereas the cost of a single sapling raised by the forest department amounted to a minimum of Rs 2 (US 15c). In addition, the forest department used fertilizers and gave tablets to saplings. The Appiko Movement's experience has brought an overuse of chemical fertilizers into the forest nursery, making it a capital-intensive, money-making program. The nursery program propagated by the forest department is really a means for utilizing village labor at cheap rates. Appiko activists have learned lessons from this experience, and they are now growing saplings only to meet their own needs, not to give to the forest department. The villagers have initiated a process of regeneration in barren common land. The Youth Club has taken the responsibility for the project and the whole village has united to protect this land from grazing, lopping and fire. The experience shows that in those areas where soil is present, natural regeneration is the most efficient and least expensive .nethod of bringing barren area under free cover. In the areas in which topsoil is washed off, tree planting-especially of indigenous, fast-growing species- is done. The irony is that the forest department is resorting to the mechanized planting of exotic species, and also uses huge amounts of fertilizers on these exotic, monoculture plantations. This work will definitely harm the soil, and eventually the tree cover, in the area. Two obvious techniques of greening are being performed: one the forest department's method, is capital intensive, and the other, the people's technique of growing through regeneration, is a natural process for sustainable development of the soil.

The third major area of activity in the Appiko Movement is related to rational use of the ecosphere through introducing alternative energy sources to reduce the pressure on the forest. The activists have constructed 2,000 fuel-efficient chulhas ("hearths") in the area, which save fuelwood consumption by almost 40 percent. The activists do not wait for government subsidies or assistance, since there is spontaneous demand from the people. Even in Sizsi town and in other urban areas, these chulhas are installed in hotels, reducing firewood consumption.

The other way to reduce pressure on the forest is through building gobar (gas plants). An increasing number of people are building bio-gas plants. However, the Appiko activists are more interested in those people who are from poorer sections- who cannot afford gas plants- so they emphasize chulhas. Some people deter the regeneration process in the forest area through incorrect lopping practices. The Appiko Movement is trying to change people's attitudes so that they realize their mistake and stop this practice.

The thrust of the Appiko Movement in carrying out its work reveals the constructive phase of the people's movement. Through this constructive phase, depleted natural resources can be rebuilt.

This process promotes sharing of resources in an egalitarian way, helping the forest dwellers. The movement's aim is to establish a harmonious relationship between people and nature, to redefine the term development so that ecological movements today form a basis for a sustainable, permanent economy in the future.

Save Silent Valley

Save Silent Valley was a social movement aimed at the protection of Silent valley, an evergreen tropical forest in the Palakkad district of Kerala, India. It was started in 1973 to save the Silent Valley Reserve Forest in from being flooded by a hydroelectric project. The valley was declared as Silent Valley National Park in 1985. None the less the controversy surrounding the valley is still on.

Background

Kuntipuzha one of the major rivers takes its origin in the flush green forests of Silent valley. In 1928 the location at Sairandhri on the Kunthipuzha River was identified as an ideal site for electricity generation. A study and survey was conducted in 1958 of the area about the possibility of a hydroelectric project of 120 MV and one costing Rs. 17 Crore was later proposed by the Kerala State Electricity Board. The Kerala State Electricity Board (KSEB) decided to implement the Silent Valley Hydro-Electric Project (SVHEP) centered on a dam across the Kunthipuzha River in 1973. The resulting reservoir would have flood 8.3 km^2 of virgin rainforest. The proposal was enquired by National Committee on Environmental Planning and Co-ordination (NCEPC) and suggested 17 safeguards to be implemented in case the project implemented. A shortage of funds delayed activity. Even then from 1974 to 1975 a very large number of trees were felled in the area.KSEB announced its plan to begin dam construction in 1973.

Beginnings

After the announcement of imminent dam construction the valley became the focal point of "Save Silent Valley", India's fiercest environmental debate of the decade. Because of concern about the endangered lion-tailed macaque, the issue was brought to public attention. Romulus Whitaker, founder of the Madras Snake Park and the Madras Crocodile Bank, was probably the first person to draw public attention to the small and remote area. In 1977 the Kerala Forest Research Institute carried out an Ecological Impact study of the Silent Valley area and proposed that the area be declared a Biosphere Reserve.

In 1978 Smt. Indira Gandhi, the Honorable Prime Minister of India, approved the project, with the condition that the State Government enact Legislation ensuring the necessary safeguards. Also that year the IUCN (Ashkhabad, USSR, 1978) passed a resolution recommending protection of Lion-tailed Macaques in Silent Valley and Kalakkad and the controversy heated up. In 1979 the Government of Kerala passed Legislation regarding the Silent Valley Protection Area (Protection of Ecological balance Act of 1979) and issued a notification declaring the exclusion of the Hydroelectric Project Area from the proposed National Park.

Participants

Kerala Sasthra Sahithya Parishath (KSSP) effectively aroused public opinion on the requirement to save Silent Valley. They also published a Techno-economic and Socio-Political assessment report on the Silent Valley Hydroelectric project. The poet activist Sugathakumari played an important role in the silent valley protest and her poem "Marathinu Stuthi" (Ode to a Tree) became a symbol for the protest from the intellectual community and was the opening song/prayer of most of the "save the Silent Valley" campaign meetings. Dr. Salim Ali, eminent ornithologist of the Bombay Natural History Society, visited the Valley and appealed for cancellation of the Hydroelectric Project. A petition of writ was filed before the High Court of Kerala, against the clear cutting of forests in the Hydroelectric Project area and the court ordered a stop to the clear cutting.

Dr. M.S. Swaminathan, the renowned Agricultural Scientist, and then Secretary to the Department of Agriculture, called at the Silent Valley region and his suggestion was 389.52 km^2 including the Silent Valley (89.52 km^2), New Amarambalam (80 km^2), Attappadi (120 km^2) in Kerala and Kunda in Tamilnadu (100 km^2)

reserve forests, should be made into a National Rainforest Biosphere *Reserve, with the aim of "preventing erosion of valuable genes from* the area". *Listen*:(8:46) to Dr. M. S. Swaminathan speaking on Sustainable Development, p.83, August 27, 2002

In January 1980 the Hon. High Court of Kerala lifted the ban on clear cutting, but then the Hon. Prime Minister of India requested the Government of Kerala to stop further works in the project area until all aspects were fully discussed. In December, the Government of Kelala declared the Silent Valley area, excluding the Hydroelectric Project area, as a National Park.

In 1982 a multidisciplinary committee with Prof. M. G. K. Menon as chairman, was created to decide if the Hydroelectric Project was feasible without any significant ecological damage. Early in 1983, Prof. Menon's Committee submitted its report. After a careful study of the Menon report, the Hon. Prime Minister of India decided to abandon the Project. On October 31, 1984 Indira Gandhi was assassinated and on November 15 the Silent Valley forests were declared as a National Park, though the boundaries of the Silent Valley Park were limited and no buffer zone was created, despite recommendations by expert committees and scientists.

Park Inaugurated

Ten months later, on September 7, 1985 the Silent Valley National Park was formally inaugurated and a memorial at Sairandhri to Indira Gandhi was unveiled by Shri. Rajiv Gandhi, the new Hon. Prime Minister of India. On September 1, 1986 Silent Valley National Park was designated as the core area of the Nilgiri Biosphere Reserve. Since then, a long-term conservation effort has been undertaken to preserve the Silent Valley ecosystem.

A New Dam Proposal

In 2001 a new Hydro project was proposed and the "Man vs. Monkey debate" was revived. The proposed site of the dam (64.5 m high and 275 m long) is just 3.5 km downstream of the old dam site at Sairandhiri, 500 m outside the National Park boundary.. The 84 km^2 catchment of the project area included 79 km^2 of the Silent

Valley National Park. The Kerala Minister for Electricity called The Pathrakkadavu dam (PHEP) an "eco-friendly alternative" to the old Silent Valley project. The PHEP was designed as a run-off-the-river project with an installed capacity of 70 MW in the first phase (105 MW eventually) and an energy generation of 214 million units (Mu) with a minimal gross storage of 0.872 million cubic metres. The claim was that the submergence area of the PHEP would be a negligible 041 km² compared to 8.30 km² submergence of the 1970s (SVHEP). However, The spectacular waterfall between the Neelikkal and Pathrakkadavu hills bordering the Silent Valley will disappear if the proposed Pathrakkadavu hydro-electric project is implemented.

During January to May 2003 a rapid Environmental Impact Assessment (EIA) was carried out during by the Thiruvananthapuram-based Environmental Resources Research Centre and its report was released in December, stating that forest lost due to the project would be just 2216 km², not including the 7.4 km approach road and land to be acquired for the powerhouse in Karapadam.

Chhattisgarh Mukti Morcha

Chhattisgarh Mukti Morcha (Chhattisgarh Liberation Front) is a political party in the Indian state of Chhattisgarh.

On the 3rd of March 1977, the Chhattisgarh Mines Shramik Sangh (Chhattisgarh Mines Workers' Union) was founded by Shankar Guha Niyogi. In 1982, CMSS formed CMM as their political front. CMM was formed to fight for the cultural identity of the region and for upliftment for the workers and peasants. CMM organized social campaigns, such as against alcohol abuse and instituted social projects, such as a workers' financed hospital.

Niyogi was murdered in Bhilai 1991. Today, Janak Lal Thakur is the president of CMM and Anoop Singh its secretary. The motto of CMMs is *Sangharsh aur Nirman* (Struggle and Construction). Another motto is *Virodh Nahi Vikalp* (Not resistance, but alternative). CMM was neutral on the issue of formation of a separate Chhattisgarh state. CMM is very active in the struggle against genetically modified seeds. In the legislative assembly elections in Chhattisgarh 2003 CMM had put up eight candidates, whom together mustered 37,335 votes.

Peasants

According to strict social science definitions, colonial India was a peasant society. By far the vast majority of the population of the subcontinent lived in villages, and well over half the working population was engaged directly in agriculture. These villages were not isolated communities: the urban population was small by comparison but substantial, and urban magnates maintained important social, economic, and political ties to the countryside to secure the steady stream of agricultural goods that sustained city life. The state was organized into territorial provinces that transcended lines of caste and clan and whose complex bureaucratic dimensions reflected the agrarian revenue potential.

Clear cultural, social, economic, and political distinctions could be and were made between town and country. Most importantly, the typical unit of production was the family household, which may or may not have owned the land upon which it worked but, regardless, directed its combined labor to the cultivation of crops. Colonial India also had a history of significant religious variety.

Indeed, few visitors to the subcontinent over the last twenty-five centuries-from Alexander to al-Biruni to Attenborough—have failed to make note of this fact. Fewer still have failed to remark upon the vast numbers of holy men who wander the subcontinent, reside in its villages, towns, and cities (often near shrines) and throng its sacred places.

These holy men, known generically as sadhus (Hindu) and fakirs (Muslim), can be described as monks inasmuch as they belong to one of many Indian monastic traditions of social detachment and spiritual discipline. As in the European tradition, however, monasticism in India encompasses a wide variety of religious experience. While frequent pilgrimage, alms, and tests of physical endurance are and have long been important aspects of the lives of many Indian monks, Indian monasticism cannot be reduced to itinerancy, begging, and asceticism. Many monks are and have long been devoted to careful study and spiritual contemplation, conducted entirely within the walls of a sanctuary in an attempt to create a paradise on earth. Still others were expert in the arts and science of warfare.

Though the institutionalized forms of charity-such as the creation of hospitals-common to western monasticism have not been nearly so prominent in India, many Indian monks were respected as able healers, and service (seva) remains a central ideal of most Indian religious traditions. Indeed, the ritual removal of Indian monks from "worldly" concerns has long presaged (and was preparatory to) their active engagement in the world, whether conducted from a religious center or as part of an itinerant or soldiering life-style.

Finally, Indian monks come from all sections of society, including the peasantry, though the degree to which monastic orders recruited from the ranks of the low-born in rural society (whether peasants or artisans) varied. However, at least one major monastic community-the Ramanandis, who look to Ramanand of fourteenth-century Banaras for religious inspiration-has long been dedicated to the recruitment of novices (both male and, to a lesser degree, female) from the entire social spectrum. Understanding how this Ramanandi recruitment philosophy has worked in historical practice, particularly during the colonial era, is one of the aims of this book.

Indian peasants and monks did not live in social and religious isolation, from the world or from each other. Indeed, the lives of peasants and monks in colonial India were (and are) intricately intertwined: monks depended on peasants for agrarian labor, material sustenance, and monastic recruitment; peasants looked to monks for spiritual guidance, religious knowledge, and ideological leadership.

Both expressed increasing concern in the colonial era with questions of religious identity and social status, in part because those questions had immediate and long-range political and economic ramifications. Peasants and monks addressed those questions by advocating both attacks on and manipulations of social hierarchy, that is, caste. The story of those attacks and manipulations, and their implications for colonial India, make up a large part of the history described in this book. However, this history also includes significant religious and cultural change, which should not be ignored.

Furthermore, the world that peasants and monks lived in, and assisted in creating, came to occupy a central place in the history of colonial and nationalist India. That world is with us still, nearly a half-century since independence from British rule, and, it can be argued, contributes to the ongoing crisis of religion and the state in north India.

But, despite the importance of radical monks who led rural rebellions, most of the social history that has described them does not explain the role of religion, or the exceptionally religious, in peasant society; rather, it merely comments upon the fact. This is as true for colonial India as it is for late antique Rome.

Peter Brown has observed that social historians of the late Roman empire have "tended to stress the spectacular occasions on which the holy man intervened to lighten the lot of the humble and oppressed: his open-handed charity, his courageous action as the spokesman of popular grievances-these have been held sufficient to explain the role of the holy man." But, Brown adds, such a view sees too little of the life of the holy man....Dramatic interventions of holy men in the high politics of the Empire were long remembered. But they illustrate the prestige that the holy man had already gained, they do not explain it. They were rather like the cashing of a big cheque on a reputation; and, like all forms of power in late Roman society, this reputation was built up by hard, unobtrusive (and so, for us, partly obscure) work among those who needed constant and unspectacular ministrations.

Certainly there are plenty of cases of peasant grievance expressed in religious language in Indian history; likewise there is no shortage of peasant movements led by holy men. Indeed, some of those grievances and movements find their way into this book.

A main purpose of this work, consequently, is to explore directly and in depth the religion that aids in defining the world of the Gangetic peasantry in colonial India. This involves broadening the working definitions of religion beyond the personal and private to include much of what is normatively considered political, social, and economic; it also involves understanding peasants in terms not only of what they do-i.e., their labor, behaviour, riots, and occasional rebellions-but also of what they believe and think and say and write. I hope that by so doing we gain a better sense of the mental worlds that produced and gave meaning to action in colonial north India, whether that action was violent or gentle, religious, social, economic or political. This recourse to culture and, ultimately, religion should not be seen as an abandonment of social history as such, but as a recognition that while social history has enabled us to ask important questions, it has not provided the tools with which to craft satisfactory answers.

Scheduled Castes, Scheduled Tribes and Other Backward Classes

We have already seen how the founding fathers of our Constitution wished to secure social, economic and political equality for all the citizens of the country. However, it was realised that this objective could not be achieved unless persons belonging to special disadvantaged groups were provided special protection to emancipate them from centuries-old prejudices and exploitation. Provisions were, therefore, incorporated in the Constitution to promote their economic, educational and social development.

It is against this background that the two types of reservations are available to the members of the backward classes under the Constitution. They are: (a) reservations of seats in the Lok Sabha, the Vidhan Sabha and the various Panchayati Raj bodies and (b) reservation in government services. While the reservations of seats in the Lok Sabha, the Vidhan Sabha and the Panchayati Raj bodies are available to the members of the SCs and STs, the provision of reservation for the OBCs is available only in the Panchayati Raj bodies. The second type of reservation is available to all the three categories of people. Moreover, under Article 244(2) special provisions have been made for the tribal areas in the states of Assam, Meghalaya, Mizoram and Tripura under the Sixth Schedule of the Constitution.

Constitutional Safeguards for the Minorities

Under the Constitution of India, certain safeguards have been granted to the religious and linguistic minorities. Articles 29 and 30 of the Constitution seek to protect the interests of minorities. They recognise the rights of the minorities to conserve their language, script or culture. They may establish and administer educational institutions of their choice. Article 350A provides for instructions in the mother tongue at the primary stage of education to children belonging to linguistic minorities. Article 350B provides for a Special Officer to investigate all matters relating to the safeguards for linguistic minorities.

It is evident from above that provisions of the Indian Constitution are exhaustive and they have helped to design a strong democratic polity under which equality and justice for all the citizens can be achieved. The Constitution has, thus, created an environment for ushering in an era of effective social change. It has acted not only as a facilitator of change but has also encouraged and promoted economic and social development.

Moreover, it has defined and guided the strategy of planning which was adopted and fostered subsequently in the country. The constitution is the driving force effecting socioeconomic reforms in the country through the process of amendment. A large number of constitutional amendments have directed, controlled and regulated almost all activities of the society. The process of social change leading to socioeconomic transformation of the Indian society was accelerated by these enactments. Some of these have influenced the lifestyle of the Indian people.

Dalit Political Movements

In addition to a growing number of lower-caste-based political parties and human rights movements, Dalits have taken part in struggles against the state and their upper-caste counterparts since the 1960s to claim their rights; several of these movements have used arms and have advocated violence. While some Dalit leaders have argued that the fundamental rights of Dalits should be addressed within a constitutional framework, many non-urbanized Dalits have taken the position that their problems cannot be resolved without a militant struggle against those in power. Mainstream political parties in India have generally adopted a top-down interventionist approach to Dalit problems, offering promises of loans, housing, and proper implementation of reservations (quotas allowing for increased representation in government jobs, education, and political bodies) as compensation for past mistreatment.

Issues of "untouchability," temple entry, violence, and economic exploitation were largely left unaddressed by the state and political parties. As the traditional political parties abandoned or avoided efforts to mobilize support among Dalits at the grassroots level, they paved the way for an autonomous Dalit leadership to emerge in the early 1990s. This new leadership has been threatening for backward and upper castes.

Dalit Panthers of India: During the 1960s and 1970s, the Dalit Panthers, and several groups with a Marxist/Leninist or Maoist orientation, emerged outside the framework of recognized political parties and parliamentary politics to confront the established powers. The Dalit Panthers were formed in the state of Maharashtra in the 1970s, ideologically aligning themselves to the Black Panther movement in the United States.

During the same period, Dalit literature, painting, and theatre challenged the very premise and nature of established art forms and their depiction of society and religion. Many of these new Dalit artists formed the first generation of the Dalit Panther movement that sought to wage an organized struggle against the varna system. Dalit Panthers visited "atrocity" sites, organized marches and rallies in villages, and raised slogans of direct militant action against their upper-caste aggressors.

The determined stance of the Dalit Panthers served to arouse and unite many Dalits, particularly Dalit youths and students. The defeat of ruling party candidates and the boycott of elections in some areas forced the government to take notice of the movement: Panther leaders were often harassed and removed from districts for speaking out against the government and Hindu religion. They also became frequent targets of police brutality and arbitrary detentions. Disagreements over the future of the movement and the inclusion of other caste groups ultimately led to a dispersal of Dalit Panther leadership.

The former aggressiveness and militancy of the Dalit Panthers have for the most part dissipated, though small splinter groups or groups that have adopted the name still survive. In Tamil Nadu, for example, the Dalit Panthers of India have thrived since the 1980s as a nonviolent awareness-raising and organizing movement concentrating primarily on women's rights and land issues and claims. They are currently led by a man named Tirumavalavan. As documented in chapters V and VIII, their members are continually harassed and detained by the police.

Naxalites: The origins of the Naxalite movement can be traced to a breakaway Maoist group in West Bengal, which in March 1967 split from the Communist Party of India (Marxist) (CPI(M)) over differences in ideology: while CPI(M) chose the parliamentary path to change, the Maoist group chose to engage in armed struggle. The group initiated a series of peasant uprisings beginning in a village in the state of West Bengal called Naxalbari, from which rebel leaders took the name "Naxalite." The peasant communities seized land, burned property records, and assassinated exploitative landlords and others identified as "class enemies." Although the uprising was brutally crushed within a few months, similar revolts broke out elsewhere in West Bengal and in other parts of India.

By 1970, Naxalite groups had expanded their efforts to large areas of the countryside stretching from West Bengal to the southern state of Kerala. They engaged in a campaign of land seizure and violence against the police and security forces, as well as against political figures, civil servants, landlords, and other civilians. In many instances, land seizures and other demonstrations of peasant resistance forced landlords to flee their lands.

The Naxalites' abuses included targeted assassinations and kidnappings of political figures and police officials. Naxalite groups also carried out bombings and arson in areas where they were likely to cause civilian casualties and summarily executed, and in some cases tortured to death, suspected police informers. All such practices constitute gross violations of international law. Although the Naxalite insurgency was brought to an end in most parts of the country by a brutal police crackdown designed to eliminate the militants and their supporters, the movement continues to survive, albeit with some splits and regroupings, in the rural areas of West Bengal, Orissa, Andhra Pradesh, and Bihar.

From the outset of the Naxalbari uprising, the government has resorted to extra-legal measures to deal with the Naxalite threat, including extrajudicial executions, torture, and forced disappearances. Most of the victims of police abuse are peasants and laborers. Members and organizers of peasant unions are automatically labelled as Naxalites. Tribal and Dalit villagers are often singled out as Naxalite sympathizers, while attacks on rural activists and striking laborers are sanctioned as part of a campaign to fight "Naxalite terrorism." Senior police officers with a record of "killing Naxalites" even receive promotions, cash rewards, and favoured postings.

4

Development Process

Poverty in India

Poverty is one of the main problems which have attracted attention of sociologists and economists. It indicates a condition in which a person fails to maintain a living standard adequate for his physical and mental efficiency. It is a situation people want to escape. It gives rise to a feeling of a discrepancy between what one has and what one should have. The term poverty is a relative concept. It is very difficult to draw a demarcation line between affluence and poverty. According to Adam Smith- Man is rich or poor according to the degree in which he can afford to enjoy the necessaries, the conveniences and the amusements of human life.

Even after more than 50 years of Independence India still has the world's largest number of poor people in a single country. Of its more than 1 billion inhabitants, an estimated 260.3 million are below the poverty line, of which 193.2 million are in the rural areas and 67.1 million are in urban areas. More than 75% of poor people reside in villages. Poverty level is not uniform across India. The poverty level is below 10% in states like Delhi, Goa, and Punjab etc. whereas it is below 50% in Bihar (43) and Orissa (47). It is between 30-40% in Northeastern states of Assam, Tripura, and Mehgalaya and in Southern states of Tamil Nadu and Uttar Pradesh.

Poverty has many dimensions changing from place to place and across time. There are two inter-related aspects of poverty- Urban and rural poverty. The main causes of urban poverty are predominantly due to impoverishment of rural peasantry that forces them to move out of villages to seek some subsistence living in the towns and cities. In this process, they even lose the open space or habitat they had in villages albeit without food and other basic amenities. When they come to the cities, they get access to some food though other sanitary facilities including clean water supply still elude them.

And they have to stay in the habitats that place them under sub-human conditions. While a select few have standards of living comparable to the richest in the world, the majority fails to get two meals a day. The causes of rural poverty are manifold including inadequate and ineffective implementation of anti-poverty programmes. The overdependence on monsoon with non-availability of irrigational facilities often result in crop-failure and low agricultural productivity forcing farmers in the debt-traps. The rural communities tend to spend large percentage of annual earnings on social ceremonies like marriage; feast etc. Our economic development since Independence has been lopsided. There has been increase in unemployment creating poverty like situations for many. Population is growing at an alarming rate. The size of the Indian family is relatively bigger averaging at 4.2. The other causes include dominance of caste system which forces the individual to stick to the traditional and hereditary occupations.

Since the 1970s the Indian government has made poverty reduction a priority in its development planning. Policies have focused on improving the poor standard of living by ensuring food security, promoting self-employment through greater access to assets, increasing wage employment and improving access to basic social services. Launched in 1965, India's Public Distribution System has helped meet people's basic food needs by providing rations at subsidized prices. Although it has affected less than 20% of the Poor's food purchases, the system has been important in sustaining people's consumption of cereals, especially in periods of drought. It has provided women and girls with better access to food and helped overcome the widespread discrimination against female consumption within households. It has also reduced the burden of women, who are responsible for providing food for the household. The largest credit-based government poverty reduction programme in the world, the Integrated Rural Development Programme provides rural households below the poverty line with credit to purchase income-generating assets. Launched in 1979, the programme has supplied subsidized credit to such groups as small and marginalized farmers, agricultural laborers, rural artisans, the physically handicapped, scheduled castes and scheduled tribes. Within this target population, 40% of the beneficiaries are supposed to be women. Although the programme has reached 51 million families, only 27% of the borrowers have been women. The programme has significantly increased the income of 57% of assisted families.

Rural poverty is largely a result of low productivity and unemployment. The Jawahar Rozgar Yojana, a national public works scheme launched in 1989 with financing from the central and state governments, provides more than 700 million person days of work a year about 1% of total employment for people with few opportunities for employment. The scheme has two components: a programme to provide low-cost housing and one to supply free irrigation wells to poor and marginalized farmers. The public works scheme is self-targeting. Since it offers employment at the statutory minimum wage for unskilled manual labor, only those willing to accept very low wages the poor are likely to enrol in the scheme. By providing regular employment and thereby increasing the bargaining power of all rural workers, the public works scheme has had a significant effect in reducing poverty. It has also contributed to the construction of rural infrastructure (irrigation works, a soil conservation project, drinking water supply). Evaluations show that 82% of available funds have been channelled to community development projects. Targeting was improved in 1996 when the housing and irrigation well components were delinked and focused exclusively on people below the poverty line.

TRYSEM (Training rural youth for self employment) was started to provide technical skills to the rural youth and to help them to get employment in fields such as agriculture, industry, services and business activities. Youth of the poor families belonging to the age-group of 18-35 are entitled to avail the benefits of the scheme. Priority is given to persons belonging to ST/SC and ex-servicemen and about 1/3 seats are reserved for women. Minimum Needs Programme was taken up as an integral part of the 5th Five Year Plan and it was intended to cater to the minimum needs of the people such as rural water supply, rural health, road building, adult education, primary education, rural electrification and improvement of the urban slums etc.With the intention of removing urban unemployment some schemes such as SEPUP (Self-employment programme for the urban poor); SEEUY (Scheme for self-employment of the educated urban youths). These schemes gives loans and subsidies for the urban unemployed youths to create or to find for themselves some jobs. The SEPUP had provided financial help for about 1.19 urban unemployed youths in the year 190-91.

The participation of civil society organizations in poverty reduction efforts, especially those directed to women, has increased social awareness and encouraged governments to provide better services. Cooperatives such as the Self-Employed Women's Association provide credit to women at market rates of interest but do not require collateral; they also allow flexibility in the use of loans and the timing of repayments. These civil society organizations have not only contributed to women's material well being; they have also helped empower them socially and politically. Such credit initiatives, by bringing women out of the confines of the household, are changing their status within the family and within village hierarchies. The demands of civil society organizations for better social services have spurred the government to launch campaigns to increase literacy and improve public infrastructure. And their calls for greater accountability and real devolution of power are increasing the likelihood that expenditures for poverty reduction will reach the needy, especially women.

The Indian state has undoubtedly failed in its responsibilities towards its citizens over the last 50 odd years. There is a need for the state to move out of many areas and the process has been started with economic liberalization. The process of decentralization should devolute lot more powers, both functional and financial, to panchayats. The lack of transparency and accountability has hampered our economic development at all levels. The problem of poverty persists because of a number of leakages in the system. New laws have to be evolved to ensure more accountability. Bodies like the Planning Commission should be modified into new constitutional bodies that can hold governments accountable for their failure to implement development programmes. A strong system of incentives and disincentives also needs to be introduced. The encouragement of non-governmental organizations and private sector individuals in tackling poverty is imperative, as the state cannot do everything.

The government has initiated, sustained, and refined many programs since independence to help the poor attain self sufficiency in food production. Probably the most important initiative has been the supply of basic commodities, particularly food at controlled prices, available throughout the country. The poor spend about 80 percent of their income on food while the rest of the population spends more than 60 percent. The price of food is a major determinant of wage scales. Often when food prices rise sharply, rioting and looting follow. Until the late 1970s, the government frequently had difficulty obtaining adequate grain supplies in years of poor harvests. During those times, states with surpluses of grain were cordoned off to force partial sales to public agencies and to keep private traders from shipping grain to deficit areas to secure very high prices; state governments in surplus-grain areas were often less than cooperative. After the late 1970s, the central government, by holding reserve stocks and importing grain adequately and early, maintained sufficient supplies to meet the increased demand during drought years. It also provided more remunerative prices to farmers.

India Poverty: In rural areas, the government has undertaken programs to mitigate the worst effects of adverse monsoon rainfall, which affects not only farmers but village artisans and traders when the price of grain rises. The government has supplied water by financing well digging and, since the early 1980s, by power-assisted well drilling; rescinded land taxes for drought areas; tried to maintain stable food prices; and provided food through a food-for-work program. The actual work accomplished through food-for-work programs is often a secondary consideration, but useful projects sometimes result. Employment is offered at a low daily wage, usually paid in grain, the rationale being that only the truly needy will take jobs at such low pay. In the 1980s and early 1990s, Indian government programs attempted to provide basic needs at stable, low prices; to increase income through pricing and regulations, such as supplying water from irrigation works, fertilizer, and other inputs; to foster location of industry in backward areas; to increase access to basic social services, such as education, health, and potable water supply; and to help needy groups and deprived areas. The total money spent on such programs for the poor was not discernible from the budget data, but probably exceeded 10 percent of planned budget outlays.

India has had a number of antipoverty programs since the early 1960s. These include, among others, the National Rural Employment Programme and the Rural Landless Employment Guarantee Programme. The National Rural Employment Programme evolved in FY 1980 from the earlier Food for Work Programme to use unemployed and underemployed workers to build productive community assets. The Rural Landless Employment Guarantee Programme was instituted in FY 1983 to address the plight of the hard-core rural poor by expanding employment opportunities and building the rural infrastructure as a means of encouraging rapid economic growth. There were many problems with the implementation of these and otherschemes, but observers credit them with helping reduce poverty. To improve the effectiveness of the National Rural Employment Programme, in 1989 it was combined with the Rural Landless Employment Guarantee Programme and renamed Jawahar Rozgar Yojana, or Jawahar Employment Plan.

State governments are important participants in antipoverty programs. The constitution assigns responsibility to the states in a number of matters, including ownership, redistribution, improvement, and taxation of land. State governments implement most central government programs concerned with land reform and the situation of small landless farmers. The central government tries to establish programs and norms among the states and union territories, but implementation has often remained at the lower bureaucratic levels. In some matters concerning subsoil rights and irrigation projects, the central government exerts political and financial leverage to obtain its objectives, but the states sometimes modify or retard the impact of central government policies and programs.

Natural Resource Degradation

Natural resource degradation in rural areas is a controversial topic. There is a wide range of opinions regarding its causes, extent, consequences, and even its definition. Narrowly defined, degradation of a natural resource can refer to a permanent, irreversible loss of its productive capacity relative to its natural state. In a broader, socioeconomic perspective, on the other hand, often human use of natural resources may be taken for granted, so the natural state is not particularly relevant. Productive capacity must be defined in terms of a given use; exploitation of a natural resource may lead to a situation in which it becomes unsuitable in one type of use yet still productive in another. Equally importantly, in some cases losses in productive capacity at one point in time may be reversed later, because human activity can also improve the productive capacity of natural resources. In discussing degradation, therefore, it is important to be explicit about what we are talking about. We follow Scherr et al (1995), who suggest that for policy purposes, a dynamic view of natural resource degradation and improvement is most useful because it allows us to examine the question of how human exploitation affects natural resource productivity under particular uses.

There are many types of natural resource degradation, such as deforestation, soil erosion and other types of soil degradation, loss or pollution of surface water or groundwater supplies, and loss of resistance to pests and diseases. All of these have some relationship to rainfed agriculture. Data on natural resource degradation are relatively sparse, and information on the implications for productivity are still more rare. We draw on a small amount of published data in this section to present some evidence about the extent and implications of various forms of natural resource degradation. Then we discuss some determinants of people's actions that lead to degradation or improvement in natural resource productivity.

Soil Degradation

Soil is the natural resource whose degradation causes the most widespread concern about rainfed agriculture in India. Soil degradation comes in several forms, including erosion by wind or water, and chemical deterioration such as loss of nutrients or salinization. Sehgal and Abrol (1994) compile the available information on soil degradation and conclude that erosion by water is the most widespread form of land degradation in India. CAR's official estimate of the distribution of lands affected by different types of degradation in the country. Water erosion is distributed throughout the country; its most severe form is found in parts of Uttar Pradesh, Madhya Pradesh, Rajasthan and Gujarat that are prone to wide, deep ravines that disfigure the land and make agriculture impossible. In other areas, erosion gradually removes topsoil and reduces yields, but it does not cause much land to be taken out of production in the short term. Wind erosion in India is confined to desert regions of Rajasthan and Gujarat, but it is not a significant problem elsewhere. Salinity is a serious problem affecting mainly irrigated areas; it causes severe productivity losses on high potential lands; some lands are even taken out of production. Lands with other nutrient losses are surprisingly small in area given the large area of drylands with soils that are naturally deficient in nutrients and receive only small applications of fertilizer and organic matter.

Degradation of Uncultivated Lands

The poor condition of India's village forest and pasture lands evoke stark images of the "tragedy of the commons." Jodha (1992) documents the breakdown of traditional mechanisms to govern use of common lands and the severe consequences in terms of decline in their area, productivity and employment generation. Area under common lands declined by 30-50 percent in 8 semi-arid states between 1950 and 1980. Bentley (1984) estimates that over 80% of India's 123 million hectares of uncultivated lands produce 20% or less of their biological potential. He argues that low productivity is particularly acute on the common lands that make up most of this area.

While about 23% of India's territory is officially classified as forested, the area actually covered by trees is no more than about 10-12% (Bentley, 1984; CSE 1982). Some forest lands have been converted to grazing pasture, but these too are unproductive (Gadgil, 1982). The resulting shortage of biomass has significant implications for the development of rainfed areas. One well-known problem is that villagers have to look for other fuel sources in addition to wood to cook meals and heat water. Chambers et al (1989) cite UNDP figures showing that the real price of firewood in rural areas doubled between 1973 and 1975. As a result, cow dung has a high opportunity cost for use as fuel, so its application to crops has declined (Motavalli and Anders 1991). Farmers correctly perceive that manure has residual productivity effects lasting up to three years, but many farmers do not apply manure so frequently. In dryland areas, irrigated plots and the most productive dry plots receive manure more manure than less productive dry plots. Motavalli and Anders found that about 70% of irrigated plots received manure at least once every three years; the figure for dryland plots was less than 20%. Biomass shortages also limit farmers' ability to retain stubble on crop lands during the dry season. Farmers cut as much stubble as possible to use as feed or fuel, and grazing animals finish what is left. The bare soil that remains is highly prone to erosion by early rains. Cogle and Rao (1993) report that applying straw mulch to alfisols greatly raises yields by increasing infiltration and reducing erosion, and that this practice would pay for itself within a few years. It is not known if farmers will be willing to adopt this practice, however, given the high, immediate demand for fodder and the scarcity of capital with which to make long term investments.

The decline in forest cover has other negative implications for rural areas. Gupta (1982) estimated that for every person directly employed in forestry, four are employed indirectly though forward linkages. Gupta (1982) also estimated that nontimber forest products generated 2 million man-years of employment in India, and that the number could be more than doubled if markets were better developed. Bentley (1984) pointed out that a much larger increase could be realized if uncultivated lands were managed for higher productivity. Jodha's (1990) finding that common lands in 24 villages in 8 semi-arid states generated an average of about 150 employment days for poor families further demonstrates their employment potential. In these same villages, the poorest families derived as much as 25 percent of their incomes from common lands.

Numerous causes underlie the decline in production of common lands; we mention them only briefly here. Repetto (1994) (citing Jodha 1992 and Agarwal 1992) outline some of the traditional mechanisms for managing village common lands in pre-colonial times and their emphasis on sustainability. The British Colonial administration usurped the ownership of these lands, managing them as a source of government revenue and natural resources to support the colonial economy (Bentley 1984, Gadgil and Guha, 1992). An adversarial relationship between villagers and Forest Departments developed as early as the late 19th century, when villagers were deprived of their traditional rights to natural resources that were an integral part of their local economy (Gadgil and Guha, 1992). Independence did not change this situation as the new government retained the same approach to forest management. Government policies also reserved many areas for forest-based industries, which received access to forest products at heavily subsidized rates and with little or no obligation to manage forest resources on a sustainable basis. People living in forest areas had little stake in the long term health of forest resources because they would be excluded from the benefits. As a result, they would intrude on the forests when they could, illegally taking what resources they could.

On common lands not managed by Forest Departments, the colonial administration nurtured relationships with large landlords (zamindars) who took responsibility for enforcing restrictions on the use of common lands. The zamindari system worked from the perspective of managing natural resources, but it was feudalistic in nature, with highly inequitable distribution of benefits. After Independence, the new government stripped zamindars of their power and with it, the effective systems for restricting the exploitation of common lands. State governments attempted to take responsibility to manage common lands but with poor results (Bentley 1984).

Development Planning

Planning in India dates back to the 1930s. Even before independence, the colonial government had established a planning board that lasted from 1944 to 1946. Private industrialists and economists published three development plans in 1944. India's leaders adopted the principle of formal economic planning soon after independence as an effective way to intervene in the economy to foster growth and social justice. The Planning Commission was established in 1950. Responsible only to the prime minister, the commission is independent of the cabinet. The prime minister is chairperson of the commission, and the minister of state with independent charge for planning and program implementation serves as deputy chairperson. A staff drafts national plans under the guidance of the commission; draft plans are presented for approval to the National Development Council, which consists of the Planning Commission and the chief ministers of the states. The council can make changes in the draft plan. After council approval, the draft is presented to the cabinet and subsequently to Parliament, whose approval makes the plan an operating document for central and state governments.

The First Five-Year Plan (FY 1951-55) attempted to stimulate balanced economic development while correcting imbalances caused by World War II and partition. Agriculture, including projects that combined irrigation and power generation, received priority. By contrast, the Second Five-Year Plan (FY 1956-60) emphasized industrialization, particularly basic, heavy industries in the public sector, and improvement of the economic infrastructure. The plan also stressed social goals, such as more equal distribution of income and extension of the benefits of economic development to the large number of disadvantaged people. The Third Five-Year Plan (FY 1961-65) aimed at a substantial rise in national and per capita income while expanding the industrial base and rectifying the neglect of agriculture in the previous plan. The third plan called for national income to grow at a rate of more than 5 percent a year; self-sufficiency in food grains was anticipated in the mid-1960s.

Economic difficulties disrupted the planning process in the mid-1960s. In 1962, when a brief war was fought with China on the Himalayan frontier, agricultural output was stagnating, industrial production was considerably below expectations, and the economy was growing at about half of the planned rate. Defence expenditures increased sharply, and the increased foreign aid needed to maintain development expenditures eventually provided 28 percent of public development spending. Midway through the third plan, it was clear that its goals could not be achieved. Food prices rose in 1963, causing rioting and looting of grain warehouses in 1964. War with Pakistan in 1965 sharply reduced the foreign aid available. Successive severe droughts in 1965 and 1966 further disrupted the economy and planning. Three annual plans guided development between FY 1966 and FY 1968 while plan policies and strategies were reevaluated. Immediate attention centered on increasing agricultural growth, stimulating exports, and searching for efficient uses of industrial assets. Agriculture was to be expanded, largely through the supply of inputs to take advantage of new high-yield seeds becoming available for food grains. The rupee was substantially devalued in 1966, and export incentives were adjusted to promote exports. Controls affecting industry were simplified, and greater reliance was placed on the price mechanism to achieve industrial efficiency.

The Fourth Five-Year Plan (FY 1969-73) called for a 24 percent increase over the third plan in real terms of public development expenditures. The public sector accounted for 60 percent of plan expenditures, and foreign aid contributed 13 percent of plan financing. Agriculture, including irrigation, received 23 percent of public outlays; the rest was mostly spent on electric power, industry, and transportation. Although the plan projected national income growth at 5.7 percent a year, the realized rate was only 3.3 percent.

The Fifth Five-Year Plan (FY 1974-78) was drafted in late 1973 when crude oil prices were rising rapidly; the rising prices quickly forced a series of revisions. The plan was subsequently approved in late 1976 but was terminated at the end of FY 1977 because a new government wanted different priorities and programs. The fifth plan was in effect only one year, although it provided some guidance to investments throughout the five-year period. The economy operated under annual plans in FY 1978 and FY 1979.

The Sixth Five-Year Plan (FY 1980-84) was intended to be flexible and was based on the principle of annual "rolling" plans. It called for development expenditures of nearly Rs.1.9 trillion (in FY 1979 prices), of which 90 percent would be financed from domestic sources, 57 percent of which would come from the public sector. Public-sector development spending would be concentrated in energy (29 percent); agriculture and irrigation (24 percent); industry including mining (16 percent); transportation (16 percent); and social services (14 percent). In practice, slightly more was spent on social services at the expense of transportation and energy. The plan called for GDP growth to increase by 5.1 percent a year, a target that was surpassed by 0.3 percent. A major objective of the plan was to increase employment, especially in rural areas, in order to reduce the level of poverty. Poor people were given cows, bullock carts, and handlooms; however, subsequent studies indicated that the income of only about 10 percent of the poor rose above the poverty level.

The Seventh Five-Year Plan (FY 1985-89) envisioned a greater emphasis on the allocation of resources to energy and social spending at the expense of industry and agriculture. In practice, the main increase was in transportation and communications, which took up 17 percent of public-sector expenditure during this period. Total spending was targeted at nearly Rs.3.9 trillion, of which 94 percent would be financed from domestic resources, including 48 percent from the public sector. The planners assumed that public savings would increase and help finance government spending. In practice that increase did not occur; instead, the government relied on foreign borrowing for a greater share of resources than expected.

The schedule for the Eighth Five-Year Plan (FY 1992-96) was affected by changes of government and by growing uncertainty over what role planning could usefully perform in a more liberal economy. Two annual plans were in effect in FY 1990 and FY 1991. The eighth plan was finally launched in April 1992 and emphasized market-based policy reform rather than quantitative targets. Total spending was planned at Rs.8.7 trillion, of which 94 percent would be financed from domestic resources, 45 percent of which would come from the public sector. The eighth plan included three general goals. First, it sought to cut back the public sector by selling off failing and inessential industries while encouraging private investment in such sectors as power, steel, and transport. Second, it proposed that agriculture and rural development have priority. Third, it sought to renew the assault on illiteracy and improve other aspects of social infrastructure, such as the provision of fresh drinking water. Government documents issued in 1992 indicated that GDP growth was expected to increase from around 5 percent a year during the seventh plan to 5.6 percent a year during the eighth plan. However, in 1994 economists expected annual growth to be around 4 percent during the period of the eighth plan.

Four decades of planning show that India's economy, a mix of public and private enterprise, is too large and diverse to be wholly predictable or responsive to directions of the planning authorities. Actual results usually differ in important respects from plan targets. Major shortcomings include insufficient improvement in income distribution and alleviation of poverty, delayed completions and cost overruns on many public-sector projects, and far too small a return on many public-sector investments. Even though the plans have turned out to be less effective than expected, they help guide investment priorities, policy recommendations, and financial mobilization.

The District Rural Development Agency

Role and Functions

If effective programme design is critical to successful implementation of rural development programmes, so is an effective delivery agency. None of the anti- poverty programmes can have impact unless they are implemented with a clarity of purpose and a commitment to the task. It is here that the DRDAs play a critical role. The DRDAs are not be implementing agencies, but can be very effective in enhancing the quality of implementation through overseeing the implementation of different programmes and ensuring that necessary linkages are provided. To this extent the DRDA is a supporting and a facilitating organisation and needs to play a very effective role as a catalyst in development process.

The District Rural Development Agency is visualised as a specialised and a professional agency capable of managing the anti- poverty programmes of the Ministry of Rural Development on the one hand and to effectively relate these to the overall effort of poverty eradication in the District. In other words, while the DRDA will continue to watch over and ensure effective utilisation of the funds intended for anit-poverty programmes, it will need to develop a far greater understanding of the processes necessary for poverty alleviation/ eradication. It will also need to develop the capacity to build synergies among different agencies involved for the most effective results. It will therefore need to develop distinctive capabilities rather than perform tasks that are legitimately in the domain of the PRIs or the line departments. The role of the DRDA will therefore be distinct from all the other agencies including the Zilla Parishad.

DRDAs must themselves be more professional and should be able to interact effectively with various other agencies. They are expected to coordinate with the line departments, the Panchayati Raj Institutions, the banks and other financial institutions, the NGOs as well as the technical institutions, with a view to gathering the support and resources required for poverty reduction effort in the district. It shall be their endeavor and objective to secure inter-sectoral and inter- departmental coordination and cooperation for reducing poverty in the district. It is their ability to coordinate and bring about a convergence of approach among different agencies for poverty alleviation that would set them apart.

The DRDAs are expected to coordinate effectively with the Panchayati Raj The institutions. Under no circumstances will they perform the functions of PRIs. The DRDAs are expected to oversee the implementation of different anti-poverty programmes of the

Ministry of Rural Development in the district. This is not to be confused with actual implementation, which will be by the Panchayati Raj and other Institutions. The DRDAs will monitor closely the implementation through obtaining of periodic reports as well as frequent field visits.

The purpose of the visit should be to facilitate the implementing agencies in improving implementation process, besides ensuring that the quality of implementation of programmes is high. This would include overseeing whether the intended beneficiaries are receiving the benefits under the different programmes. The DRDAs shall keep the Zilla Parishad, the State and the Central Government duly informed of the progress of the implementation of the programmes through periodic reports in the prescribed formats. Special report, as and when called for, shall be provided.

It shall be the duty of the DRDAs to oversee and ensure that the benefits specifically earmarked for certain target groups (SC/ST, women and disabled) reach them. They shall take all necessary steps to achieve the prescribed norms. The DRDAs shall take necessary step to improve the awareness regarding rural development and poverty alleviation particularly among the rural poor.

This would involve issues of poverty, the opportunities available to the rural poor and generally infusing a sense of confidence in their ability to overcome poverty. It would also involve sensitizing the different functionaries in the district to the different aspects of poverty and poverty alleviation programmes.

The DRDAs will strive to promote transparency in the implementation of different anti- poverty programmes. Towards this end, they shall publish periodically, the details of the different programmes and their implementation. Keeping in view, the substantial investment that are being made in poverty alleviation programmes, the DRDAs shall ensure financial discipline in respect of the funds received by them, whether from Central or State Governments. They shall also ensure that the accounts are properly maintained including in respect of the funds allocated to banks or implementing agencies in accordance with the guidelines of different programmes.

Thus the role of the DRDA is in terms of planning for effective implementation of anti-poverty programmes; coordinating with other agencies- Governmental, non-Governmental, technical and financial for successful programme implementation; enabling the community and the rural poor to participate in the decision making process, overseeing the implementation to ensure adherence to guidelines, .quality, equity and efficiently; reporting to the prescribed authorities on the implementation; and promoting transparency in decision making and implementation. In addition the DRDAs shall coordinate and oversee the conduct of the BPL Census and such other surveys that are required from time to time.

The DRDAs shall also carry out/ aid in carring out action research/ or evaluation studies that are initiated by the Central/ State Governments. The DRDAs should deal only with the anti-poverty programmes of the Ministry of Rural Development. If DRDAs are to be entrusted with programmes of other ministries or those of the State Governments, it should be ensured that these have a definite anti-poverty focus. Entrusting of any programme to the DRDAs, other than anti- poverty programmes of the Ministry, be it of any other Ministry of Government of India or the respective State Government will have to be done with the approval of the Secretary, Rural Development of the respective State(s), who should examine such request in consultation with the Ministry of Rural Development, Government of India, In such cases, it must be ensured that adequate provision is made for requisite staffing needed for proper implementation of the programme.

Organizational Structure

In order to be effective, the DRDA must have an appropriate staffing structure as well as suitable personnel policy. Keeping in view the role and functions of the DRDA listed in the previous chapter, the staffing structure of DRDA must include positions for Planning for poverty alleviation, Project formulation, Social organisation and Capacity building, Gender concerns, Engineering supervision and Quality control, Project monitoring, Accountancy and Audit functions as well as Evaluation and Impact studies. An indicative staffing structure is given in Annexure and is also detailed below. The State Government may modify the structure suitably, but without altering the basic design, to take care of the needs of individual districts keeping in view their size as well as specificity. However, this will also be subject to the overall ceiling of administrative costs admissible to the DRDAs in the State. By and large the staff appointed should be dedicated to DRDA- related works and should not be frequently transferred.

National Integration

The euphoria of independence was short-lived as partition brought disastrous consequences for India in the wake of communal conflict. Partition unleashed untold misery and loss of lives and property as millions of Hindu and Muslim refugees fled either Pakistan or India. Both nations were also caught up in a number of conflicts involving the allocation of assets, demarcation of boundaries, equitable sharing of water resources, and control over Kashmir. At the same time, Indian leaders were faced with the stupendous task of national integration and economic development.

When the British relinquished their claims to paramountcy, the 562 independent princely states were given the option to join either of the two nations. A few princely states readily joined Pakistan, but the rest—except Hyderabad (the largest of the princely states with 132,000 square kilometers and a population of more than 14 million), Jammu and Kashmir (with 3 million inhabitants), and Junagadh (with a population of 545,000)—merged with India. India successfully annexed Hyderabad and Junagadh after "police actions" and promises of privileges to the rulers. The Hindu maharajah of predominantly Muslim Jammu and Kashmir remained uncommitted until armed tribesmen and regular troops from Pakistan infiltrated his domain, inducing him to sign the Instrument of Accession to India on October 27, 1947. Pakistan refused to accept the legality of the accession, and, as a result, war broke out. Kashmir remains a source of friction between the neighbors. The assassination of Mahatma Gandhi on January 30, 1948, in New Delhi, by a Hindu extremist opposed to Gandhi's openness to Muslims ended the tenuous celebration of independence and deepened the hatred and mutual suspicion in Hindu-Muslim relations.

Economic backwardness was one of the serious challenges that India faced at independence. Under three successive five-year plans, inaugurated between 1951 and 1964 under Nehru's leadership, India produced increasing amounts of food. Although food production did not allow self-sufficiency until fiscal year (FY) 1984, India has emerged as the nation with the seventh largest gross national product (GNP) in the world.

Linguistic regionalism eventually reached a crisis stage and undermined the Congress' attempts at nation building. Whereas in the early 1920s, the Congress had deemed that the use of regional vernaculars in education and administration would facilitate the governance of the country, partition made the leaders, especially Nehru, realize how quickly such provincial or subnational interests would dismantle India's fragile unity. However, in the face of widespread agitation for linguistic separation of states, beginning with the Telangana Movement in 1953, in 1956 Nehru reluctantly accepted the recommendations of the States Reorganisation Commission, and the number of states grew by reorganization along linguistic lines. The states became the loci for democratization of political processes at district levels, for expression of regional culture and popular demands against a national culture and unity, for economic development at strategic localities in the rural areas, and for proliferation of opposition parties that ended the possibility of a pan-Indian two-party system.

Communalism in India

Communalism emerged as a consequence of the emergence of modem politics, which marked a sharp break with the politics of the ancient or medieval or pre-1857 periods. Communalism; as also other modem views such as nationalism and socialism could emerge as politics and as ideology only after politics based on the people, politics of participation and mobilization, politics based on the creation and mobilization of public opinion had come into existence. In pre-modem politics, people were either ignored in upper class based politics or were compelled to rebel outside the political system and, in case of success, their leaders incorporated into the old ruling classes. Many perceptive Indians recognized this. Jawaharlal Nehru, for example, noted in 1936: 'One must never forget that communalism in India is a latter-day phenomenon, which has grown up before our eyes.' Nor was there anything unique about communalism in the Indian context. It was not an inevitable or inherent product of India's peculiar historical and social development. It was the result of conditions which have in other societies produced similar phenomena and ideologies such as Fascism, anti-Semitism, racism, Catholic-Protestant conflict in Northern Ireland, or Christian Muslim conflict in Lebanon.

The communal consciousness arose as a result of the transformation of Indian society under the impact of colonialism and the need to struggle against it. The growing economic, political and administrative unification of regions and the country, the process of making India into a nation, the developing contradiction between colonialism and the Indian people and the formation of modem social classes and strata called for new ways of seeing one's common interests. They made it necessary to have wider links and loyalties among the people and to form new identities. This also followed from the birth of new politics during the last half of the 19th century. The new politics was based on the politicization and mobilization of an ever-increasing number of the Indian people.

The process of grasping the new, emerging political reality and social relations and the adoption of new uniting principles, new social and political identities with the aid of new ideas and concepts was bound to be a difficult and gradual process. The process required the spread of modem ideas of nationalism, cultural-linguistic development and class struggle. But wherever their growth was slow and partial, people inevitably used the old, familiar pre-modem categories of self-identity such as caste, locality, region, race, religion, sect "and occupation to grasp the new reality, to make wider connections and to evolve new identities and ideologies. Similar developments have occurred all over the world in similar circumstances. But often such old, inadequate and false ideas and identities gradually give way to the new, historically necessary ideas and identities of nation, nationality and class. This also occurred on a large scale in India, but not uniformly among all the Indian people. In particular, religious consciousness was transformed into communal consciousness in some parts of the country and among some sections of the people.

This was because there were some factors in the Indian situation which favored its growth; it served the needs of certain sections of society and certain social and political force. The question is why did communalism succeed in growing during the 20th century? What aspects of the Indian situation favored this process? Which social classes and political forces did it serve? Why did it become such a pervasive part of Indian reality? Though it was not inherent or inevitable in the situation, it was not a mere conspiracy of power-hungry politicians and crafty administrators either. It had socioeconomic and political roots. There was a social situation which was funneling it and without which it could not have survived for long. Above all, communalism was one of the by-products of the colonial character of Indian economy, of colonial underdevelopment, of the incapacity of colonialism to develop the Indian economy. The resulting economic stagnation and its impact on the lives of the Indian people, especially the middle classes, produced conditions which were conducive to division and antagonism within Indian society as also to its radical transformation.

Throughout the 20th century, in the absence of modem industrial development and the development of education, health and other social and cultural services, unemployment was an acute problem in India, especially for the educated middle and lower middle classes who could not fall back on land and whose socioeconomic conditions suffered constant deterioration. These economic opportunities declined further during the Great Depression after 1928 when large-scale unemployment prevailed.

In this social situation, the nationalist and other popular movements worked for the long-term solution to the people's problems by fighting for the overthrow of colonialism and radical social transformation. In fact, the middle classes formed the backbone both of the militant national movement from 190.5 to 1947 and the left-wing parties and groups since the 1920s. Unfortunately there were some who lacked a wider social vision and political understanding and looked to their narrow immediate interests and short-term solutions to their personal or sectional problems such as communal, caste, or provincial reservation in jobs or in municipal committees, legislatures, and so on.

Because of economic stagnation, there was intense competition among individuals for government jobs, in professions like law and medicine, and in business for customers and markets. In an attempt to get a larger share of existing economic opportunities, middle class individuals freely used all the means at their disposal-educational qualifications, personal merit as also nepotism, bribery, and S.J on. At the same time, to give their struggle a wider base, they also used other group identities such as caste, province and religion to enhance their capacity to compete. Thus, some individuals from the middle classes could, and did, benefit, in the short run, from communalism, especially in the field of government employment. This gave a certain aura of validity to communal politics. The communalist could impose his interpretation of reality on middle class individuals because it did have a basis, however partial, perverted and short-term, in the social existence and social experience of the middle classes.

Gradually, the spread of education to well-off peasants and small landlords extended the boundaries of the job-seeking middle class to the rural areas. The newly educated rural youth could not be sustained by land whether as landlords or peasants, especially as agriculture were totally stagnant because of the colonial impact. They flocked on the towns and cities for opening in government jobs and professions and tried to save themselves by fighting for jobs through the system of communal reservations and nominations. This development gradually widened the social base of communalism to cover the rural upper strata of peasants and landlords.

Thus, the crisis of the colonial economy constantly generated two opposing sets of ideologies and political tendencies among the middle classes. When anti-imperialist revolution and social change appeared on the agenda, the middle classes enthusiastically joined the national and other popular movements. They then readily advocated the cause and demands of the entire society from the capitalists to the peasants and workers.

Individual ambitions were then sunk in the wider social vision. But when prospects of revolutionary change receded, when the anti-imperialist struggle entered a more passive phase, many belonging to the middle classes shifted to short-term solutions of their personal problems, to politics based on communalism and other similar ideologies. Thus with the same social causation, large sections of the middle classes in several parts of the country constantly oscillated between anti-imperialism and communalism or communal-type politics. But there was a crucial different in the two cases. In the first case, their own social interests merged with the interests of general social development and their politics formed a part of the broader anti-imperialist struggle. In the second case, they functioned as a narrow and selfish interest group, accepted the socio-political status quo and objectively served colonialism.

To sum up this aspect: communalism was deeply rooted in and was an expression of the interests and aspirations of the middle classes in a social situation in which opportunities for them were grossly inadequate. The communal question was, therefore a middle class question par excellence. The main appeal of communalism and its main social base also lay among the middle classes. It is, however, important to remember that a large number of middle class individuals remained, on the whole, free of communalism even in the 1930s and 1940s. This was, in particular, true of most of the intellectuals, whether Hindu, Muslim or Sikh. In fact, the typical Indian intellectual of the 193 Os tended to be both secular and broadly left wing. There was another aspect of the colonial economy that favored communal politics. In the absence of openings in industry, commerce, education and other social services, and the cultural and entertainment fields, the Government service was the main avenue of employment for the middle classes.

Much of the employment for teachers, doctors and engineers was also under government control. As late as 1951, while 1.2 million persons were covered by the Factory Acts, 3.3 millions got employment in government service. And communal politics could be used to put pressure on the Government to reserve and allocate its jobs as also seats in professional colleges on communal and caste lines. Consequently, communal politics till 1937 was organized around government jobs, educational concessions, and the like as also political positions-seats in legislative councils, municipal bodies, etc.-which enabled control over these and other economic opportunities. It may also be noted that though the communalists spoke in the name of their 'communities,' the reservations, guarantees and other 'rights' they demanded were virtually confined to these two aspects. They did not take up any issues, which were of interest to the masses.

Above all, communalism developed as a weapon of economically and politically reactionary social classes and political forces-and semi feudal landlords and ex-bureaucrats (whom Dr. K.M. Ashraf has called thejagirdari classes) merchants and moneylenders and the colonial state. Communal leaders and parties were, in general, allied with these classes and forces. The social, economic and political vested interests deliberately encouraged or unconsciously adopted communalism because of its capacity to distort and divert popular struggles, to prevent the masses from was a specific feature of Indian social development-in several parts of the country. The religious distinction coincided with social, and class distinctions.

Here most often the exploiting sections-landlords, merchants and moneylenders,-were upper caste Hindus while the poor and exploited were Muslims or lower caste Hindus. Consequently, propaganda by the Muslim communalists that Hindus were exploiting Muslims or by the Hindu communalists that Muslims were threatening Hindu property or economic interests could succeed even while wholly incorrect. Thus, for example, the struggle between tenant and landlord in East Bengal and Malabar and the peasant-debtor and the merchant-moneylender in Punjab could be portrayed by the communalists as a struggle between Muslims and Hindus.

Similarly, the landlord-moneylender oppression was represented as the oppression of Muslims by Hindus, and the attack by the rural poor on the rural rich as an attack by Muslims on Hindus. For example, one aspect of the growth of communalism in Punjab was the effort of the big Muslim landlords to protect their economic and social position by using communalism to turn the anger of their Muslim tenants against Hindu traders and moneylenders, and the use of communalism by the latter to protect their threatened class interests by raising the cry of Hindu interests in danger. In reality, the struggle of the peasants for their emancipation was inevitable. The question was what type of ideological political content it would acquire. Both the communalists and the colonial administrators stressed the communal as against the class aspects of agrarian exploitation and oppression. Thus, they held that the Muslim peasants and debtors were being exploited not as peasants and debtors but because they were Muslims.

In many cases, a communal form is given to the social conflict not by the participants but by the observer, the official, the journalist, the politician, and, finally, the historian, all of whom provide a post-facto communal explanation for the conflict because of their own conscious or unconscious outlook. It is also important to note that agrarian conflicts did not assume a communal color until the 20th century and the rise of communalism and that too not in most cases. In the Pabna agrarian riots of 1873, both Hindu and Muslim tenants fought zamindars together. Similarly, as brought out in earlier chapters, most of the agrarian struggles after 1919 stayed clear of communal channels. The peasants and workers and the radical intelligentsia succeeded in creating powerful secular peasants' and workers' movements and organizations, which became important constituents of the anti-imperialist struggle.

It is important to note in this context that Hindu zamindars in Bengal had acquired control over land not because they were Hindus but as a result of the historical process of the spread of Islamic religion in Bengal among the lower castes and classes. Hindu zamindars and businessmen acquired economic dominance over landed capital in Bengal at the beginning of the 18th century during the rule of Murshid Quli Khan, religiously the most devout of Aurangzeb's officials and followers.

Under his rule, more than seventy-five per cent of the zamindars and most of the taluqdars were Hindus. The Permanent Settlement of 1793 further strengthened the trend by eliminating on a large scale both the old Hindu and Muslim zamindar families and replacing them with new men of commerce who were Hindus. Similarly, the predominance of Hindus among bankers, traders and moneylenders in northern India dated to the medieval period.

The dominance these strata acquired over rural society under British rule was the result not of their being Hindu but of the important economic role they acquired in the colonial system of exploitation. In other words, colonial history guaranteed the growth and economic domination of merchant-moneylenders; medieval history had guaranteed that they would be mostly Hindus. Communalism represented, at another level, a struggle between two upper classes or strata for power, privileges and economic gains. Belonging to different religions (or castes) these classes or strata used communalism to mobilize the popular support of their co-religionists in their mutual struggles. This was, for example, the case in Western Punjab where the Muslim landlords opposed the Hindu moneylenders 'and in East Bengal where the Muslimjotedars (small landlords) opposed the Hindu zamindars.

Secularism in India

Secularism in India has very different meaning and implications. The word secularism has never been used in Indian context in the sense in which it has been used in Western countries i.e. in the sense of atheism or purely this worldly approach, rejecting the other-worldly beliefs.

India is a country where religion is very central to the life of people. India's age-old philosophy as expounded in Hindu scriptures called Upanishad is sarva dharma samabhava, which means equal respect for all religions. The reason behind this approach is the fact that India has never been a mono-religious country. Even before the Aryan invasion India was not a mono-religious country. There existed before Aryan invasion numerous tribal cults from north-western India to Kanya Kumari most of whom happened to be Dravidians. Thus certain languages in North West of Pakistan even today contain some words of Dravidian origin. However, with the invasion of Aryans people of Dravidian origin were driven down south and today we find all Dravidian people in four southern states of India.

Aryans brought new religion based on Vedas and Brahmins dominated intellectual life of north India. But a section of Brahmins also migrated to south and evolved new cults marrying Vedic cults with Dravidian ones. Thus it is said that Hindu Indians worship more than 33 hundred thousand gods and goddesses. Thus even before advent of Christianity and Islam India was multi-religious in nature. Christianity and Islam added more religious traditions to existing Indian traditions. Thus it would be correct to say that India is bewilderingly diverse country in every respect – religious, cultural, ethnic and caste.

India is one country where caste rigidity and concept of untouchability evolved and still plays a major role in religious, social and cultural matters. Caste dynamics in Indian life, even in Christian and Islamic societies, plays larger than life role. Since most of the conversions to Christianity and Islam took place from lower caste Hindus, these two world religions also developed caste structure. There are lower caste churches and mosques in several places.

Under feudal system there was no competition between different religious traditions as authority resided in sword and generally there were no inter-religious tensions among the people of different religions. They co-existed in peace and harmony though at times inter-religious controversies did arise. However, there never took place bloodshed in the name of religion. There was also tradition of tolerance between religions due to state policies of Ashoka and Akbar. Ashoka's edicts clearly spell out policy of religious tolerance and Akbar used to hold inter-religious dialogue among followers of different religions and he also followed the policy of tolerance and even withdrew the jizya tax (poll tax on Hindus which was an irritant. Thus both Ashok and Akbar have place of great significance in religious life of India. No doubt they have been designated as 'great' i.e. they are referred to as Ashoka the Great and Akbar the Great.

Also, India had Sufi and Bhakti traditions in Islam and Hinduism respectively. Both Sufism and Bhakti traditions were based on respect for different religions. The poorer and lower caste Hindus and Muslims were greatly influenced by these traditions. Unlike 'ulama and Brahmans the Sufi and Bhakti saints were highly tolerant and open to the truth in other faiths. They never adopted sectarian attitudes and were never involved in power struggles. They kept away from power structures.

Nizamuddin Awliya, a great Sufi saints of 13-14th century saw the times of five Sultans but never paid court to a single one. When the last Sultan of his life sent a message requesting him to come to the court, he refused. Then he sent the message that if Nizamuddin does not come to my court, I (the Sultan) will come to his hospice. He replied that there are two doors to my hospice; if Sultan enters by one, I will leave by the other. Such was the approach of Sufis and Saints to power structure of their time.

Dara Shikoh, was heir apparent to Shajahan, the Moghul Emperor but had sufi bent of mind and was also a great scholar of Islam and Hinduism. He wrote a book Majmau'l Bahrayn (Co-mingling of Two Oceans Islam and Hinduism) and quoting from Hindu and Islamic scriptures showed both religions had similar teachings. The difference was of languages (Arabic and Sanskrit) and not teachings. Thus Dara Shikoh also contributed richly to inter-religious harmony in India.

Most of the conversions to Islam and Christianity took place through Sufis and missionaries with a spirit of devotion. Even today in India most of the Christians and Muslims belong to these lower caste strata. Even centuries after conversion their caste status and economic status has not changed.

Emergence of Competitive Politics

However, the entire social, economic and political scenario changed after advent of the British rule in 19th century. Differences between Hindu and Muslim elite began to emerge for various reasons – socio-cultural, economic and political. The British rulers adopted the policy of divide and rule, distorted medieval Indian history to make Muslim rulers appear as tyrants to the Hindu elite. This distorted history was taught in new school system, which was established by the British rulers. Also there developed economic and political competition between Hindu and Muslim elite leading to communal tensions. The Hindu elite was quick to adjust to new realities and took to modern education and commerce and industries. The Muslim ruling elite resisted new secular education system and also could not take to commerce and industry. They were thus left far behind in the race for progress.

Sir Syed Ahmad Khan had a perceptive mind. He understood importance of modern education system and founded Mohammedan Anglo Oriental College (MAO College) which became fulcrum of modern education for North Indian Muslim elite. The orthodox Ulama, however, vehemently opposed modern secular education and declared Syed Ahmad Khan as kafir (unbeliever) as he was supporting modern secular education.

Initially Hindu and Muslim elite cooperated with each other and Syed Ahmad Khan always emphasised Hindu-Muslim unity but the competitive nature of political and economic power drove wedge between the two elites and communal tensions began to emerge. When Indian National Congress was formed in 1885, it adopted secularism as its anchor sheet in view of multi-religious nature of Indian society.

India could not head towards Hindu Rashtra (Hindu Nation) as India was not merely a Hindu country. In pre-partition period Muslims were 25% besides Christians, Sikhs, Buddhists and Jains. However, Hindu society was highly fragmented society and far from monolithic. The dalits (low caste people) refused to call themselves as Hindus (subsequently their leader B.R.Ambedkar) adopted Buddhism in protest).

Muslims too, though not monolithic, had semblance of unity and this was used by communal Hindus to try to unite Hindus as one community. However, it is also true that the Hindu elite was more confident than the Muslim elite in the emerging new power-structure and felt more secure. Muslim elite felt less secure and they hitched their wagon with the British rulers. They wanted to share power-sharing arrangement before the British left the country. Thus secularism in India was more a political than philosophical phenomenon. The Indian National Congress adopted secularism, not as this worldly philosophy but more as a political arrangement between different religious communities. As power-sharing arrangement could not be satisfactorily worked out between the Hindu and Muslim elite the country was divided into two independent states of India and Pakistan, Muslim majority areas of North-West going to Pakistan.

After independence and partition a large body of Muslims were left in India and hence the leaders like Gandhi and Nehru preferred to keep India secular in the sense that Indian state will have no religion though people of India will be free both in individual and corporate sense to follow any religion of their birth or adoption. Thus India remained politically secular but otherwise its people continued to be deeply religious. In India right from the British period main contradiction was not between religious and secular but it was between secular and communal. In the western world main struggle was between church and state and church and civil society but in India neither Hinduism nor Islam had any church-like structure and hence there never was any such struggle between secular and religious power structure.

The main struggle was between secularism and communalism. The communal forces from among Hindus and Muslims mainly fought for share in power though they used their respective religions for their struggle for power. Even after partition communal problem did not die. It raised its head again within few years. The RSS (Rashtriya Swayam Sevak Sangh), which is mainspring of Hindu right remained in existence and at its instance a new political outfit, which was communal in nature came into existence called Jan Sangh. In independent India the Jan Sangh was mainspring of communal problem and it kept on denouncing secularism as western concept alien to the Indian ethos.

Jawahar Lal Nehru, the first Prime Minister of India was great champion of secularism and secular politics. Theoretically speaking the Congress Party was also committed to secularism. However, the Congress Party consisted of several members and leaders whose secularism was in doubt. But it was due to Mahatma Gandhi, Nehru, Maulana Abul Kalam Azad and B.R.Ambedkar that India committed itself to secularism and its Constitution was drafted on secular lines.

Secularism in India, as pointed out before, meant equal respect for all religions and cultures and non-interference of religion in the government affairs. Also, according to the Indian Constitution no discrimination will be made on the basis of caste, creed, gender and class. Similarly all citizens of India irrespective of ones religion, caste or gender have right to vote. According to articles 14 to 21 all will enjoy same rights without any discrimination on any ground. According to Article 25 all those who reside in India are free to confess, practice and propagate religion of one's choice subject of course to social health and law and order. Thus even conversion to any religion of ones choice is a fundamental right. But the BJP (Bhartiya Janta Party) and RSS are opposed to all this. According to them there should be Hindu Rashtra (Hindu Nation) in India and Muslims and Sikhs should be secondary citizens without any political right.

Since the BJP is a political party it cannot say so openly and publicly. It also has to take pledge of secularism for contesting election. But since it is integral part of RSS ideology it is also responsible for RSS beliefs. In fact all secular forces in India consider the BJP as a communal party. It always takes anti-minority stance and accuses the Congress, supposedly a secular party, of 'appeasement' of minorities. It also describes the Congress and other secular parties as indulging in 'pseudo-secularism'.

The RSS and BJP also known as the Sangh Parivar, not only reject secularism but provoke violence against minorities. Since independence several major communal riots have taken pace in India. The first such riot took place in Jabalpur in Central India and last major riot took place in Gujarat in Western India in 2002 in which more than 2000 Muslims were killed and several women were raped. When the Gujarat carnage took place in 2002 BJP was ruling over Gujarat.

According to the filed evidence Chief Minister of BJP party Mr. Narendra Modi was involved along with the entire governmental machinery in the carnage and on this basis the US Government denied him visa in early 2005. The BJP was directly involved in high pitch propaganda against the historic mosque called Babri Mosque and ultimately demolished it claiming it to be a birth-place of Lord Ram, a Hindu god. Mr. Lal Krishna Advani who was then the President of BJP spearheaded the campaign against Babri Mosque and the mosque was demolished right in his presence. He later became Home Minister in the National Democratic Alliance (NDA) ministry. He is known as hardliner Hindu. Shri Vajpayee who became Prime Minister of India in NDA Government, is known as the moderate face of BJP though one can say there is hardly any ideological difference between the two.

Secular and Unsecular People

Now question arises how many Indian people are secular and how many unsecular? Since secularism does not mean being this worldly in India, one cannot say how many are believers and how many unbelievers? On the contrary in Indian context what it means how many people are against people of minority religions like Islam and Christianity and how many people respect them. In fact in India an overwhelming majority of people are religious but tolerant and respect other religions and are thus 'secular' in Indian context. Even Sufis and Bhakti Saints are considered quite secular in that sense. The followers of RSS and the BJP are very few, not more than 5-10 per cent. India has remained secular and democratic for its entire post-independence period (more than 58 years).

There is no doubt India has witnessed much communal violence but only due to involvement of RSS and BJP and occasionally the Congress in some places. Communalism is a powerful political weapon used by politicians of different hues. The Hindu masses are generally not to be blamed for such violence. However, few fanatics under the influence of RSS ideology are involved along with anti-social elements. It is also true that on certain major issues like birth place of Ram people get misled by powerful communal propaganda and may side with the BJP but that does not mean they are for violence and bloodshed. If they are properly informed they withdraw their support. However, secular forces are not as pro-active as communal forces are. Communal forces are actively working spreading communal poison round the year whereas secular forces become active only after communal violence and once peace is established they become nonchalant. It is their nonchalance which, benefits communal forces.

The communal forces thus came to power through false propaganda but were exposed during this five-year rule and were voted out of power as they were perceived to be behind communal carnage in Gujarat in 2002. No less than a person like Vajpayee, the former Prime Minister of BJP, himself admitted that people rejected us because we were held responsible for the Gujarat carnage. This confession on the part of ex-Prime Minister of BJP itself clearly establishes that people of India are by and large secular and do not like killing of others just because they are not Hindus. Not only the BJP lost the election but also its allies, which are otherwise considered secular. The BJP is today being deserted by its former allies as they realised that association with communal dispensation is not approved by the people of India.

There are some rationalists and secularists who reject religion in its entirety but such rationalists or secularists are extremely few. Though there are no census figures available but one can safely say they are less than 0.1% in India. Also, there are extremely orthodox people who exhibit rigidity and intolerance towards other faiths though of course not on communal grounds but on the grounds of religious orthodoxy but they too are in miniscule minority. Tolerance in India among people of all religions is widely prevalent. It is perhaps due to influence of ancient Indian doctrine that truth is one but is manifested in different forms, and on the other hand due to the Sufi doctrine of wahdat al-wujud (Real Being is one) that implies that there is only One Real Being and all of us are mere manifestations of that real being. As the ancient Hindu doctrine leads to inclusiveness and peaceful coexistence so does the Sufi doctrine. For peaceful co-existence another Sufi doctrine of sulh-i-kul i.e. total peace and peace with all is very important. Sufism left deep influence on Hindu masses as much as on Muslim masses.

Thus the real spirit of secularism in India is all inclusiveness, religious pluralism and peaceful co-existence. However, it is politics, which proved to be divisive and not religion. It is not religious leaders by and large (with few exceptions) who divide but politicians who seek to mobilise votes on grounds of primordial identities like religion, caste and ethnicity.

In a multi-religious society, if politics is not based on issues but on identities, it can prove highly divisive. Politicians are tempted to appeal to primordial identities rather than to solve problems. The former case proves much easier. The medieval society in India was thus more religiously tolerant as it was non-competitive. The modern Indian society, on the other hand, has proved to be more divisive as it is based on competition. This competition becomes more acute if development is uneven and unjust. Thus in case of India one can say by and large it is secular in as much as it is religiously plural and tolerant but there are politically divisive forces quite active and create communal pressure and widen the gap between religious community thus bringing Indian secularism under threat.

Different types of Secularism in India

The Hindi word that is commonly albeit incorrectly used for "secularism" in India is *dharmanirapekshata* and which ought to mean "indifference towards religion" but actually means "indifference to duty or Justice" The word Dharma is not to be confused with religion, it implies a broader definition encompassing duty, Justice and virtuousness. The correct Hindi term is 'Panthnirpekshta' meaning "indifference towards matters of faith".

The state cannot be Dharma neutral as that would imply abdication of duty. The usage itself denotes the understanding of secularism as more a policy of political practice than a philosophy in itself. The other Sanskrit word that is used for it is *dharmanirapekshavada* where the suffix *vada* is the same as *ism* and denotes the philosophical aspect of secularism. However, the plurality of religions, religious pluralism (the view that all religions are equally valid), and cultural (and communal) concerns greatly influence the various ways in which secularism has developed and is looked at on in India. Prominently in Indian soil, secularism is more a subject of politics than of metaphysics or even values, at present. The other philosophical viewpoint that is often confused with secularism is religious pluralism, or the view that all religions are equally valid ways of religious expression or salvation.

The Preamble of the Constitution of India declares that India is a secular state. The term secularism in politics refers to the governmental practice of indifference towards religion. Though such bifurcation is not totally possible, still, secular politics attempts to prevent religious philosophies or bodies from influencing governmental policies. The philosophy that the Indian constitution upholds on to is a kind of secular humanism made relevant through a historical development of the ideology within the context of religious pluralism in India.

History

The history of Indian secularism has roots in the protest movements in the 5th century B.C. The three main protest movements were by the Charvakas (a secularistic and materialistic philosophical movement), Buddhism, and Jainism. All three of them rejected the authority of the Vedas and any importance of belief in a deity. However, it was in the 18th century, when the British East India Company began to gain total control over India that ideas of secularism began to have impact on the Indian mind. Until then, religion was considered to be inseparable from political and social life. On the other hand, the British codified laws pertaining to practices within religions on the sub-continents. To this effect they instituted separate laws for Hindus, Muslims, Christians, Sikhs, Parsis and others. In doing so they laid the foundation for a civil code which remains largely unchanged to date. This is a major grouse for the Hindu right wing politicians who insist that there should be a uniform civil code for all citizens. For example, believers of all faiths other than Islam are legally bound to be monogamous while those who practice or convert to Islam are permitted up to four marriages.

Religious Laws

On Conversions

Religious conversions are a contentious issue in India. It is opposed mainly by the right wing organizations like the Rashtriya

Swayamsevak Sangh, the Vishwa Hindu Parishad, and the Bajrang Dal. States such as Orissa, Madhya Pradesh, Tamil Nadu, Gujarat, and Arunachal Pradesh have passed bills that have criminalized forced religious conversions.

On Marriage

As the Shah Bano case demonstrated, successive governments have failed to enact a uniform civil code as regards to marriages, and in this case, the dissolution thereof. A significant observation from this case was that despite a direct ruling from the Supreme Court of India, the Rajiv Gandhi government, in pandering to the Muslim vote bank not only failed to protect the interests of a divorced female in a secular and even handed manner (Shah Bano was 62 and a mother five when her husband divorced her), the Muslim Women (Protection of Rights on Divorce) Act, 1986 was enacted, further exacerbating Muslim women's plight.

Views

While the pluralist view of Mahatma Gandhi, that all religions are equal, has a strong impact, there are movements like those of the dalits (depressed classes) and the communists who have criticized such a view. Gandhi himself was a devout man and instilled devotion in the Independence Struggle. The Sikhs are as well (except for the Khalistani Sikh Extremists). However, the certain sections of Indian society including the Hindutva movement have always opposed the form of secularism in India as really being pseudo-secularism.

However, there is obvious difference between secularism practised in India and elsewhere. The western model of secularism means that religion and politics are separate from each other (Caesar and God theory). In other words, polity does not enter in religious affairs and religion in political affairs. This also means that political mechanism cannot correct problems inside a religious group. However, Indian society being a mixture of religions, is always prone to dominance and conflicts. Moreover, the issues such as casteism is particularly of religious origin. In order to mitigate the harmful effects of casteism and other source of conflicts and human right violations arising out of religions, it is necessary that polity/government be able to meddle with religious affairs. As a result of several year's efforts to detoxify the religions, Government has been able to reduce the effects of casteism and modernize the Hindu personal laws. However, the country is far from having a common civil code. As far as other religions are concerned, government has only limited success in correcting human right violations such as atrocities against women in Islam.

However, ability of Government to indulge in religious affairs also boomeranged. Religions and castes increased their influence on political parties. As a result, politico-religio-regional chauvinism is becoming more common in contemporary Indian Politics. Thus, practising the Indian Brand of secularism (mutual tolerance instead of mutual respect) in the last 60 years, failed to produce communal harmony and trust. Liberhann Commission which investigated the Babri Masjid Incident, has recommended that religion be delinked from politics and that Politicians must not garner votes preaching religion or caste. The Indian experiment on secularism is here to continue.

Foreign Relations

India's foreign relations reflect a traditional policy of nonalignment, the exigencies of domestic economic reform and development, and the changing post-Cold War international environment. India's relations with the world have evolved considerably since the British colonial period (1757-1947), when a foreign power monopolized external relations and defence relations.

On independence in 1947, few Indians had experience in making or conducting foreign policy. However, the country's oldest political party, the Indian National Congress (the Congress), had established a small foreign department in 1925 to make overseas contacts and to publicize its freedom struggle. From the late 1920s on, Jawaharlal Nehru, who had the most long-standing interest in world affairs among independence leaders, formulated the Congress stance on international issues. As a member of the interim government in 1946, Nehru articulated India's approach to the world.

During Nehru's tenure as prime minister (1947-64), he achieved a domestic consensus on the definition of Indian national interests and foreign policy goals—building a unified and integrated nation-state based on secular, democratic principles; defending Indian territory and protecting its security interests; guaranteeing India's independence internationally through nonalignment; and promoting national economic development unencumbered by overreliance on any country or group of countries. These objectives were closely related to the determinants of India's foreign relations: the historical legacy of South Asia; India's geopolitical position and security requirements; and India's economic needs as a large developing nation. From 1947 until the late 1980s, New Delhi's foreign policy goals enabled it to achieve some successes in carving out an independent international role. Regionally, India was the predominant power because of its size, its population (the world's second-largest after China), and its growing military strength. However, relations with its neighbors, Pakistan in particular, were often tense and fraught with conflict. In addition, globally India's nonaligned stance was not a viable substitute for the political and economic role it wished to play.

India's international influence varied over the years after independence. Indian prestige and moral authority were high in the 1950s and facilitated the acquisition of developmental assistance from both East and West. Although the prestige stemmed from India's nonaligned stance, the nation was unable to prevent Cold War politics from becoming intertwined with interstate relations in South Asia. In the 1960s and 1970s, New Delhi's international position among developed and developing countries faded in the course of wars with China and Pakistan, disputes with other countries in South Asia, and India's attempt to balance Pakistan's support from the United States and China by signing the Treaty of Peace, Friendship, and Cooperation with the Soviet Union in August 1971. Although India obtained substantial Soviet military and economic aid, which helped to strengthen the nation, India's influence was undercut regionally and internationally by the perception that its friendship with the Soviet Union prevented a more forthright condemnation of the Soviet presence in Afghanistan. In the 1980s, New Delhi improved relations with the

United States, other developed countries, and China while continuing close ties with the Soviet Union. Relations with its South Asian neighbors, especially Pakistan, Sri Lanka, and Nepal, occupied much of the energies of the Ministry of External Affairs.

In the 1990s, India's economic problems and the demise of the bipolar world political system have forced New Delhi to reassess its foreign policy and to adjust its foreign relations. Previous policies proved inadequate to cope with the serious domestic and international problems facing India. The end of the Cold War gutted the core meaning of nonalignment and left Indian foreign policy without significant direction. The hard, pragmatic considerations of the early 1990s were still viewed within the nonaligned framework of the past, but the disintegration of the Soviet Union removed much of India's international leverage, for which relations with Russia and the other post-Soviet states could not compensate.

Pragmatic security, economic considerations, and domestic political influences have reinforced New Delhi's reliance on the United States and other developed countries; caused New Delhi to abandon its anti-Israeli policy in the Middle East; and resulted in the courtship of the Central Asian republics and the newly industrializing economies of East and Southeast Asia. Although India shares the concerns of Russia, China, and many members of the Nonaligned Movement about the preeminent position of the United States and other developed countries, different national interests and perceptions make it improbable that India can turn cooperation with these countries to its advantage on most international issues. Furthermore, although Cold War politics have ceased to be a factor in South Asia, the most intractable problems in India's relations with Pakistan—conflict over Kashmir, support for separatists, and nuclear and ballistic missile programs—still face the two countries.

Role of the Prime Minister

Nehru set the pattern for the formation of Indian foreign policy: a strong personal role for the prime minister but a weak institutional structure. Nehru served concurrently as prime minister and minister of external affairs; he made all major foreign policy decisions himself after consulting with his advisers and then entrusted the conduct of international affairs to senior members of the Indian Foreign Service. His successors continued to exercise considerable control over India's international dealings, although they generally appointed separate ministers of external affairs.

India's second prime minister, Lal Bahadur Shastri (1964-66), expanded the Office of Prime Minister (sometimes called the Prime Minister's Secretariat) and enlarged its powers. By the 1970s, the Office of the Prime Minister had become the de facto coordinator and supraministry of the Indian government. The enhanced role of the office strengthened the prime minister's control over foreign policy making at the expense of the Ministry of External Affairs. Advisers in the office provided channels of information and policy recommendations in addition to those offered by the Ministry of External Affairs. A subordinate part of the office—the Research and Analysis Wing—functioned in ways that significantly expanded the information available to the prime minister and his advisers. The Research and Analysis Wing gathered intelligence, provided intelligence analysis to the Office of the Prime Minister, and conducted covert operations abroad.

The prime minister's control and reliance on personal advisers in the Office of the Prime Minister was particularly strong under the tenures of Indira Gandhi (1966-77 and 1980-84) and her son, Rajiv (1984-89), who succeeded her, and weaker during the periods of coalition governments under Morarji Desai (1977-79), Viswanath Pratap (V.P.) Singh (1989-90), Chandra Shekhar (1990-91), and P.V. Narasimha Rao (starting in June 1991). Although observers find it difficult to determine whether the locus of decision-making authority on any particular issue lies with the Ministry of External Affairs, the Council of Ministers, the Office of the Prime Minister, or the prime minister himself, nevertheless in the 1990s India's prime ministers retain their dominance in the conduct of foreign relations.

Ministry of External Affairs

The Ministry of External Affairs is the governmental body most concerned with foreign affairs, with responsibility for some aspects of foreign policy making, actual implementation of policy, and daily conduct of international relations. The ministry's duties include providing timely information and analysis to the prime minister and minister of external affairs, recommending specific measures when necessary, planning policy for the future, and maintaining communications with foreign missions in New Delhi. In 1994 the ministry administered 149 diplomatic missions abroad, which were staffed largely by members of the Indian Foreign Service. The ministry is headed by the minister of external affairs, who holds cabinet rank and is assisted by a deputy minister and a foreign secretary, and secretaries of state from the Indian Foreign Service.

In 1994 the total cadre strength of the Indian Foreign Service numbered 3,490, of which some 1,890 held posts abroad and 1,600 served at the Ministry of External Affairs headquarters in New Delhi. Members of the Indian Foreign Service are recruited through annual written and oral competitive examinations and come from a great variety of regional, economic, and social backgrounds. The Foreign Service Training Institute provides a wide range of courses for foreign service officers, including a basic professional course, a comprehensive course in diplomacy and international relations for foreign service recruits, a refresher course for commercial representatives, and foreign language training.

The Ministry of External Affairs has thirteen territorial divisions, each covering a large area of the world, such as Eastern Europe and the post-Soviet states, or smaller areas on India's periphery, such as Afghanistan, Iran, and Pakistan. The ministry also has functional divisions dealing with external publicity, protocol, consular affairs, Indians abroad, the United Nations (UN) and other international organizations, and international conferences. Two of the eighteen specialized divisions and units of the ministry are of special note. The Policy Planning and Research Division conducts research and prepares briefs and background papers for top policy makers and ministry officials. The briefs cover wide-ranging issues relating to India's foreign policy and role in the changing international environment, and background papers provide information on issues concerning international developments.

The Economic Division has the important task of handling foreign economic relations. This division augments its activities to reflect changes in the government's economic policy and the international economic environment. In 1990 the division established the Economic Coordination Unit to assess the impact on India of the Persian Gulf crisis arising from Iraq's invasion of Kuwait, changes in Eastern Europe and the Soviet Union, and formation of a single market in the European Economic Community (after 1993 the European Union), as well as to promote foreign investment. The Economic Division also runs India's foreign aid programs, including the Indian Technical and Economic Cooperation Programme, the Special Commonwealth African Assistance Programme, and aid to individual developing countries in South Asia and elsewhere. The ministry runs the Indian Council for Cultural Relations, which arranges exhibits, visits, and cultural exchanges with other countries and oversees the activities of foreign cultural centers in India.

The Ministry of External Affairs had a budget of Rs.8.8 billion (for value of the rupee) for fiscal year (FY) 1994. The largest single expense was the maintenance of missions abroad: Rs.3.8 billion, or close to 44 percent of the ministry's expenditures. Foreign aid totaled Rs.1.3 billion, or 15.1 percent of the ministry's expenditures. The single largest recipient—as in most previous years—was Bhutan (Rs.690 million), whose government operations and development are heavily subsidized by India.

Bibliography

Campbell-Johnson, Alan: *Mission with Mountbatten*. London: Hale, 1982.

Chopra, P. N.: Towards Freedom: Documents on the Movement for Independence in India, 1937. Delhi: Oxford UP, 1986.

Ghanshyam Shah: Social Movements and the State : Readings in Indian Government and Politics, Sage, Delhi, 2002.

Gupta, P. S.: Towards Freedom: Documents on the Movement for Independence in India, 1942-1944. Delhi: Oxford UP, 1997.

Hasan, Mushirul: India's Partition: Process, Strategy and Mobilization. New Delhi: Oxford UP, 1993.

Mahendra Prasad Singh and Satish Kumar Jha: Professor Chetakar Jha's Indian Government and Politics : A Political Commentary, Research Press, Delhi, 2006.

Manoranjan Mohanty: Class, Caste, Gender : Readings in Indian Government and Politics, Sage, Delhi, 2004.

Moon, Penderel: *Divide and Quit*. Delhi: Oxford UP, 1998.

Peter Ronald deSouza and E. Sridharan: India's Political Parties : Readings in Indian Government and Politics, Sage, Delhi, 2006.

S A Palekar: *Indian Government and Politics,* ABD Pub, Delhi, 2008.

Jarillo, J.C.: *Creating the Borderless Organization*, Oxford, Butterworth-Heinemann, 1993.

Keane J.: *Democracy and Civil Liberty*, London, Verso, 1988.

Kenneth C. Wheare: *Modern Constitutions*, New York, Oxford University Press, 1951.

Lenneal, J. : *Urban Administrators: The Politics of Role Elasticity*, Westport, CT, Greenwood Press, 1988.

Lipietz A.: *Mirages and Miracles*, London, Verso, 1987.

Lucian, W. : *Asian Power and Politics: the Cultural Dimensions of Authority*, Cambridge, Belknap Press, 1985.

Manpong, C. M.: *District Administration in Arunachal Pradesh*, New Delhi, Omsons Publications, 1993.

Michael, B.: *The Politics of Succession in India*, Connecticut, Greenwood, 1976.

Norman, Uphoff: *Local Organizations: Intermediaries in Rural Development*, Ithaca, Cornell University Press, 1984.

Politt. C: *Managerialism and the Public Services*, Oxford, Blackwell, 1993.

Riggs, F.: *Administrative Reform and Political Responsiveness*, Beverly Hills, Sage Publications, 1970.

Rosen, P.: *Societies and Military Power: India and its Armies*, Ithaca, Cornell University Press, 1996.

Rourke, E.: *Bureaucratic Power in National Politics*, Boston, Little Brown and Company, 1978.

Simon, D. : *Public Administration*, New York, Knopf, 1950..

Sudarshan, R. : *Human Development and Structural Adjustment*, New Delhi, McMillan, 1993.

Thomas, R. : *Elements of Government*, New York, Random House, 1960.

Thompson, V.: *Public Administration*, New York, Knopf, 1950.

Vincent, R.: *The French in India: From Diamond Traders to Sanskrit Scholars*, Bombay, Popular Prakashan, 1990.

Whicker, L.: *Handbook of Research Methods in Public Administration*, New York, Marcel Dekker, 1999.

Ziring, L.: *An Introduction to Asian Politics*, N.J., Prentice-Hall, 1977.

Index

A

Accountability, 232, 233.
Agreements, 77, 80.
Ambedkar, 3, 5, 7, 14, 15, 16, 17, 28, 52, 55, 69, 151, 160, 201, 257, 258.
Appiko Movement, 213, 215, 216, 217.
Approaches, 85, 207.
Arthashastra, 167.

B

Block Samitis, 140, 141, 142.
British Parliament, 6, 13.
Buddhism, 201, 257, 263.
Bureaucracy, 213.

C

Central Government, 53, 64, 149, 167, 233, 234, 235.
Chandra Shekhar, 268.
Charan Singh, 179, 186.
Chhattisgarh Mukti Morcha, 195, 221.
Chipko Movement, 195, 205, 206, 207, 210.
Civil Servant, 1.
Civil Service, 192.
Civil Society, 25, 206, 232, 258.
Commissions, 71, 147, 155.
Committees, 14, 15, 16, 17, 27, 28, 56, 135, 140, 141, 142, 147, 156, 157, 220, 250.
Constituent Assembly, 1, 2, 4, 5, 6, 7, 8, 13, 14, 15, 16, 17, 19, 27, 28, 55, 69, 70, 151, 160, 168.
Constitution of India, 8, 9, 14, 16, 17, 27, 28, 30, 34, 53, 54, 59, 99, 160, 225, 263.
Constitutional Machinery, 74.
Constitutional Provisions, 75, 151, 152, 191.
Constitutional Safeguards, 225.
Constitutional System, 9.
Council of Ministers, 18, 101, 102, 104, 119, 120, 122, 167, 268.
Cultural Diversity, 71, 72.

D

Dalit Movement, 201.
Dalit Political Movements, 226.
Democracy, 1, 21, 22, 26, 29, 38, 41, 47, 54, 56, 57, 66, 68, 83, 147, 148, 149, 153, 166, 169, 171, 176, 178.
Deputy Commissioner, 145.
Development Agency, 242, 243.
Development Planning, 149, 230.
Directive Principles, 18, 19, 27, 41, 42, 43, 45, 47, 48, 49, 52, 53, 64, 151.
Distribution, 23, 27, 43, 59, 60, 79, 92, 175, 214, 222, 251, 270.

District Rural Development Agency, 242, 243.
Drafting Committee, 5, 8, 14, 15, 16, 28, 56, 69.

E

Economic Justice, 42, 52.
Economic Planning, 239.
Election Commission, 20, 126, 134, 155, 188, 189, 191, 193, 194.
Electoral Laws, 191.
Emergency Provisions, 27.
Executive Branch, 57.

F

Fascism, 26, 248.
Federalism, 4, 69, 72, 73, 75, 76.
Federation, 69, 70, 167, 201.
Finance Commission, 71, 152, 155.
Financial Relations, 71.
Financial Resources, 155.
Foreign Investment, 270.
Foreign Policy, 265, 266, 267, 268, 269.
Foreign Relations, 265, 266, 267, 268.
Freedom, 4, 13, 29, 30, 32, 34, 35, 38, 45, 47, 53, 54, 56, 57, 59, 60, 61, 62, 64, 65, 67, 78, 135, 168, 174, 177, 178, 184, 187, 198, 265.
Fundamental Duties, 28, 38, 55.
Fundamental Rights, 9, 10, 28, 30, 38, 41, 46, 47, 48, 49, 53, 54, 56, 57, 64, 65, 66, 226.

G

Governance, 14, 41, 46, 153, 167, 247.
Government Revenue, 238.
Governments, 2, 22, 40, 49, 75, 95, 98, 141, 143, 147, 150, 154, 168, 194, 203, 231, 232, 233, 234, 239, 244, 245, 264, 268.
Gram Sabha, 143, 144, 152, 158.

H

Hierarchy, 89, 200, 201, 223.
Human Rights, 54, 56, 201, 203, 226.

I

Indian Constitution, 3, 27, 30, 32, 33, 61, 69, 160, 164, 166, 225, 259.
Indian Foreign Service, 268, 269.
Indian Polity, 17, 21, 27, 44.
Indian Press, 178, 186.
Indira Gandhi, 177, 178, 179, 185, 186, 187, 211, 218, 219, 220, 268.
Investment, 242, 244, 270.

J

Jawaharlal Nehru, 19, 55, 247, 265.
Jayaprakash Narayan, 178, 208.
Judicial system, 197.
Justice, 13, 19, 42, 43, 44, 52, 68, 95, 105, 107, 108, 112, 113, 115, 116, 118, 144, 156, 158, 168, 178, 181, 184, 186, 225, 239, 262.

K

Karl Marx, 25.

L

Lal Bahadur Shastri, 185, 268.
Leadership, 3, 26, 70, 72, 74,

75, 91, 147, 173, 177, 178, 185, 187, 197, 201, 223, 226, 227, 247.
Legislative Powers, 104.
Local Government, 26, 71, 152.
Lok Sabha, 18, 65, 140, 142, 150, 154, 163, 164, 178, 195, 225.

M

Mahatma Gandhi, 8, 26, 29, 180, 184, 185, 195, 201, 246, 258, 264.
Maintenance, 36, 37, 45, 64, 144, 145, 270.
Management, 34, 42, 44, 72, 83, 145, 146, 193, 195, 213, 238.
Morarji Desai, 179, 268.
Multi Party System, 174.

N

Narmada Bachao Andolan, 201, 203, 204, 205.
National Integration, 69, 75, 246.
Natural Resource Degradation, 235.
Non-governmental Organizations, 233.
Nyaya Panchayats, 146.

O

Occupations, 201, 230.
Opposition Parties, 72, 247.
Organization, 44, 167, 177, 180, 184, 185, 201.

P

Panchayati Raj, 4, 140, 142, 143, 146, 147, 148, 149, 150, 151, 153, 154, 155, 225, 243, 244.
Panchayati Raj System, 140.
Parliamentary Democracy, 54, 83.
Party Members, 174, 178, 182, 186.
Party System, 24, 169, 171, 172, 173, 174, 247.
Peasant Movement, 197.
Philosophy, 13, 14, 16, 43, 52, 147, 166, 180, 187, 223, 254, 257, 262, 263.
Policy, 11, 18, 19, 24, 27, 41, 42, 45, 46, 47, 51, 52, 55, 64, 81, 82, 151, 165, 170, 173, 175, 178, 179, 184, 186, 203, 209, 214, 235, 242, 245, 255, 256, 262, 270.
Political Parties, 7, 8, 52, 54, 55, 73, 76, 77, 80, 81, 86, 87, 88, 150, 169, 170, 171, 175, 176, 177, 179, 183, 185, 195, 198, 204, 226, 265.
Political System, 23, 24, 84, 90, 247, 267.
Politics, 22, 24, 25, 49, 79, 80, 87, 88, 89, 90, 91, 159, 169, 170, 171, 172, 174, 177, 187, 195, 224, 226, 247, 248, 250, 251, 252, 256, 258, 261, 262, 263, 264, 265, 266, 267.
Power of Parliament, 36, 190.
Powers, 9, 13, 14, 15, 22, 27, 36, 41, 55, 64, 67, 71, 75, 76, 97, 100, 104, 107, 108, 110, 111, 112, 114, 134, 135, 136, 139, 143, 144, 147, 149, 151, 152, 154, 155, 159, 160, 161, 165, 166, 167, 168, 191, 226, 232, 268.
Private Enterprise, 242.
Production, 25, 42, 44, 113, 141, 142, 197, 212, 221, 233, 236, 238, 240, 247.

Protection, 16, 30, 33, 43, 44, 53, 56, 57, 59, 60, 61, 151, 217, 218, 225, 264.
Provisions, 2, 3, 4, 15, 16, 17, 18, 20, 21, 27, 28, 34, 35, 37, 39, 46, 57, 58, 60, 62, 64, 66, 69, 70, 73, 75, 94, 97, 99, 100, 101, 102, 108, 110, 111, 112, 113, 114, 115, 117, 118, 119, 120, 123, 125, 126, 129, 130, 131, 134, 135, 136, 138, 139, 143, 151, 152, 159, 160, 161, 162, 189, 190, 191, 225.
Public Interest Litigation, 56.
Public Sector, 239, 240, 241, 242.

R

Rajiv Gandhi, 149, 151, 180, 187, 220, 264.
Rajya Sabha, 65, 140, 142, 150, 162, 163, 164.
Reform Movements, 196.
Relationship, 18, 22, 67, 197, 207, 217, 235, 238.
Research, 84, 203, 218, 220, 245, 268, 269.
Resistance Movement, 196.
Revolutions, 46.
Round Table Conference, 10.
Rural Development Agency, 242, 243.

S

Sarkaria Commission, 71, 73, 75.
Save Silent Valley, 195, 217, 218, 219.
Scheduled Castes, 17, 31, 45, 51, 119, 141, 142, 152, 224.
Scheduled Tribes, 21, 31, 45, 51, 141, 142, 152, 224.
Security, 30, 32, 44, 45, 59, 63, 64, 228, 230, 266, 267.
Single Party System, 171, 172.
Social Movements, 196.
Social Movements Types, 196.
Social Security, 44.
Social Welfare, 35, 63, 142.
Society, 7, 22, 23, 25, 26, 42, 58, 67, 68, 155, 172, 179, 196, 197, 198, 206, 208, 219, 221, 222, 223, 224, 226, 227, 232, 248, 249, 250, 254, 257, 258, 262, 264.
Soil Degradation, 235, 236.
State Policy, 18, 19, 27, 42, 45, 151.
Sustainable Development, 219.

T

Traditions, 222, 255, 256.

U

Union Judiciary, 105, 162.
Union Public Service Commission, 115.
Untouchability, 29, 30, 54, 55, 57, 58, 201, 226, 255.

W

Warfare, 222.
Welfare, 22, 35, 41, 43, 44, 49, 50, 51, 57, 63, 67, 119, 141, 168, 172, 173, 187, 198.
Welfare State, 41.
World War II, 239.

Z

Zilla Parishad, 140, 141, 142, 143, 147, 155, 156, 157, 243, 244.

❑❑❑